the Bully at Work

What You Can Do to Stop the Hurt and Reclaim Your Dignity On the Job

Gary Namie, Ph.D.
and Ruth Namie, Ph.D.

SOURCEBOOKS, INC.
NAPERVILLE, ILLINOIS

Published by Sourcebooks, Inc.
P.O. Box 4410
Naperville, IL 60567-4410
630.961.3900
Fax: 630.961.2168

Library of Congress Cataloging-in-Publication Data
Namie, Gary.
   The bully at work: what you can do to sop the hurt and reclaim your dignity on the job / Gary Namie, Ruth Namie.
      p. cm.
   Includes bibliographical references and index.
   ISBN 1-57071-534-3 (alk. paper)
   1. Bullying in the workplace. I. Namie, Ruth. II. Title.

HF5549.5.E43 N348 2000
650.1'3—dc21
                                                                00-024737

Printed and bound in the United States of America
BG   10 9 8 7 6 5 4 3 2

In memory of Lillian and Florence and to Pat,
the three women who always gave unconditional love and support.

In memory of Heinz Leymann and Andrea Adams, pioneers.

*Each time a man stands up for an ideal, or acts to improve the lot
of others, or strikes out against injustice, he sends forth a tiny ripple of
hope, and crossing each other from a million different centers of energy
and daring, those ripples build a current which can sweep down the
mightiest walls of oppression and injustice.* —Robert F. Kennedy

Disclaimer

. . . .

Dear Reader:

This book contains information, suggestions, and opinions about improving the quality of people's lives from the authors. The use, misuse, understanding, or misunderstanding of the material, in whole or part, is the sole responsibility of the reader.

Neither the publisher nor authors assume responsibility or liability, jointly or individually, to any person, group, organization, or entity regarding any emotional or material loss, damage, or injury caused or alleged to be caused directly or indirectly by the information contained in this book.

Readers are advised to use this material in a safe and logical manner. In some cases, this material is most effective when used in conjunction with professional legal and/or counseling services.

Table of Contents

. . . .

Acknowledgments

. . . .

Some of the most beautiful things in Nature are the giant Sequoia and Redwood trees that grow in Ruth's native California. Nature, in her wisdom, only allows new growth of these trees to come from destruction of the seed pod by fire. It was through personal destruction and pain our cause was born.

At the top of the list to thank are the thousands of anonymous people who visit with us virtually at the website or by telephone to share their stories, seek advice, or look for support. They, in turn, launched the U.S. anti-bullying movement with their sacrifices.

Special thanks go to Daniel Levine, Employee Advocate extraordinaire, and Gary Purece for his insights. We are blessed with experts who encourage the introduction of bullying to the U.S.—Andy Ellis, Susan Marais-Steinman, and Tim Field from overseas and academic affiliates of the Campaign Against Workplace Bullying—David Yamada, Loraleigh Keashly, and Joel Neuman. Mindy Werner-Crohn, M.D., June Chewning, and Carol Fehner help in special ways beyond description. April Harper, Australian eagle eye and advocate, improved the text with her insightful, sensitizing comments.

We acknowledge the support of those closest and dearest to our hearts: Helen Williams, who has been with us since the beginning and our sons, Sean, Rob, and Macario.

Special thanks to the Sourcebooks team are extended to Dominique Raccah for embracing the significance of the anti-bullying movement, to Todd Stocke and Jennifer Fusco for strengthening the manuscript, and to all the clever, creative, and committed production and promotion people—Eric O'Malley, Todd Schuetz, and Vicki Frye.

Finally, thanks for the steadfast love from Ike Namie. He made the Campaign, the book series, and the future all possible.

Preface

· ·

The Campaign Against Workplace Bullying was begun in January 1, 1998, on the Internet (www.bullybusters.org) and incorporated as a nonprofit education, research, and advocacy organization on November 4, 1998. It was immediately recognized as the national clearinghouse for learning about bullying. Targets seeking advice came by the thousands; reporters broke the silence about bullying with facts, people, and outrage found at the site.

The San Francisco Bay Area-based Campaign grew from Ruth and Gary Namie's employee advice and coaching service begun in 1996, itself an extension of their consulting work begun in 1985. Dr. Ruth, a psychotherapist with a doctorate in clinical psychology, directs the individual support projects. Dr. Gary is a social-organizational psychologist with a background in university teaching, behavioral research, and workplace consulting.

The Campaign talks to more Targets than anyone in America. We have personally coached thirty-seven hundred people. The lessons from those conversations, coupled with the research we conduct, gives us a unique perspective of the bullying phenomenon.

The cause, in general, and the Campaign Against Workplace Bullying, in particular, owe much to progress made by sexual harassment advocates.

We also have borrowed wisdom from the child abuse and domestic violence movements. The victims in each situation and Targets have much in common. Child and spousal abuse are more relevant than the multitude of business and management fads that dot the consulting landscape. Bullying truly crosses traditional boundaries of work, life, leisure, pathology, the law, and organizational dysfunction.

The Mission of the grassroots Campaign is twofold:

1. to raise public awareness (of bullying) and initiate a national dialogue, and
2. to create and promote solutions for individuals and workplaces.

Focus areas for the Campaign are:

- Public Awareness Education
  (the U.S. National Conference, public Town Hall Meetings, promotion of Freedom From Bullies At Work Week, BullyBuster Awards, this book series, and the website)
- Support for Bullied Individuals
  (telephone coaching, grassroots peer support network)
- Research
  (online surveys, presentations at scientific and professional conferences)
- Guidance for Employers
  (design of integrated solutions to address bullying)
- Social Change
  (support for public policy and law reform)
- Alliances with Organizations and Individuals
- The Work Trauma Institute
  (continuing professional education for attorneys, physicians, and mental health professionals)

The First Campaign Survey

On Labor Day 1998, the Campaign released results from its first online survey. In all, 154 Targets and 46 witnesses completed surveys. Sixty-six Targets also completed a questionnaire about the aftermath of their bullying situations.

Though the sample was not a randomly representative group, thus rendering the study a "non-scientific" one, it was a rare look inside many of our unhealthy workplaces.

Major Survey Findings

1. Bullying is different from the more recognizable issues that plague the workplace—sexual harassment, racial discrimination, and violence. Both women and men are victimized as Targets and serve as perpetrators.
2. Falling prey to a bully's destructive tactics is a career hazard; it is not about gamesmanship or a fair competition among equals. Bullies commonly adopt surprise and secrecy to gain leverage over Targets.
3. Targets are a diverse group of normal, talented people.
4. Bullying devastates the Target's emotional stability and can last a long time.
5. The employer, as an organization, bears partial responsibility for the systematic disassembly of a once productive employee by a mean-spirited, one-person wrecking crew.

The expanded set of findings appears in the Appendix. Key findings are sprinkled throughout the text.

Introduction

. . . .

A simple truth: to stop a bully from turning you into a Target, just firmly announce that her behavior (when she decides to test your resistance) will not be accepted without her running the risk that it will be reported immediately to both a private lawyer and the company's legal team. Gesture that she has one chance to stop now (palm of your raised hand facing her) and that she consider the consequences of continuing her childish, embarrassing behavior.

Easy to say, right? Easy to understand and dream about, too. But nearly impossible to do. If it were *just that simple*, you would have done it in the first place and skipped all the misery from being the bully's Target.

All the pain now felt comes not from that single missed opportunity alone, but from the postponement of taking action to right the wrong. Nipping it in the bud, people call it. But using another old saying, *it's all water under the bridge*, the current situation requires you to stop the hurt now however you can.

BullyProofing Comes First

Based on the thousands of individuals we have coached and have spoken with through the first Internet site in the U.S. dedicated to workplace bullying, we at the Campaign Against Workplace Bullying developed a two-phase approach for individuals:

Phase 1: BullyProofing to Stop the Hurt

Phase 2: BullyBusting to Topple the Tyrant

By first becoming proficient at BullyProofing yourself, you can prevent the bully from getting inside your head, of convincing you that lies are truths. Going to work need not jeopardize your health.

Once you've restored your self-respect and dignity at work, you then have to decide how to get the bully off your back now and forever. Some people are ready to begin bringing the bully down when first assaulted because they were more enraged than wounded. This does not make them superior, smarter, stronger, better, or more valuable. Those rare birds simply have a different way of responding to nasty, brutal attackers.

Caution: if you are not one of those who can go directly to Phase 2 (and most of us are not), do not try to take action while still vulnerable or reeling from assaults from the bully. If you do, you will most probably fail. There is a time to counterattack and a time to heal.

Phase 1 is about regrouping, healing, and retaking what was stolen from you—self-confidence, the belief in your competence, and goodness. BullyProofing can be accomplished alone or with trusted family and friends. It does not require a public commitment to action.

After BullyProofing yourself, you are less likely to be a future Target.

Phase 2 is the public reclaiming of your dignity. You will need all the energy your mind and soul can muster to rid the workplace of the creep who makes life miserable for you. BullyBusting requires incredible organization and selling skills.

How the Book Is Organized

Section One: Workplace Bullying

Chapters 1 through 6 define the phenomenon. We introduce the players—bullies, those who cause misery in the workplace, and Targets, the recipients of the misery. We attempt to explain why bullying occurs in the first place and why witnesses are so reluctant to act swiftly to stop it.

We provide an elementary history of the anti-bullying movement begun in Europe. The international and domestic legal landscape is then surveyed. Here in the U.S., the picture is bleak if you are counting on the current justice system to help. Instead of waiting for a future law to appear, the final chapter in this section suggests how others who want to help can do so and what you need to know to act as a smart consumer of help offered by "institutional helpers."

Section Two: BullyProof Yourself to Stop the Hurt

This section is a cluster of chapters describing various techniques and tools that can overcome self-defeating traps that bullied Targets fall into. Most of the chapters have practical exercises to guide individuals from the negative to the positive. It is the toolkit part of the book, the heart of BullyProofing yourself. To be BullyProof is to reclaim stolen dignity and denied self-respect.

Section Three: BullyBusting to Topple the Tyrant

First, the targeted person's readiness is questioned. Fighting back too early in the cycle of emotional reactions to bullying can worsen matters. Next, we detail our approach to BullyBusting, to be undertaken only if and when you're ready. It is an elaborate process to make your case internally, either before or without a legal case. There are vast resources organized against the individual employee and the likelihood of success is low, but we also review the personal reasons to engage in the battle. Finally, we address the question of leaving a job when personal sacrifices are unreasonably high.

If you have a spouse or life-partner who also shares the experience, the journey out of Targethood must be taken by you both. Therefore, it is a good idea to have that person and caring acquaintances become familiar with the first section of the book, to be able to share the terminology and to appreciate the seriousness of your situation.

You Are Not Alone!

. . . .

Workplace Bullying: Silent Epidemic, National Scandal

Chapter One:

Bullying at Work

. . . .

All the great things are simple, and many can be expressed in a single word:
freedom, justice, honor, duty, mercy, hope. —Sir Winston Churchill

Bullying at work is the repeated, malicious verbal mistreatment of a Target (the recipient) by a harassing bully (the perpetrator) that is driven by the bully's desire to control the Target. That control is typically a mixture of cruel acts of deliberate humiliation or interference and the withholding of resources and support preventing the Target from succeeding at work. The most important defining characteristic is that the bully's actions damage the Target's health and self-esteem, relations with family and friends, economic livelihood, or some combination of them all.

Bullying encompasses all types of mistreatment at work. All harassment is bullying as long as the actions have the effect, intended or not, of hurting the Target. Without harm felt, the tyrant's maneuvers are not bullying.

Perpetrators are women and men who torment women and men of all races and ages, in all workplaces, regardless of size or type of business.

Though bullying begins as one-on-one harassment, troubles for Targets are complicated by each inappropriate or inadequate response to the cruelty by employers, institutional helpers, and the legal system. All contribute to sustaining the cruelty. Remarkably, the organization's resources are predictably marshaled in support of the bully instead of the wronged Target. From the Target's perspective, the work world has colluded against her to do her harm.

Unchecked one-on-one bullying quickly escalates into a hostile, poisoned workplace where everyone suffers. If ignored long enough, the entire organization is placed at risk, facing preventable trauma or litigation.

Understanding BullySpeak

BullySpeak is a vocabulary that we deliberately choose to use so that we neither offend crusaders for other social justice causes nor confuse the individuals we attempt to support through the Campaign Against Workplace Bullying.

Female is the preferred gender

We use the pronoun "she" throughout the text to describe both the Target, the recipient of mistreatment at work, and the bully, the perpetrator. We need to expand harassment's definitional boundaries beyond the narrow "protected class" Equal Employment Opportunity categories of female, minority, older, and disabled workers. Also, the majority of advice seekers who contact us are women who are stalked by women bullies. We are not ignoring men. Male Targets, a large 30 percent minority, need only mentally substitute pronouns throughout the text. They can ask a woman for help seeing the world from the other side; she's been doing it for a lifetime.

Targets and bullies

Out of respect to Targets, with whom we sympathize, we always capitalize the word "Targets." We capitalize the word "bullies" if the word happens to begin a sentence.

Targets merely had the bad fortune to run into a bully too lazy to acquire the insight about her personal list of deficiencies, her lack of self-esteem. A Target drifts in, and hopefully out of, the crosshairs of the bully's scope. Target status can be temporary or it can drone on for years.

Targets, not victims

Bullies select Targets to harm. Targets are recipients of unrelenting verbal assaults that cut to the core of the Target's being. Over time, the Target's personality gets trampled, bent out of recognition even to herself. When Targets see themselves as victims, two undesirable things can happen:

1. if they have a personal history of being exploited by others in their family or in other relationships, victimhood lures them back to a painful time. Once there, victims find it harder to act to reverse their situation. Bullying is certainly re-traumatizing for those with prior experience. This affects the intensity of the damages done; it does not justify the bully's actions nor relieve the employer of responsibility for putting the Target in harm's way and not protecting her when the bullying is reported.

2. victimhood begets powerlessness, helplessness, and an inability to change matters for the better.

BullyProofing is about reclaiming dignity and self-respect. We are eternally optimistic that the situations Targets find themselves in get better.

Targets Don't Deserve or Want What They Get

Bullies Are Liars and Cowards!

Bullying, not abuse

Abusers have victims. Battered spouses and children deserve to have the terms abuse and victim reserved for them because they suffer physical violence unlike

Targets of bullying. Workplace bullying involves abuse of power, but we shy away from using the term abuse whenever possible.

Cheerleaders for corporate competition are quick to denigrate victims as deserving their fate. Wrong! Bullied Targets no more like the torment they endure than rape victims are likely to invite the rapist. The anti-bullying movement is not asking for pity from the morally bankrupt.

Folks in Britain coined the phrase "Workplace Bullying." It is an instantly recognizable term to Americans. Every time we stand in line at a store, sit at an airport, or talk to a reporter, we get to hear someone's memory of torment at work, either theirs or a friend's. It is that common, a "silent epidemic" ready to be pushed into the light of day (or to face press and media scrutiny as defined in the modern world).

Bullying—Familiar Yet Different

Illegal sexual harassment is a special type of harassment. All sexual harassment is also bullying. Bullying, defined as "generalized workplace abuse," was four times more prevalent than sexual harassment in a study of several work-related groups at the University of Illinois at Chicago (J. Richman, *American Journal of Public Health*, 1999).

Bullying is rarely illegal. Either the law does not apply at all or the legal options make the case too difficult to build. Harassment or discriminatory treatment—if unrelated to gender, race, age, or any of the other Title VII (of the Civil Rights Act) protected class categories—are invisible in the eyes of current U.S. law.

"Protection" is a misnomer. Laws on the books are routinely ignored in the American workplace anyway. Sexual harassment and the hostile work environment are pervasive. The hostility continues despite millions of dollars invested in corporate training claiming to prevent or stop it. The attitude seems to be a challenge to "sue me" by employers who can outspend and outlast any lone plaintiff.

The presence of a law simply gives one the "right to sue." In turn, that means placing yourself in financial jeopardy at the hands of an attorney, pro-corporate judge, or jury whose decisions can be overruled easily over the course of several years. Even when the settlement or award is paid, the payoff hardly justifies prolonging the agony that bullying started. Legal solutions are rarely satisfying.

Schoolyard bullying—the torment of one child by another—is often compared to workplace bullying. Both types share common underlying principles—the desperate grab for control by an insecure inadequate person, the exercise of power through the humiliation of the Target. School-age bullies, if reinforced by cheering kids, fearful teachers, or ignorant administrators, grow up as dominating people. If it works for them, there is no reason to change. At work as adults, they do what they do best—bully others. An unknown percentage of workplace bullies have a lifelong record of disrespecting the needs of others. Of course, the cues given off in a super-competitive workplace will draw out the dark side of many others who were not bullies in a prior life, witnesses perhaps, but rarely Targets.

The stakes for workplace bullying are more serious than in the school. Bullying threatens the economic livelihood not only of the Target but the Target's family. When a bully decides to capriciously untrack a Target's career, years of investment in terms of time and money are at risk. Finally, the most important difference—the one that distinguishes our approach to solutions—is that the child Target *must* have the help and support of third-party adults to reverse the conflict. Bullied adults have the primary responsibility for righting the wrong, for engineering a solution. When others intervene on their behalf—as when a more aggressive, well-intentioned spouse takes over finding the solution—the Target suffers additional consequences from giving away her independence.

Incivilities and rudeness rarely trigger stress in the people who experience them. Toe picking, knuckle cracking, belching, and nostril reaming are all offensive and undignified. However, they reflect only on the socialization of the picker, cracker, belcher, and reamer. It's not bullying until the bully does something to the Target. If the bully picks the Target's toes (against her wishes) or picks her nose (without permission) and this offensive behavior hurts her emotionally, it could be bullying. Social mistakes not expressly done to affect another person may be cute to talk about, but they do not qualify as bullying according to our criteria.

Chris Pearson, Ph.D., is an "incivilities" researcher. Her survey of workers who admitted they were the targets of rudeness or disrespect revealed that 12 percent felt compelled to leave their jobs. Our survey of bullied Targets demonstrated that 75 percent had to leave their jobs to make the bullying go away.

When employers complain of incivility, they can dodge responsibility for establishing the toxic culture at work. It is easy then to blame troubles on the conflicting personality of "those" employees.

Workplace violence certainly grabs headlines, but they are misleading. Workers face the greatest risk of assault from customers, clients, robbers, scorned lovers, and strangers. Violence between workers, of the same or different rank, accounted for only 11 percent of workplace homicides, according to the University of California-Berkeley Labor Occupational Health Program's 1997 findings. How is bullying related to this dramatic, albeit rare, worker-on-worker violence?

A bully-tolerant workplace can be quite pathological, gripped in fear, with everyone, including management, too petrified to hold the bully accountable for her unforgivable behavior. The bully routinely practices psychological violence against her Target. Yet, she rarely has to resort to physical violence or threats of it to satisfy her control needs. Violent outbursts follow frustration about not having some needs met. Bullies are in charge and rarely frustrated. Some bullies do threaten violence, but nearly all bullies are content to damage people without fists or weapons.

There is a highly profitable workplace violence "industry" created by management consultants who don't want employers to hear the 11 percent figure. They want employers to fear employees. That illogical fear convinces employers to pay huge fees for psychological testing of non-supervisory employees and of pre-hire job applicants. Testing is wrong for two reasons. First, an uncritical acceptance of testing places a premium on personality as the cause of all action. In reality, hostile workplaces, in other words, situations and circumstances, coerce people to do strange things. A second error is to omit testing management, who comprise 89 percent of the pool of bullies according to our research. Therefore, the perpetrators are exempt from having their own aggressive impulses detected.

The industry experts, acting as sycophants for management, busily and expensively ferret out lower-level workers who appear to pose a potential risk to become violent and affix the scarlet letter "V." Many ex-law enforcement types work in the "industry" which helps maintain the notion that employees are fraudulent, not trustworthy, and simply are waiting to explode with guns blazing. Zero-tolerance clauses also enable a manager to provoke a worker over the course of several years and to terminate her immediately if she dares to react emotionally with a verbal threat. The workplace has become a police state for some based on irrational fears.

> One federal worker, a mother with kids in child care, was dragged away unceremoniously from work in handcuffs when she innocently commented that since her workplace was hell (and she had her bully to blame for that) she could sympathize with postal workers who had become violent because no one listened to them either. She not only lost her job, she was prohibited to contact her children while she wrangled with law enforcement that night.

Are bullied Targets a violence risk? In the rarest of circumstances, a Target, after years of mistreatment at the hands of tyrant and inaction by the employer, saw no alternative and turned to violence.

> One man killed himself and his branch manager of the state agency on the day of his return from recuperation from a heart attack induced by that manager. The manager greeted him in the parking lot and provoked him before entering the office. The man, described as very gentle and caring by all who knew him, got in his car and drove away, only to return minutes later with a loaded gun. His co-workers considered the killings a tragedy only because of the suicide. It turns out that the branch manager was a favorite in the state capitol. His reputation was as a "turnaround guy" who cracked the whip in each of the several offices to which he was assigned. Staff turnover, workers' compensation, and disability claims were his legacy. He was hated by employees, though encouraged and respected by the folks in the central office who generally disrespected their workforce.

Post-shooting analysts carefully have to dissect each episode of workplace violence. If the shooter selects certain people, then we at the Campaign are reasonably sure that those victims had previously frustrated the person by ignoring or denying repeated complaints about mistreatment at work. That is, when the victims are an EEO officer, a human resources staffer, or the boss of the bully, then we can attribute the violence to unaddressed bullying. Sadly, the knee-jerk, simplistic story told is that the shooter was a wacko. Reporters interview the bullying supervisor who defames the employee as a poor performer "with troubles" as the body is being loaded into the coroner's wagon.

It is more likely that Targets direct the violence inward and commit suicide. Given the roles shame and humiliation play in their lives, Targets have great difficulty getting out of bed and often suffer from depression. By the time they kill themselves, they have lost their marriages, their homes, their children, and all hope of surviving economically. It was bullying that probably drove them out of the job and started the decline in the quality of their lives in the first place. Unfortunately, the link between the suicide and the cruel mistreatment and subsequent loss of the job is less obvious than the trail of bodies in a public shooting rampage. A federal agency union representative knew of nine suicides in one year in her region directly attributable to bullying.

On a scale of damage one could suffer at work, incivilities would fall near the low end. Bullying would cover a wide middle range of destructive, intimidating workplace practices. Physical violence appears at the high end, score 10.

Severity of Damage

The most important difference between workplace violence and bullying is that the latter is a daily occurrence for many. Violence is rare, but bullying is estimated to affect one in five workers in the U.S. workforce (according to Keashly, "A Year 2000 Scientific Survey of Michigan Residents"). Headlines about violence regrettably distract the public from addressing the more prevalent phenomenon of bullying that destroys the lives, careers, and families of millions.

The Campaign, Catalyst for Change

Workplace bullying is a serious threat to:

- Freedom from fear and trauma
- Employee health and safety
- Civil rights in the workplace
- Dignity at work
- Personal self-respect
- Family cohesion and stability
- Workteam morale and productivity
- Employment practices liability
- Retention of skilled employees
- Employer reputation

Bullying is a multi-faceted problem which requires multi-disciplinary solutions:

- Behavioral and organizational researchers
- Medicine
- Mental health practitioners
- Legal resources
- Organized labor
- Employee advocates
- Management and human resources
- Dispute-resolution specialists
- Education
- Government

It is an uphill fight to be sure. In our media-saturated world, messages for and about regular workers are rare. One former business reporter was so frustrated by the fawning over CEOs, investors, entrepreneurs, and consumers that he started an online magazine—www.disgruntled.com. There, he is able to tell stories from the employee's point of view. Daniel Levine is one of those rare advocates for employees. His 1998 book, *Disgruntled: The Darker Side of the World of Work*, speaks with a candor rarely seen in the mainstream press or heard in broadcasts. We join *Disgruntled* in the fight.

Silence and shame ensure that bullying will never stop. We must work to uncover and reverse the atrocities, one person, one company, and one law at a time.

Do not wait for leaders; do it alone, person to person.   ——Mother Teresa

Chapter Two:

Understanding Bullies

. . . .

*There is overwhelming evidence that the higher the level of
self-esteem, the more likely one will be to treat others with
respect, kindness, and generosity.* ——Nathaniel Branden

It normally takes two to make a relationship grow from an initial spark. This is true for love and for some exploitative relationships, too. In most couples, each person wants something. Otherwise nothing develops. Ideally, in a partnership, each person needs the other in some way.

However, the Target-bully pathological "relationship" is different because:

- the Target is swept into the relationship involuntarily simply because the employer put the Target in harm's way by work assignment and then insisted that the battered partner not be allowed to escape without significant sacrifice.
- the bully controls every aspect of the reign of terror—when to attack, when to hold back, the place, and the audience.
- mutual benefit or gain is not the goal, control is, and the Target wants none of it.
- the undermining, scheming bully's tactics are so unwelcome, inappropriate, and undeserved that in no way can the Target be held responsible, even partially responsible.

- it is impossible to rationalize that the Target benefits.
- bullies need Targets to live; Targets find it hard to live when bullies intrude in their lives.

The people have always some champion whom they set over them and nurse into greatness....This and no other is the root from which a tyrant springs. —Plato

Origins of Bullies

People arrive at bullyhood by at least three different paths: through personality development, by reading cues in a competitive, political workplace, and by accident.

Chronic Bullies

The chronic bully tries to dominate people in nearly every encounter— at work and away from work. She bullies waitresses at restaurants as well as workplace Targets. She says, "I can't help it. It's just who I am. Don't like it? Leave," always believing that she does not have to change. Who could argue with her "success"?

The chronic bully's motivation is her own failure to confront her deepest feelings of personal inadequacy, her self-loathing. Unfortunately, she was not raised to analyze herself with the goal of improving herself. The self-control required to admit and overcome her shortcomings is applied painfully to those she seeks to dominate. She invents flaws in others (which are mirror images of her own), then irrationally attacks them to feel good about herself.

Bullies Are Inadequate, Defective, and Poorly Developed People

Targets Are Empathic, Just, and Fair People

She probably was a brash, bratty kid at school. Schoolyard bullies who were never stopped in childhood grow up to bully others in the workplace. Because people react to her either with fear or indifference, she's used to getting her way in every situation in which she exerts herself. It's a self-reinforcing cycle. She dominates, others submit or turn away in silence, so she dominates more. In companies that promote cutthroat competition, chronic bullies are over-represented. They are seen as "leaders."

Chronic bullies are trapped by their personality honed over a lifetime. At this late in the game, they couldn't change even if they wanted. It is true that some chronic bullies have certifiable character disorders—either Antisocial or Narcissistic Personality disorders. In the general population, these types of people are statistically rare, hovering around 2 to 3 percent, according to the DSM-IV, the classification guide to mental disorders published by the American Psychiatric Association.

These are the most malevolent, mean-spirited, and nasty people at work. They manipulate everyone on some level. They inflict harm on others. Chronic bullies end careers and shatter the emotional lives of their targets. And Targets tell us frequently that staring into the face of their bully, they swear they are looking at the devil personified. Some bullies delight in humbling other people into subservience. Their cruelty is so satisfying, they cannot stop their evil smirk when they sense public victory. A small number of bullies are undeniably sadistic. They love torturing others.

Targets should know that simply labeling the bully a sociopath or psychopath does not change the situation or excuse the bully. Most important, dwelling on the bully's relatively permanent personality distracts Targets and those who want to help them from changing the work environment. Except for the rare personality disordered types, all bullies can be made to respond to workplace rewards and punishment.

As a Target, you need to be less concerned with *why* bullies do what they do and most concerned with how to stop the hurt they inflict (BullyProofing yourself) or how to bring them down (BullyBusting).

Opportunist Bullies

The opportunist bully is the one you're most likely to encounter at work. She is a master at reading cues from the workplace. If competition is encouraged, she knows that beating up other people will lead to winning. Only "wimps" would stand in a competitor's path and have her slow down to pay attention to how people might be injured. Opportunists are the "climbers."

The opportunist differs from the chronic bully in that when she is away from work, she's able to suspend her competitive nature. She's capable of being charming and supportive—she might even host a youth group meeting in her home. She's a great mother, churchgoer, neighborhood activist, and good citizen.

At work, when the opportunity presents itself to compete to move ahead, she steps over a Target who she thinks might be a contender for the same prize or a person blocking her success. She justifies her behavior to herself as her survival instinct kicking in. She believes, "It's all part of the game." But to the opportunist bully, games are serious business. Careers are built with political gamesmanship.

She is likely to be well-connected up the chain of command, to have allies willing to shield her from punishment for her malicious behavior. Her supporters think she can do no wrong. Targets have a hard time having their case heard against her. Accusations are written off as "sour grapes" by "wimps" or "losers." After all, this bully is the personification of "the American dream."

Though companies preach cooperation and teamwork, the opportunist knows what is actually rewarded. Like the chronic bully, her behavior is governed by reinforcement. Unlike the chronic bully, she will stop hassling others if the organization began to punish the mistreatment of others. The opportunist is a keen reader of signals in her environment. By changing the workplace culture, opportunist bullies can be stopped.

When companies lay off ten thousand employees to maintain their profit margins to satisfy Wall Street investors—a deliberate act of malice—how do they justify it? With the belief, "It's just business, nothing personal." Those moments of seizing market opportunities without regard to consequences for humans make organizations just like opportunist bullies.

Accidental Bullies

Bullies by accident are benign. The benign accidental bully is simply a social fool. The accidental bully is truly *unaware* of the effect of her actions on other people. She operates as if the rest of the world does not exist. She's awkward and child-like.

She hurts others with inappropriate comments or actions. She insults with sexist or personal affronts. She starts to show you how to do something new, then does the job herself because she lacks the patience to wait. She never learned the subtlety of social interactions.

The remarkable thing about the benign accidental bully is that when confronted, she retreats immediately and apologizes. She never does it again. She *can* learn social skills.

Substance Abusing Bullies

The substance abusing bully is very dangerous and threatening because she may not be in control of her decisions at all. According to experts, 74 percent of substance abusing Americans are employed. They do not live on sewer grates or in homeless shelters. They go to cubicles, stores, and factory floors just like regular people do.

When drugs enter the picture, all assumptions about rationality and logic are tossed out the window. The bully who snorts powder up her nose as routinely as she puts on lipstick is a potentially crazed animal. Most substances that hook people are disinhibiting. That means the control mechanism that monitors social politeness and decorum is shut off. Anything goes for the person under the influence. Unpredictable mood swings become commonplace. Marijuana and alcohol are depressing and induce lethargy and paranoia. Has your bully been a bit too morose, too bug-eyed? Stimulants like methamphetamines create psychotic-like episodes, true craziness, with a healthy dose of paranoia. Cocaine habits are expensive. It's not the rank-in-file Suzy six-pack that drives from the 'burbs into the downtown ghetto in Beamers and Mercedes to buy her supplies. Rank, which begets higher salaries, enables higher-ups to maintain a life of using.

We know that 89 percent of bullies are bosses. Drug testing is ordered by management for their subordinates. Therefore, most drug-using bosses whose altered states may account for much of the chaos and madness Targets endure remain undetected, free from the privacy-robbing experience of peeing in a cup.

Bullies: Types, Tactics, and Tips for Handling

The Campaign Survey Says . . .

Top Ten Bullying Tactics

1. Blame for "errors"
2. Unreasonable job demands
3. Criticism of ability
4. Inconsistent compliance with rules
5. Threatens job loss
6. Insults and put-downs
7. Discounting/denial of accomplishments
8. Exclusion, "icing out"
9. Yelling, screaming
10. Stealing credit

Bullies are workplace politicians. Their goal is simple—to control people they target. To do this, they engage in a variety of tactics. Regardless of the tactics adopted, they all serve to shame, humiliate, and treat the Target like a powerless person. In a bully's mind, Targets are powerless. This distorted thinking is the only way bullies know how to survive the work world, at someone else's expense.

Bullies Start All Conflict and Trouble.

Targets React.

Bullies can be categorized. But individuals who choose to bully can adopt any tactic at any time to accomplish their goal. They are not restricted to neat categories. They adopt one or more styles, as needed. A short list of illustrative tactics accompanies each type of bully. The list is not meant to be exhaustive. You can probably think of many more tricks each type plays.

Constant Critic

Extremely negative. Nitpicker. Perfectionist. Whiner. Complainer. Fault finder. Liar. Masks personal insecurity with public bravado. Loved by senior management because of her ability to "get those people to produce." Plays parent to your child (as she sees it). Aims to destroy confidence, encourages self-doubt. Satisfies her need to control with obsession over others' performance.

- put-downs, insults, belittling comments, name-calling
- constant haranguing about Target's "incompetence"
- makes aggressive eye contact, glaring at the Target; demands eye contact when she speaks but deliberately avoids eye contact when Target speaks
- negatively reacts to Target contributions with sighs, frowns, peering over top of eyeglasses to condescend, sour face (the "just sucked a lemon" look)
- accuses Target of wrongdoing, blames Target for fabricated errors (doctored documents, compromised databases, fake witness accounts)
- makes unreasonable demands for work with impossible deadlines, applies disproportionate pressure, expects perfectionism
- sends signals of disrespect through over-confident body language—sitting at a desk with feet up, showing Target bottom of shoes and talking to Target through feet, grooms self (hair, nails) while ignoring the Target; making target sit while bully stands, hovering over, staying above

- overuses memos, e-mails, messages to bury Target in correspondence requiring replies
- personally criticizes aspects of the Target's life that are irrelevant to work—appearance, family, friends
- excessively or harshly criticizes Target's work or abilities
- engages Target in intense cross-examination to belittle and confuse

Why the Constant Critic Acts As She Does

Many of us work with someone who is extremely negative and nit-picking, someone who never seems satisfied. It might be a perfectionist who relentlessly finds fault or an insecure colleague who criticizes your work with the intention of making you feel small. She uses whining, complaints, and criticism to make everyone else feel insecure. How do you deal with someone whose faultfinding is hard to take and stop them from undermining you own sense of competence?

To improve your situation with a critic at work, it is critical to uncover and understand why she acts this way. Then it will be easier to stand up to her and not get destroyed by her negativity.

Four things most often seen in the Constant Critic are:

1. The person who deliberately sees that they have an obligation, a reason for living, that states they must find something wrong with everything everyone else does. You will find that this person once had someone in their life who was extremely critical and demanding. This may have been a father, mentor, or boss. From these experiences, the Constant Critic has the impression that an intelligent person naturally acts this way. Perhaps this critic once was humiliated or lost a job or business because they were too tolerant of other people's mistakes. In either case, the Critic then made a conscious decision to be sure they are always on top of things in the future.

2. It is essential to remember that no matter what originally made this person so finicky and unpleasant, she cannot rest or relax until some probing uncovers something for her to complain or worry about.

3. The Critic has a tone of voice or a way of speaking that is hard to take. When she finds fault with your work for the umpteenth time, it is not just the words that hurt, it is the tone of the voice or way of speaking that cuts to the bone. Whether it is a whiny tone, a flat monotone or a staccato way of snapping out criticisms.

4. Because the Critic constantly struggles to stay in control of every situation, it is almost impossible for her to feel that someone else might also be right. It is more important for her to defend her position than to sit down and brainstorm about solutions to the immediate problem. A constant state of worry and dissatisfaction feels normal to her. She is extremely resistant to change and you will never be able to satisfy her.

Handling Tips

Humor: Using humor can work wonders for you as you go head-to-head with the Constant Critic. As soon as she starts to ask probing, fault-finding questions or begins to make critical remarks, take a deep breath and let it out as you say to yourself, "Thank goodness! My life would not be complete without this person's criticism." Don't say it out loud, only several times to yourself.

This simple phrase can prove to be a tool to take the sting out of potentially invalidating remarks. Using your own wit and sarcasm—in a safe and unspoken way, of course—gives you a protective distance that can't be taken away. Using your sense of humor also prevents the launch of your biochemical "fight or flight" stress response. Most importantly, this allows you to remain in control, to remain intelligent, and to preserve the dignity she desperately wants to take away.

Get a Second Opinion: When confronted by an Constant Critic who picks apart both your work and your worthiness, it's hard to not believe she is right. She seems to know exactly how to make you feel small, incompetent, or unworthy.

The most important thing for handling a nitpicker is to get a *reliable* second opinion to assess the Critic's criticisms and to identify:

- What part of her feedback is accurate and what is just her negative way of complaining about everything?
- What part of her feedback is useful to your work, and what part is incorrect, misinformed or just plain whiny?

Some possible sources for quick and useful second opinions are:

- a good friend or respected ally at work who could help you determine if any of the criticism is useful.
- someone you work with whom you can call in a crisis to give you reliable information about the accuracy of the Critics's comments and suggestions.
- a close friend, family member, counselor, or therapist who can help you regain your sense of self-confidence and professionalism even when you have just been torn apart.

When soliciting help from others, it is critical to identify the situation and ask exactly what you are looking for. As soon as possible after a Critic has belittled you or your work, call this supportive individual and explain, "I just left a meeting where I had a boom dropped on my head by (the bully). Would you please remind me that I do have the qualifications to be doing this work, and that I am an adult, and I do deserve to hold my head up even though (the bully) thinks I am an idiot."

Don't be afraid to ask for support. Whether looking for a second opinion or an emotional boost, be sure to make the phone call and get the support you need. People usually like to be asked for their expertise and their guidance. If the person you call is too busy at that moment to listen to your situation, find a more convenient time to talk or call another person who can give you the information you require.

Two-Headed Snake

Passive-aggressive indirect, dishonest style of dealing with people and issues. Pretends to be nice while sabotaging you. "Friendliness" serves only to decrease resistance to giving information she may later use against you. Smile hides naked aggression. Assassinates reputation with higher-ups. Plays favorites. Satisfies need for control by managing the image of the Target in other people's minds.

- ensures that the Target does not have the resources (time, supplies, help) to do work
- demands that co-workers provide damning "evidence" against Target, uses lies or half-truths, threatens non-cooperators (the "divide and conquer" technique)
- discriminates against smokers by requiring they gather trash from the parking lot while taking a smoke break
- assigns meaningless or "dirty" tasks as punishment
- makes nasty, rude, hostile remarks directly to Target while putting on a rational "face" for others
- breaches confidentiality; shares private information about the Target with co-workers or other bosses
- discriminates against non-smoking Target by permitting breaks only for smokers
- creates a special personnel file kept in bully's car or locked in her office full of defamatory information to sabotage Target's career inside or outside the organization
- steals credit for work done by the Target

Snakes pretend to be nice, but actually work against you. Beware! She is selfish and needs to be handled very carefully. Not at all a friend or mentor, the Snake's "friendliness" masks her attempts to gain control.

Two-Headed Snakes come in three varieties:

1. The "Backstabber" Snake: Quite simply, this person tells you one thing and then says something entirely different behind your back. They kiss up the ladder and attack those below. She tells you you're wonderful while telling her boss that she needs help getting rid of you because you cannot perform.

2. The "Jekyll and Hyde" Snake: This Snake's sweetness mask alternates with her mean streak. She tends to be vicious one minute, human and encouraging the next. Unfortunately, you may be the only one who sees both sides of this controller. Others who only see the sweet side are unsympathetic to your complaints.

3. The "No Problem, Don't Bother" Snake: These words, spoken by certain individuals, are often a warning that trouble follows. Snakes tell you "no problem" after they have violated the rules and they want to cover it up. They are unethical creatures and expect help carrying out their unethical plans.

Handling Tips

Enlist Supporters: Don't feel alone and unsupported when someone mistreats you at work. Don't dismiss everyone around you as dishonest. However, take time to talk with a trusted friend or counselor to help you sort out your feelings. When talking to your supporters at work (the ones you know you can trust and the ones you have decided you can talk to) you will probably find you are not the only one who has been mistreated by the Two-Headed Snake. Carefully identify a supporter by asking:

- Have they ever experienced any similar problems with this Snake?

- Are they willing to brainstorm with you on ways to improve the situation without anyone having to take on the Two-Headed Snake alone?
- Would they be willing to back you up if you stood up to the Snake? Get clear about supportive action you expect.
- Would they be willing to join you in a meeting to confront the situation directly?

Do's and Don'ts When Jousting with the Snake: Resist lowering yourself into a dirty, nasty street fight. Snakes are obsessed with appearances—they want to appear cool and collected most of the time. Staying emotionally in control is easier with Snakes than with other bully types.

Be clear that you will not tolerate or cooperate with misleading or dishonest statements to help the Snake lie.

Be prepared for this person to argue, threaten, lie, or try most anything to coerce you into cooperating with her. Keep repeating what you consider unacceptable behavior and what you will and what you will not do.

Avoid waiting too long to bring up the problem or trying to transform or "fix" this bully.

The right words to say to a Snake often require practice. By practicing, you appear less defensive and are more likely to prevent yourself from verbally attacking the Snake (although it might feel good). Some discussion starters that allow you to maintain control:

"I want us to work together. Here's what we can do to make that happen..."

"There's a specific problem you and I can solve if we remember to..."

"There's something you do that I need to ask you to try to do a little differently next time..."

"There's a way you and I can improve our work situation. Are you interested?"

Though the above statements are rational and do not attack or criticize, don't be surprised when the Snake slips into denial. Snakes are bullies. Bullies are illogical. At least you tried.

When working with a Snake, you need to act the minute you suspect that she might be manipulating you. Ask for clarification regarding the specific procedures and results she is after. Your demand for clarity will frustrate the person who relies on clouding every interaction to feel in control. Clarity cuts through confusion. Others will respect you for it. In the process, the Snake's deviousness can be revealed to her supporters as well as enemies.

Gatekeeper

Most transparent of the controllers. She needs to establish herself as "one up" on you, to order you around or to control your circumstances. To her, control of all resources (time, supplies, praise, approval, money, staffing, help) is the most important aspect of work. She satisfies her need for control by putting herself in the middle of everything, making her feel important.

- deliberately cuts the Target out of the communication loop—stops mail, email, memo distribution, doesn't return calls
- refuses to make "reasonable accommodation" for a Target returning to work with a disability
- refuses to follow internal policies and government-mandated employee protections for Target
- denies privileges and rights to Targets who file complaints against the bully, either an internal complaint or a lawsuit or with the EEOC, DOL
- ignores the Target; gives the "silent treatment," and models isolation/exclusion for others
- sets office clocks fifteen minutes ahead of "real" time, then punishes Target for being late at start of day, while not allowing her to leave before quitting time according to "real" time
- makes up new rules on a whim, Target expected to follow, but bully is exempt

Handling Tips

There will be some time in every job when you are ignored. One of the games people play at work is the game of exclusion. Not inviting you to an important meeting, not sending a copy of an important memo, not letting you know about ongoing work in progress, or not including you in an important social gathering. This treatment is designed to make you feel invalidated and worthless.

This situation is quite different than dealing with a specific personality style who is difficult to work with. The Gatekeeper is not always a boss, but she might be someone you once considered a friend. By some change of circumstance, you and this person used to see eye to eye but now you are being treated with coldness or disrespect.

Why has this person changed?

Try and recall:

- What was it like when you initially met this person? How did you get along then?
- What changed?
- Did something change in the other person's workload or status at work thus making her more cold and rigid?
- Did something change in the other person's personal life— perhaps a financial situation making her more secretive or unapproachable?
- Was there an incident between you that left bad feelings?
- In what ways have your needs begun to clash with hers?
- Why does this bully feel the need to put up a wall or keep you at a distance?

Try to take her perspective:

- Were there clues early on that this individual was going to put up barriers toward you or others?
- Is this bully threatened by you being rewarded at work and is shutting you out of the loop?

- If you were in her shoes, would you have any reason to exclude others at work?
- Could you possibly remind this individual of someone else—a parent, sibling, spouse, ex-spouse, boss, or ex-boss—who gave this individual a hard time?
- In what way did you also put up a wall and feel the need to keep the other person at a distance?

In most cases it is not just the bully who has changed. Her actions could have caused you to put up your own wall:

- Does this bully irritate you or cause you to feel cold or distant?
- Does this person remind you of someone else—a parent, sibling, spouse, ex-spouse, boss or ex-boss—who gives you a hard time?
- Has something happened in your life that has made you a little more rigid or judgmental toward others?
- Is there something about the other person's style of doing things that you find frustrating, building tension between you?

To answer these questions, you will need to do more than just feel hurt. Talk to friends and co-workers about how they see your actions. If your first reaction is that this person doesn't like you or doesn't respect you, try and find out from colleagues if she has been under pressure lately. Maybe she is putting up a wall for reasons that have nothing to do with you. The more you find out about the way you are being treated, the more clarity you will have about the situation. Use a personal journal to detail your feelings.

Once you have a good handle on your feelings, find a way to actually discuss your feelings with the Gatekeeper. This heart-to-heart discussion may be hard to do, but it is the clearest way to find out what is happening. Plan where you want to stage this talk. The best place usually isn't at work. Try to plan a quiet time away from the office.

When you finally get to the point of staging this meeting, don't be discouraged if the Gatekeeper puts up resistance. Remember, this is a person you need to work with on a daily basis and conflicts need to be resolved. Don't be discouraged if it takes more than one try to set up a meeting.

Expect the beginning of the meeting to be awkward. Remember—this is why you are here. Once the ice is broken, address the problems you are having with the coldness you feel between the two of you. The success of this meeting will depend on your honesty and sincerity. Stating the issues simply and calmly will allow the Gatekeeper to listen to your words without becoming antagonistic and feeling the need to defend herself.

If the Gatekeeper will never agree to meet with you, much less listen to your feelings or needs, you will need to enlist the aid of someone in the office who will tell you when the Gatekeeper leaves you out of the loop. A co-worker who has good rapport with the Gatekeeper can act as a conduit or mediator. Don't be afraid or ashamed to ask this person to help you. Consider using a phrase such as, "I need a favor, (the bully) is giving me the cold shoulder and you seem to be on good terms with both of us. Can you help me arrange a meeting for the three of us to get together and clear this up?"

Dealing with a Gatekeeper can trigger feelings left from your past experiences—monitor your own reactions when you feel left out. Even if you think these past hurts are long forgotten and in your past, a frustrating situation can trigger emotions from long ago. You might need to work through the emotional issues through your personal journal, with a close friend, or a therapist. What did you do in the past at work when you have encountered a Gatekeeper? In the past, how did you get a Gatekeeper to take you seriously and stop excluding you? Thinking about and answering these questions should give you some good insight about your situation.

Remember that timing is everything and the situation can be resolved, but there are seldom overnight changes.

Screaming Mimi

Stereotypical, but statistically rare. Controls through fear and intimidation. Emotionally out of control. Impulsive. Volatile. Explosive. Threat of physical violence becomes issue. Wants to instill sense of dread. Overbearing. Self-centered, insensitive to needs of others. Very worried about being detected as imposter. Bombast masks incompetence. Satisfies need for control by dictating the emotional climate in front of audiences who are expected to tremble as a result.

- yells, screams, curses
- barks out loud often that "I AM THE BOSS!!!!" and "DO WHAT I TELL YOU!!!"
- poisons workplace with angry outbursts, tantrums
- intimidates through gestures: finger pointing, slams things down, throws objects
- crowds the Target's personal space, moves close to threaten or to make the Target anxious, hovers over, sneaks up from behind to startle
- constantly interrupts the Target during meetings and conversations
- discounts and denies Target's thoughts or feelings
- threatens job loss or punitive transfer
- traps Target by insisting that complaints go "up the chain of command," starting with her

Handling Tips

The Screaming Mimi can launch at any time. You immediately feel scolded or judged, as if you were a child. When you attempt to ignore or avoid conflict with a Screaming Mimi, she only sees your passivity as a welcome mat. The more you try to avoid her wrath, the more she will target you. Physical reactions are common in those who work with the Screaming Mimi. Complaints include:

- stomachaches
- headaches
- back spasms
- skin reactions

These symptoms frequently increase with prolonged exposure.

Your productivity decreases and costly mistakes occur more often when an angry person is breathing down your neck. The Screaming Mimi can make you hate your job, make you dread even going to work. A job you love can become a source of depression and this may lead to thoughts of career change. Work frustrations might carry over to your family life.

Protect yourself if someone attacks you personally. Convert feelings of powerlessness into a source of inner strength.

Here are five protection techniques to try:

The Silent Mantra: In meditation, the mantra is one of the most powerful ways to relax and stay centered in the midst of chaos. Find a yoga group or start your own meditation program. Then, as soon as the angry person starts to speak, repeat this mantra:

> *Hear the valuable stuff.*
> *Ignore the anger. It's not yours.*

This takes a little practice. Repeating this phrase silently to yourself when confronted by a verbal attack helps you to deflect the anger and maintain your inner strength. Each time you repeat the silent mantra, you will feel a little less affected by the Screaming Mimi.

Find the Vulnerable Spot: A second way to protect yourself and regain your composure is to find the vulnerable spot. Find and focus your attention on the most humorous spot of this person's appearance. Without letting the Screaming Mimi know what you are doing, simply think about the one feature of the bully's physical appearance you find most awkward. Remember to do this silently. Thus, instead of feeling intimidated or afraid of the bully's outburst, you can feel a renewed sense of inner strength because you are not taking her too seriously.

Keep a Journal: Whether or not anyone sees what you write, keep a journal. You need to get your anger out by writing phrases such as:

1. I hate you! You bitch!
2. You have no right to talk to me like that!
3. I am a team player. I'm not a sick workaholic like you.
4. Don't ever talk to me that way again in front of so
   many people.

Similarly, you could make entries like these:

1. I don't have to apologize for taking a vacation.
2. This storm will pass and, once again, people will remember
   that I've been doing a great job here.

Just remember to focus on what you can change and don't get overwhelmed by what you can't change.

Find the Right Words: Most people who are confronted by a Screaming Mimi tend to freeze without any idea of what to say. There are some specific ways in which you can respond in a professional way.

First response: "Stop! I don't appreciate being talked to like this."

This statement doesn't criticize the Bully, but states in an assertive and straightforward manner how you feel. It announces to her that you are a person with self-respect and professionalism. It also lets the other person know that you won't let her tromp all over you.

Second response: "Time out! I want to hear what you're saying,
but I've got to ask you to slow down a bit."

This gentler, more specific line is intended to be an invitation to the angry person. It is a way to encourage a non-critical response. Sometimes calling *time out* while putting your left hand facing down in a flat horizontal position with your right hand pointing up into the middle of your left hand you can remind the bully that she is dealing with a reasonable person rather than just someone to yell at.

Third response: "Let's talk about this. You go first and I won't interrupt.
Then when you're done, I'll see if I have any questions."

This line is more direct and managerial in nature. It sounds professional. You regain control of the situation instead of just becoming someone's verbal punching bag. You stop seeming like a victim and become the facilitator/director of the conversation. By letting the Screaming Mimi go first and assuring her that you won't interrupt, you can often short circuit a bully's anger. It also sets ground rules—if you courteously declare you won't interrupt them, it will be harder for them to interrupt you.

Understand Your Own Anger: This is the time to uncover your own anger-handling style. Many times, we hold back from being strong or effective with Screaming Mimis because anger stirs up some inner turmoil in ourselves that needs to be resolved. Growing up in a family where anger was not expressed can leave you without the confidence to deal with others' anger. Be sure to read the BullyProof toolkit chapter on anger. Become an expert at predicting your style of responding to angry others.

Workplaces Where Bullies Thrive

Much is made about the role of workplace culture in determining the level of satisfaction or dissatisfaction an employee experiences. Of course, the culture may be as sprawling as the company is large. Or culture can be contained within a single work group of employees under the control of one supervisor.

Companies and agencies whose main characteristic is denial about any problems give themselves the chance to avoid ever addressing problems because they simply do not exist. People addicted to drugs think like this. In Anne Wilson Schaef and Diane Fassel's classic *The Addictive Organization*, the point is amply illustrated that firms can operate with a common mindset not unlike that of an addict:

Good Employers Purge Bullies, Bad Ones Promote Them

1. *Denial of problems:* "We may have a minor problem, but not a major one."
2. *Confusion:* Company has trouble trying to predict what will happen next and how to deal with it.
3. *Dishonesty:* Company is focused on appearance—it is more about "packaging" and putting on a good front.
4. *Perfectionism:* Management pretends to know all possible solutions.
5. *Illusion of control:* Employees' feelings are seen as weaknesses.
6. *Scarcity principle:* Company encourages hoarding, getting more for yourself, cutthroat behavior.
7. *Ethical deterioration:* Company displays a spiritual void from the habits of lying, cheating, and stealing.
8. *Communication difficulties:*
   - Indirect—talking about a person through others rather than to that person
   - Abundant, but ineffective—lots of memos, but little is learned from them and the messages are not to be trusted
   - Secretive—about salaries, promotions, hiring, etc., "for their own good"
   - Skilled incompetence—excessive meetings, constant planning, no action
   - Preference for logical, rational, dualistic style— supposedly the facts only, black or white only
9. *Poor Thinking:*
   - Bad memory—lessons never learned, mistakes repeated
   - Tolerance for individuals dumping on others, instead of working out personal problems
   - Norm of dishonesty based on the belief that

in the organization, one can't succeed if honest
- Judgmental—people become bad, not their ideas or performance, a dread of evaluations
- Crisis orientation—distracts from doing routine work, initially exhilarating, but eventually exhausting
- Forcing people to take sides on issues—encourages co-dependent behavior

In workplaces characterized by the above list, an opportunistic bully could practice her craft without calling attention to herself. The company becomes the bully's accomplice. We know from our survey results that employers were seen as playing a vital role in sustaining, even if not directly contributing to, the bullying.

The Campaign Survey Says . . .

Targets Divide Responsibility for Bullying

Bullies:	59.5 percent responsible
Employer:	24 percent
Law/Society:	8.3 percent
Targets:	8.2 percent

This finding parallels the "hostile work environment" basis for sexual harassment charges. Any workplace that fosters bullying is certainly hostile.

Chapter Three:

Targethood:
An Undeserved Burden

. . . .

That's what it takes to be a hero, a little gem of innocence inside you
that makes you want to believe that there still exists a right and wrong,
that decency will somehow triumph in the end. —— Lise Hand

Bullies don't usually torment everyone. The factors that affect Target selection include: the depth of the bully's inadequacy, her own fluctuating self-esteem at any given moment, position at work, ability to bully without being punished, the Target's resistance, the amount of road rage siphoned off during the morning commute, time in the lunar calendar, and the Target's personality.

Are You Being Bullied?

__ 1.   Your co-worker or supervisor seems irritated or angry with you at least two times a week, although you always try your best to do quality work on time.

__ 2.   You often feel confused because she responds to your work efforts with criticism even when you have tried your hardest to do things "her" way.

__ 3.   You are upset with your working relationships. Your attempts at communication are constantly misunderstood and degraded.

    4. You constantly wonder, "What's wrong with me? No matter how hard I try to please her, I always feel that I have done something wrong."

    5. She rarely includes you in her plans for work although she expects you to fully understand what she wants you to do.

    6. She is either angry or "doesn't know what you are talking about" when you try to discuss work issues with her.

If you agree with two or more of these statements, you are probably bullied at work.

As bad as being bullied feels, it is natural to downplay its impact on your life for many reasons.

Target Types

The Campaign Survey Says...

Targets are Everywoman, Everyman

- ✓ 29.5 percent of Targets held a graduate or professional degree; 27.5 percent had a four-year college degree
- ✓ 78 percent of those surveyed were twenty-four to forty-six years old
- ✓ Employers were divided among private sector (59.3 percent), 25.3 percent in government, and 15.4 percent nonprofit firms

Ethical, Just, and Fair People

Targets don't have an integrity problem. Hypocrisy is a workplace and societal problem. Institutions fill their hallways with framed testaments spouting noble notions about "respect for individuals" and "courtesy and dignity for all." Yet, most ring hollow when employees pass daily and can snicker under their breath "nice frame." People working in the culture can tell anyone who bothers to ask if there is a fit between what really happens and the glowing phrases crafted at an expensive off-site retreat for executives and consultants. Employees know that integrity is about fit, of not having to falsify.

Targets who work in schools, in medical centers, in research university labs, in churches, and in nonprofit organizations dedicated to improving public health seem to expect their employers to both proclaim and act in accordance with higher moral goals than an auto shop. Of course, they are routinely disappointed. The school district may be honored with a Presidential award for excellence based on the work of a man who was chased away. The man's health was damaged and his career tossed to the rocks, but the tormenting district superintendent accepted the plaudits anyway. Bullies have no shame.

Nurses call the Campaign help line regularly. The same people tasked with saving lives of strangers turn on their own if they don't like someone's makeup or the car she drives.

The ethics gap deserves a fancy name, but there is none. It is the primary malady from which Targets suffer. It is clear that no workplace is immune to bullying. It happens in the "best" companies and in the ones where we might expect it for some stereotypical reason.

Targets have non-political, and therefore impractical, expectations about how organizations and people should treat each other with integrity. Whistleblowers take seriously the responsibility to see that schools funded to care for special kids not misuse the money. Tobacco industry insiders went public with information that belied the falsehoods the industry wanted the public to believe. Integrity is a very personal decision. Organizations get involved when someone in power wants to silence the one with integrity. The bullying starts small between two people. The entire organization enlists its goon squad when the morally superior whistleblower refuses to back down. Character assassination begins; the Target loses her job, family, friends, and her health. Was the Target's decision worth it?

Whistleblowers would tell you they'd do it all again given a chance. The truth compels them.

Targets also prize equity and justice. They believe that rewards should be proportional to talent. That's why it's so irksome when incompetent bullies steal ideas and get promoted. As you see below, Targets are almost always smarter than their bullies. It's not fair.

Justice is a principle that causes Targets limitless pain. The entire complaint-response system disappoints the person hoping to see justice done. When bullies are confronted about their misconduct, they lie. This outrages the Target who may have taken great risks to have the bullying surface in public. Targets make difficult clients for attorneys. Though it is the law that does not provide protection, Targets hold attorneys accountable for not being able to do more.

Targets driven by a strong sense of equity, justice, and integrity do make life challenging for those who wish they simply would disappear. Maybe they make us uncomfortable because they remind us of how we all should be, of what we should aspire to become. It is that guilt that allows witnesses to the bullying to abandon the principled, passionate, and driven Target.

Independent, Skilled, and Bright People

The Campaign Survey Says . . .

No. 1 Reason For Being Bullied

✓ Target's refusal to be subservient, to not go along
   with being controlled (reported by 31 percent of
   respondents)

Paradoxically, bullies also target strong people for assault. Remember that bullies are, by nature, creatures haunted by their own inadequacy. On one level, they realize this, but the public persona they present is a mask of bravado and superiority. Rather than undertake an introspective analysis and personal re-socialization plan (as if one could redo childhood later in life to get it right), bullies prefer to lash out at others who threaten their presumption of superiority.

Into their work world come genuinely bright, creative, self-assured people. Since these people are a threat, bullies work hard to undermine them.

They sabotage them through myriad covert means. They spread rumors and misrepresent the accomplishments of this group of Targets. If the bully is a subordinate or co-worker, the rumor mill of disinformation is the only means by which the desperate bully can claw her way back into control.

If the bully is the boss of the independent and skilled Target, all she has to do is constrain her creativity, pile on impossible burdens, or steal credit for the Target's work. These Target types will leave the job or stay to outwit the bully because, thanks to their self-confidence, they have a low threshold for the lies bullies dish out.

If the bright Target chooses not to compete with the bully, she could be untracked and walk away from a job in disbelief about the banishment. All she wanted was "to be left alone to do the job I was hired to do, as best as I could do it." There is a naiveté about these Targets. They are highly proficient in the work to be done, but oblivious to office politics (the sole reason to exist according to the bully's world view).

The Campaign Survey Says...

No. 2 Reason For Being Bullied

✓ "Bully Envy" of the Target's skill, knowledge, or ability to work with people (reported by 21 percent of respondents)

Cooperative, Nice People

Bullies eat "nice" people alive. Bullies are competitors and live for the opportunity to work with a bunch of cooperators—people who can willingly be bossed around. Imagine the glee of a sadistic supervisor who inherits a group of positive, non-confrontational people to manage.

In light of all the talk about "team-ness" being central to successful work performance in most contemporary American workplaces, it is ironic that the people with a more advanced stage of human development (the ability to cooperate) fall prey to the primitive, Neanderthal bullies.

Research shows that when everyone cooperates, groups maximize benefits to each person. They get more goodies, whatever goodies there are. But the human tendency to grab the most for oneself prevails in studies with groups that have chances to build a collective cash pool. The rules typically call for a doubling of the amount of cash in a bowl if no one person withdraws money from the bowl during a round of a game.

Unfortunately, groups in U.S. psychological studies break the bank and rarely play more than one round. This happens because greedy individuals (from a random group of people sitting around the table) snatch the money bowl for themselves, ruining the game for others. They do this despite being free to talk out loud, to formulate a strategy, to agree to keep doubling money that could be split.

The reality of the workplace is no different. The formal, written rules call for teamwork, dangling the biggest prizes to groups that cooperate with each other. Operating rules, however, undermine cooperation. Bullies, as strong competitors, know that if they grab "goodies" at the expense of Targets, they win. The cooperators are left to watch the competitor dictate the outcomes (gains or losses) they will experience.

It is clear in the competitive workplace populated with bullies, cooperators are second-class citizens. Americans hate being second. In the face of a winner-take-all world, cooperators don't stand a chance without a concerted institutional effort to wrest control of the rules away from greedy bullies.

Cooperators are not weak; they are simply over-optimistic that goodwill will naturally and automatically prevail. Bullies interpret "nice" as the unlikeliness to confront or to stop them.

Vulnerable People

Bullies scan groups for the weakest. Maybe it is an evolutionary remnant of our place in the animal kingdom. All predatory species select and attack the weakest prey. It's done for food. Barely human, bullies only symbolically eat their prey. They are gratified by the fear they instill in Targets.

Bullies test the field, especially with new employees. They look for the Targets who put up no resistance to attacks. Approximately 75 percent of the workforce does not tolerate being controlled by another person. The bully backs off when resisted. Behavioral researchers speak of an aggressor's mental calculation of her effort/benefit ratio. The people who require more effort to aggress against than is considered worth it to the aggressor are no longer seen as Targets. That is, bullies are lazy. They want an easy mark.

Many of us hate conflict and confrontation. We want peace and quiet. Being non-confrontational when provoked makes Targets look and sound non-threatening. This is done with both words and nonverbal messages communicated to the bully.

Vulnerability Through Words

Self-effacing statements can be a sign of humility or civility. In those instances, we hear lots of praise heaped on others from the Target, a genuine desire to deflect credit that she herself deserves. "I could not have done this alone. There are many others to thank. My co-workers made it impossible for anyone to fail." "I owe my success to everyone around me." The person may not intentionally be choosing to defame herself, she may simply be choosing to not draw any attention to herself.

However, self-denigrating, self-defeating statements are tell-tale signs of a deeper insecurity. There is evidence that the seed of self-doubt was planted long ago, in one's childhood, and has reared its ugly head through conflict with a bully. All of us have doubts at one time or another, but most believe that we are inherently capable of overcoming obstacles. Those with historical doubts are always more susceptible to spiraling into despair whenever confronted by powerful people who only criticize and demean them.

It's one thing for the horrific bully to put down the Target, but when the Target does it to herself, it's painful to witness. For instance, it hurts to hear someone say:

- "I only slow the others down."
- "I never was good at this sort of thing."
- "You all should go on, I can't help. I'd only make it worse for you all."
- "I never learned how to work computers. My kids are much smarter than me. I'm such a dolt."
- "You may be right that I screw up a lot, but I'll try harder next time."

In addition, there are aspects of speech that provide nonverbal clues to a hovering predator. Relevant paralinguistic cues (all aspects of speech except the words themselves) include tone of voice (mousy, timid), rate of speech (either slow enough to be interrupted or too fast and flurried to mask a fear of being detected as less than competent), and showing a tolerance for interruptions by the bully, all combine to convey a general lack of confidence.

Vulnerability Through Action

The way the Target walks, carries herself, sits, stands, uses hands, and uses interpersonal space is scrutinized by the bully, perhaps without the Target's awareness. Fear or intimidation can be signaled by a hesitant walking pace, short stride, or actually walking backwards to attend to what the more powerful person is saying. Confident people typically gesture with their hands to punctuate speech. The absence of gestures does not necessarily indicate poor confidence. It does, however, convey a reticence either learned in a family that discouraged free expression or a deliberate delay in taking action. In either case, the bully pounces on the quiet, non-expressive person, assuming that she will not fight back when attacked.

Finally, bullies exploit personal space to their advantage. They stand too close, hover over your shoulder in your cubicle when your back is turned, and touch you to signify control rather than compassion. Whenever a Target fails to back the bully off, to re-establish a comfortable distance, she risks having the invasion of her personal space wreak havoc over her own sense of control. Cowering or tolerance of invasion often indicates submission to the bully.

A Private Vulnerability

Some Targets carry a private burden inside. Somehow and by someone they have been previously traumatized. Though years may have passed, the memory never dies. The Campaign has talked with many victims who have shared horrific stories of such traumatization. For many, the cycle is hard to break. For instance, when she was a child, her parents may have undergone a divorce that caused deep feelings of resentment, abandonment, or loss. She may have been sexually abused as a child, and as an adult, told to keep secrets about embezzlement by a bank manager. She may have seen her young daughter killed by a reckless driver as she crossed the street and spent years healing, only to have her gay male boss demand that she "make a beautiful baby" for him and his partner. A woman who was shamed into tears daily as a child by a domineering father may jump from one demeaning boss to another.

We have learned that the previously traumatized Targets:

- are more reluctant to tell others about their torment
- lack confidence that the bully is the reason for the harsh treatment
- tolerate much more craziness and instability at work because they are accustomed to chaos
- experience so much shame that it is especially hard to ask for help or to talk about it, even to spouses
- appear angry to co-workers and management when finally speaking up about the bullying—pent-up resentment toward the bully comes spewing out angrily and unfiltered

- are more susceptible to the uninvited assaults by a bully because of the re-traumatization effect
- experience an emotional setback from re-living deep memories at each step of the fighting back process—with each repeating of the story to a bureaucrat, a psychologist, a lawyer

This knowledge about previously traumatized Targets is offered to help them and their families understand why the healing process takes so long. Healing cannot begin until there is separation from the bully and her supporters. If a lawsuit is begun, it postpones indefinitely the end of the bullying situation. It can take years. Sometimes, well-intentioned family members get frustrated that the Target doesn't simply "let it go." It is not that easy. Spouses may not know about the Target's early-life experiences. The bullying episode provides a chance for starting that intimate, private discussion.

In no way does an increased susceptibility excuse the bully's unconscionable, despicable behavior. Prior traumas are none of the bully's or employer's business. Unfortunately, if they learn about prior trauma, they will use that information against the Target. In that case, she will need the unconditional support of her family more than ever.

Denial

Is it possible to not know that you are the target of a bully's assaults? As odd as it sounds, yes. Self-denial allows it to happen. Denial is a process we use to protect ourselves from something that we think is so personally threatening that we could be immobilized if we face it head-on. Denial blocks our awareness of a painful reality. It is important to realize that denial in its various forms is not deliberately deceitful. It is automatic. It is a useful unconscious safety-valve that the mind invokes to keep from being overwhelmed by circumstances.

Denial is adopted by individuals, both Targets and bullies, groups, work units, entire organizations, and even nations. For brevity here, let's talk only about the

Target's denial, a self-denial of an unacceptable, painful reality. Co-workers and the organization itself use the same techniques.

The term "denial" encompasses many forms that serve to protect us. All involve self-talk, adopting a script that when repeated serves to convince our own minds that the denial is the right thing to do. Some common forms are:

Simple denial

Maintaining that bullying is not happening despite evidence that it is and that it is also perceived by others. This is the "see, hear, and speak no evil" approach. When the group discusses what the bully does, you leave the room, believing that when it is out of sight, it will be out of mind.

Minimizing

Admitting to bullying, but downplaying it in such a way that it appears to be much less serious than it is. The lines "tough times build character" and "I have to grow a thicker skin, that's all" run through your mind.

Rationalizing

Offering other reasons or justifications for the behavior of the bully. To make the insane appear normal, you convince yourself that the bully's tactics are somehow justified. This leaves the Target with no one to blame but herself. "I must have done *something* to cause her to launch on me."

Intellectualizing

Avoiding the hurtful effects of the bully by dealing with it on the basis of generalization, intellectual analysis, or theorizing. This is the "macro" approach. The justification sounds something like: "Worldwide competition has driven my company offshore," or, "I'm lucky to have a job at all," "The pressure the poor CEO feels is more than a person should bear," "She has no choice, she's merely going with the flow," or finally, "I have to accept a lean and mean environment so the company can remain competitive, because this is an economic necessity."

Healthy Self-Denial

When we are hurting from the effects of bullying and we feel vulnerable, we want the pain to stop. When we feel threatened or vulnerable after yet another round of bullying, it is sometimes important to deny the situation. It is too much to comprehend all at once. It's as if we are wearing a blindfold. We refuse to take it off to see what has happened.

This often works in the short term so we can finish what we need to do. It helps you limp to the planned vacation, to time off. When you are ripped by the boss, you use denial to get through the afternoon until you can get home and verify her craziness with your family and friends.

Without denial, the trauma from bullying could overwhelm you and render you inactive and immobile. Losing a job or constant harassment from a boss or co-worker can lead to shock. Denial is the defense we use to avoid the flooding of emotions after the initial shock wears off.

Everyone uses some sort of denial when in pain. If you come from a background where there was a lot of pain, you may have learned to use denial often to escape that pain.

Origins of Self-Denial

In the Target's family-of-origin, no one calls bullying what it is. The bully herself encourages and sustains denial by everyone.

In childhood, you may have often heard the words, "You have nothing to cry about." This teaches the Target to not trust her feelings. When someone denies your right to feel and express a genuine emotion that you feel, it is called discounting. Having one's personal perspective disregarded while growing up explains why Targets would accept similar verbal taunts from the bully. Adult Targets simply do not trust or value their own version of events. Bullies always try to invalidate what you know to be true.

When the bully is confronted about her unacceptable behavior, she may say it never happened or that the Target "provoked" it. The Target who thinks she has no right to dispute those lies may instinctively search for a rational explanation, believing the bully has a logical reason for acting as she did. She may think, "There must be some reason she is mad at me," or, "If she thinks my work isn't good, it probably isn't."

The Target spirals into a trap of self-defeat, acting on a script rehearsed since childhood. The bully's work is perpetuated by the Target herself.

The Target's belief that the bully is behaving logically is one of the main sources of confusion. The bully may bring her an important work project and calmly explain what is to be done, only to be screaming at her when it is not done in ten minutes. This rapid change from rational to irrational behavior increases the Target's confusion, driving the logic-hungry Target to look for sanity in an insane world. Denial minimizes pain from the confusion.

The Target may never have asked the question, "Am I being bullied?"

Many people have never heard of bullying and they do not know what it is. In many cases, the concept is totally new to them. It is amazing how many people have said to us that just having a name, a label, for what they were going through helped them start to do something about it. It helps pierce the veil of secrecy and shame imposed by bullies.

Denial postpones putting a name to intolerable mistreatment, which delays counterattacking.

Bullying is wrong because of the unilateral decisions bullies make. Targets do not invite, provoke, desire, approve of, nor prosper as a result of the bully's assaults.

Daily torment from a bully also encourages self-denial by Targets. She is told that she is too sensitive, too competitive, and trying constantly to have her own way. It is akin to brainwashing and can even extend beyond work to encompass her family and her life.

Bullying Is NOT The Target's Fault!

Denial Cycles

Denial can come and go after bullying as a way to avoid acknowledging pain. This is demonstrated by psychologist Lenore Walker, who has researched domestic violence. Her model of the cycle of abuse from domestic violence fits well with the concept of bullying.

Applying Dr. Walker's model to the work world goes like this: first, everything seems to be going well at work. Then, tensions begin to rise as the Target experiences stress from the bully's undermining tactics. This is then followed by a verbal, destructive incident of bullying, causing the Target confusion. She wonders how she can change herself to make her boss or co-worker happy. The Target's attempts to change (to meet the bully's standards) to appease the bully are at first met with approval. Things around the office are quiet for a while—until the bully feels out of control, and then the cycle begins again.

For the cycle of bullying to stop, denial must be broken. The Target must recognize the bullying and begin to intervene on her own behalf. Taking control of your life and your destiny is the only way to stop bullying.

Prolonged Denial Worsens Situations

Denial is acceptable as a short-term strategy only. While the Target is in denial, she remains stuck in circumstances of her mind's invention that prevent a realistic assessment of the situation. Without taking that first appraisal step, no action to restore dignity at work can or will be started. Prolonged denial is a dead end.

Psychologist Jerry Harvey, author of *The Abilene Paradox and Other Meditations on Management*, blames the over-reliance on denial on people's overblown negative fantasies. That is, they imagine the worst possible, albeit unlikely, outcome from confronting the bully—they would lose their jobs, the bully would turn on them, they would have a heart attack, the bully would kill their children, and so on. With a mind full of negative thoughts like these (mostly about events that would never occur) individuals act very conservatively. People want to take no risk.

Our aversion to risk coupled with an exaggerated imagination that limits thinking about possibilities allows the Target-bully relationship to grow even stronger with time.

Further, the longer a confrontation with the source of your pain at work is postponed, the less likely that action ever taken will stop the bully. Prolonged denial is a form of distraction which, over time, actually loses its only usefulness—the power to mask depression and self-doubt.

> ### *Ironic Reality:* Failing to Confront Costs a Procrastinating Target and Family More Than the Worst Imagined Consequence

It's Always about Control

Control is the central underlying theme, the ultimate basis of bullying. Dealing with the chaotic co-worker or boss, the out-of-control corporate environment, and the rigid rules of the business world are all closely linked to the theme of control. The need for control is always there. Worries about losing control are the core issue for both Targets and bullies.

For the Target, the need for control is great. The fear of appearing too open, too needy, too aggressive, or too angry is linked to every aspect of work. Seen from the other side, control means being dominant, demanding, aggressive, and totalitarian. Targets believe that the only way to protect themselves is to maintain control. The issue becomes black-or-white. This emphasis on control leaves the Target vulnerable to bullies who start the entire bullying melodrama in order to appease their own need for control.

Stephanie Brown, in her book *Safe Passage: Recovery for Adult Children of Alcoholics*, draws a distinction between coping and being defensive. She states that coping creates problems in that situations (with bullies) are never resolved. Thus, using denial as a coping strategy only leads to escalating problems—it never solves the problem. Without resolution of some sort, Targets find their pain prolonged indefinitely.

Chapter Four:

Work Trauma

. . . .

The soul of man is immortal and imperishable. — Plato

Targets bear the brunt of job stress in America. Our society has a split personality about psychological pain. At times, we seem enlightened. We joke about Prozac and the growing family of anti-depressants, but its familiarity is testament to the prevalence of depression and the numbers of people who seek help for it. Then, we act stupid about psychological processes when we callously discount those asking for help as being "weak" or "needing a crutch." Despite the extensive body of pharmacological research about brain chemistry and the biological bases of diseases like depression, we still expect people to "tough it out."

Personal experience breeds tolerance, however. The concept of bullying is immediately recognized by anyone who has been through it or knows someone who has—there are no more than two degrees of separation.

There are several diseases or disgraceful habits once accepted as "the way things are done" that are no longer taboo. We've learned to talk freely about impotence, incontinence, sexual harassment, domestic violence, child abuse, drunk driving, and a host of cancers—breast, prostrate, colorectal. We at the Campaign predict an end to taboo status for workplace bullying.

Work Shouldn't Hurt

The first step is to raise public and lawmaker awareness of the damage bullies inflict on the quality of the Target's life. Americans should be intolerant of such unwanted, harmful invasions of a worker's life. Its constituency is diverse and large, including people of all races, income levels and political persuasions. Bullying unites its veterans. There is an untapped reservoir of American support for public policy and law reform concerning this subject.

Only corporate defense lawyers believe that employees deserve a traumatizing workplace if that's what ownership wants. We have federal and state laws ensuring physical workplace safety. Shouldn't there also be freedom from psychological injury, too?

For workplace bullying to be taken seriously by policymakers and people who naturally repel bullies, Targets must be able to demonstrate that harm has occurred. For any law proposed, the employer lobby will demand documentation of extensive damage. The current tort most closely related to bullying is Intentional Infliction of Emotional Distress (IIED). In order for a Target to sue and win a legal case, she must prove to the court that the injury has been severe. Courts mirror the "get tough" public judgment, underestimating the severity of emotional distress claimed by Targets in lawsuits.

Not everyone at work is targeted for mistreatment by bullies at work. Of those targeted, the harm they suffer ranges from mild to severe. Same bully, same tactics, different Targets, different types and severity of damage. Individual differences determine whether the Target loses sleep or spirals down into a deep depression, reduced to an essentially traumatized life.

As a more severe example, the Swedish ordinance outlawing "victimization" at work requires the employee to be "placed outside the workplace community." In other words, the worker has to lose the job to have been damaged.

The Many Faces of Hurt

Emotional-Psychological Health Damage

- Poor concentration, forgetfulness
- Loss of sleep, fatigue
- Stress, irritability
- Mood swings, bursts of anger
- Spontaneous crying, lost sense of humor
- Indecisiveness
- Panic attacks, anxiety
- Clinical depression
- Feelings of insecurity, being out of control
- Nightmares about the bully
- Obsessive thinking about the bully
- Always anticipating the next attack (hyper-vigilance)
- Shattered faith in self-competence, feelings of worthlessness
- Shame, embarrassment, and guilt
- Self-destructive habits: Substance abuse, workaholism
- Altered personality, unrecognizable to family & friends
- PDSD/PTSD (stress disorders detailed below)
- Suicidal thoughts
- Violence: suicide or violence against others

**Bullying Can Be Hazardous to Your Health!
It Causes Psychological INJURY.

Targets Are Not Mentally Ill!**

Psychological pain should not be minimized or denied by Targets themselves or by others. Stoic bravery or toughness are no match for suicidal thoughts or feelings of terror when you turn into the company parking lot in the morning. Seek help. You owe it to yourself and the people who love you. They recognize and want the very real pain you endure from bullying to stop.

The greater the severity of psychological pain, the more dangerous and the longer the effects seem to last. It is a fact that those exposed to domestic violence are hurt more by the verbal abuse than the physical wounds, which heal easily.

Physical Health Damage

- Reduced immunity to infection: more colds, flu
- Menstrual difficulties
- Itching, skin disorders
- Stress headaches
- Increased allergies, asthma
- Indigestion, colitis, irritable bowel syndrome
- Rheumatoid arthritis, fibromyalgia
- Hair loss
- Weight swings
- Hyperthyroidism: overactive thyroid gland
- Migraine headaches
- Hypertension: high blood pressure
- Diabetes mellitus
- Peptic ulcers
- Heart palpitations
- Heart attack
- Micro-shredding: weakened heart

Micro-shredding was defined by Robert S. Elliot, M.D, a cardiologist hired by NASA to find out why many of their young engineers were dying mysteriously. It was determined that they had experienced micro-shredding (stewing) of the heart muscle caused by stress. The symptoms are a sudden burning sensation of "heartburn" that is not due to gases in the stomach. What really happens is that the person is experiencing a special type of heart attack caused by excessive long-term stress.

Dr. Elliot discovered that NASA had employed a negative incentives policy in the workplace. At the end of every successful rocket project, NASA terminated 15 percent of the engineers. This policy caused deep anxiety within an engineer's mind that he or she could contribute to project's success and yet be part of the group to be terminated.

As the study found, this type of anxiety caused many heart failures. Age, incidentally, was not a factor as many of these engineers were in the thirty- to forty-year age group.

Damage to Social Relations

- Co-worker isolation from personal fear
- Parents encourage compromise with bully
- Co-worker resentment, attempts to silence you
- Spouse questions your role in dispute with bully
- Children and friends outside work show strain
- Wavering support from family
- Abandonment/Betrayal by co-workers
- Separation/Divorce by immediate family
- Abandonment by friends outside work

Economic-Financial Damage

- Sympathetic medical provider recommends halted work hours for job stress
- Paid time off (PTO) accounts begin to be used
- Sick leave exhausted, switch to short-term disability
- Employer encourages unpaid leave under FMLA (Family Medical Leave Act)

- Employer orders you to choose termination vs. workers' compensation (WC)
- PTO accounts exhausted, no days left
- Placed on long-term disability, income cut
- Personal savings tapped
- Creditors renegotiate payment structure
- File for WC, potentially lose right to sue
- Formally terminated in a way so employer can deny unemployment compensation
- Disability payments run out
- House and property sold
- Personal savings depleted

In a matter of a few months, it is possible that a vibrant, healthy, competent employee can be driven to ruin—economic, physical, and emotional. And this is all due to the unilateral decisions made by an incompetent, insecure, vicious individual backed by the power of an employer who did not want to get involved in a "personality conflict" between two people.

Stages of Stress

The bully is the source of the Target's stress—she and the havoc she wreaks is the stressor. It is the responses of your body and mind to stressors that determines the extent of damage inflicted. The sequence of biological stress is well known. There are three stages, as described by Hans Selye:

1. Alarm—the turning on of the entire body's defense systems, designed to be brief—it enables the "flight or fight" response in the face of danger, physical or psychological. Unfortunately, the body reacts to fright from the impending pounce of a tiger the same way it does to an insult from the bully. Alarm triggers the sympathetic nervous system that releases adrenaline to deal with the stressor.

2. Resistance—the maintenance of an alert stage that usually stops after the alarm. The body expects, and needs, this reaction to be turned off so that normal functions can resume. Resistance to the bully, however, is continuous, and that depletes the body's defenses. If you stay in resistance too long, the body rebounds and the actual damage occurs even when the stressor is gone.

3. Exhaustion—a full system breakdown, mental and physical. It demands that the stressor be removed or it will claim your life. To get to exhaustion, you have to ignore all the warning signs that your body gives. These can lead to death if the stressor never disappears and the body and mind continue to fight indefinitely.

Stress Is Real

According to the American Institute of Stress:

✓ Job stress is far and away the leading source of stress for adult Americans. Seventy-eight percent of Americans describe their jobs as stressful.

✓ Seventy-five to 90 percent of visits to primary care physicians are for stress-related problems.

✓ The National Safety Council estimates that one million employees are absent on any average workday because of stress-related problems.

✓ Job stress is estimated to cost American industry $200 to $300 billion annually, as assessed by absenteeism; diminished productivity; employee turnover; accidents; direct medical, legal, and insurance fees; workers' compensation awards; etc. Put into perspective, that's more than the price for all strikes combined, and the total net profits of the Fortune 500 companies.

✓ Sixty to 80 percent of accidents on the job are stress related.

✓ Forty percent of worker turnover is due to job stress.

✓ Workers' compensation claims for job stress have skyrocketed—California employers shelled out almost $1 billion for medical and legal fees alone.

One reporter asked us why we take Targets at their word. "Aren't you concerned that they are making it up?" was her concern. Why would they? People lie about beauty, wealth, and health. There is no reason to fabricate a tale about strokes, heart attacks, and immobilizing anxiety.

Symptoms of Stress

Here are some very common signs of a stress reaction in a traumatized person.

Physical Indicators

- Nausea, tremors of the lips, hands
- Feeling uncoordinated
- Profuse sweating
- Chills
- Diarrhea
- Dizziness
- Rapid heart beat
- Chest pain (have a physician examine you)
- Rapid breathing
- Increased blood pressure
- Muscle aches
- Uncontrollable crying
- Headaches

Thinking-Cognitive Indicators

- Mental slowness or confusion
- Indecisiveness

- Trouble with problem solving
- Time/place disorientation
- Poor concentration
- Memory problems
- Difficulty naming objects
- Nightmares
- Self-blame
- Minimizing the experience
- Sense of an unfair world

Emotions as Indicators

- Anxiety
- Fear
- Guilt
- Grief
- Depression
- Sadness
- Wanting to hide
- Feeling lost, abandoned, or isolated
- Anger
- Feeling shocked
- Numbness
- Wild mood swings
- Shame

The Campaign Survey Says . . .

Top 8 Effects of Bullying on Targets

1. Stress, anxiety
2. Depression
3. Exhaustion
4. Insecurity, self-doubt
5. Shame, embarrassment, guilt
6. Obsessive thinking, nightmares
7. Poor concentration
8. Sleeplessness

Harvey Hornstein, author of *Brutal Bosses and Their Prey*, surveyed nearly a thousand people for his book. Especially interesting were the health consequences for people subjected to disrespect. There were meaningful and statistically significant correlations between disrespect and depression ($r = .64$), anxiety ($r = .58$), and the loss of self-esteem (self-respect) ($r = .45$).

The Campaign Survey Says . . .

The Target's Emotional Instability Persists

Survey respondents were divided into:
- Short-term (≤ 1 year since bullying stopped)
- Long-term (18 months to 10 years)

> ✓ 81.25 percent of short-termers still had frequent or constant intrusive thought about the bullying.

> ✓ 23.5 percent of long-termers suffered similarly.

> ✓ 58 percent of all those who completed the Aftermath survey said they were still troubled by bullying.

Post-Traumatic Stress Disorder (PTSD)

The American Psychiatric Association recognizes a condition called acute stress disorder with symptoms that include disorientation, confusion, intense agitation, and dazed detachment, sometimes followed by amnesia. This reaction apparently makes the development of PTSD more likely. The risk is also high when the stress is sudden and severe, prolonged and repetitive, humiliates the victim, or destroys the victim's community and support system. Bullying does this!

PTSD is the injury that results from an overwhelming assault on the mind and emotions. A trauma is an event beyond the range of ordinary human experience—something that would be overwhelmingly terrifying for almost anyone. Even hearing about the suffering of another person is sometimes enough. Bullying often qualifies as a trauma, repeated over time.

The immediate response to a trauma can be intense fear, helplessness, or horror. The reaction may be delayed by days, weeks, months, or even years, and can last for a long time. There are three classes of symptoms:

Hyper-alertness: People often are edgy, irritable, easily startled, and constantly on guard. They sleep poorly, become easily agitated, have trouble concentrating, are aggressive, and are easily startled.

Thought Obsessions: An involuntary reliving of the traumatic event in the form of memories, nightmares, and flashbacks that may recreate the responses and feelings of the actual event. Sufferers may act as though the event were recurring (these episodes may or may not be recalled), and may display anxiety symptoms when exposed to anything that resembles some aspect of the trauma.

Emotional Flatness: A need to avoid feelings, thoughts, and situations reminiscent of the trauma, a loss of normal emotional responses, feelings that seem unreal.

- Not caring about the ordinary business of life, feeling cut off from the concerns of others, an inability to trust others.
- Sensing that there is no future, anger at those responsible for the traumatic experience while feeling ashamed of their own helplessness, or guilty about what they did, or what they failed to do. Sufferers feel demoralized and isolated.
- Suppressing anger that might lead to an explosion of violence. They no longer are able to use their feelings as cues to pay attention to their needs. Trauma victims habitually respond either too intensely or not at all.

Prolonged Duress Stress Disorder (PDSD)

It is important to know that PTSD was first introduced to the medical community in 1980. Its purpose was to provide a diagnosis and treatment for Vietnam veterans and those who had suffered a great trauma (seeing a child killed, surviving a fire, etc.). However, for most of the cases of workplace bullying, their experience is different. The Target usually experiences the symptoms described above but the one-time, traumatizing stressor is usually not present.

According to two English psychologists, Michael Scott and Stephen Strandling (*British Journal of Clinical Psychology*, 1994), most people traumatized at work suffer from all the symptoms of PTSD. The symptoms, however, do not result from a single traumatic episode but rather from the last in a series of cumulative bullying events. Thus, these two researchers feel that Targets of bullying suffer from PDSD. Most bullies assault their Targets over a long period with no single episode seemingly harsh enough to disrupt the Target's life. The damage comes from the accumulation of hurtful assaults.

Although PDSD is the best description of what develops after you have experienced harassment and bullying at work, it is not yet officially in the medical or psychological lexicon. What is most important to remember is that the resulting symptoms are similar to PTSD and need to be treated by a professional who is knowledgeable about the effects of stress and PTSD after trauma. A mental health practitioner without an understanding about the possibilities for harm by prolonged exposure to verbal attacks can do more harm than good.

You might suggest that your therapist get a copy of the 1994 Donald Michenbaum, Ph.D. book, *A Clinical Handbook/Practical Therapist Manual for Assessing and Treating Adults with PTSD*.

Treating Work Trauma

Borrowing from the suggestions of William Wilkie, M.D., in the Australian book *Bullying from Backyard to Boardroom*, we propose treating PTSD using the following method.

1. The foremost thing to do is to reassure the Target that she did nothing to cause her own victimization. She is not to blame. The most severe damage a bully can cause is to undermine the individual's confidence in her competence.

Targets often blame themselves for the bullying, for lacking courage, for being weak, or for feeling defective when hurt by criticisms (however unwanted, unprovoked, and undeserved). Above all, the Target is to be held blameless.

2. Assure the person that she is an injured person, not a mentally ill one. She should receive treatment for the injury just as certainly as if she had fallen and broken an arm at work. She's not crazy.

3. Targets do not have to find a rational meaning for the bully's inane actions. If no reason can be found, she might have to come to grips with the reality that the bully's behavior is unwarranted and irrational.

Michenbaum and his colleagues have provided information about how most people react when suffering from PTSD or PDSD. There are predictable reactions and some stages you may go through.

People who have been exposed to a traumatic or series of traumatic events have a difficult time letting go of the memories of the event(s). Hence the obsessiveness of Targets that appears to tax the patience of family and friends. This is not unusual because the nature of the bullying is meant to be degrading and mean. Because this trauma attacks not only your work, but questions your very existence, this can become the only thing you think about. It hurts when someone sets out to destroy you both at work and at home.

Bev is a forty-four-year-old medical assistant who has worked for more than twenty years. She is in a stable personal relationship of eleven years with a supportive partner. She is a gentle, nice woman who truly believes that if you work hard at a job you will be liked and your talents will be acknowledged.

When Bev began working, she was eager to learn and in her career has worked for many different doctors. She has always sought out new experiences and new information to learn. She also has done temp work which attests to her ability to come into a office and quickly adjust to differing needs of different doctors.

Last year, after a series of temp positions, she decided to look for a permanent job. She received several offers and decided to accept a job in an office where the last assistant had stayed for seventeen years. Bev welcomed the chance to use her skills in this new setting.

Bev quickly learned the office procedure—but that wasn't good enough. Within the first week, the physician began to find fault with her work. At first it was simple things. He told her she didn't work fast enough. She didn't perform certain procedures "his" way. He would trap her in one of the patient rooms during her half hour lunch and she would lose the only time she had for herself. There were no breaks and only severe disapproval if she asked for time to go to the bathroom.

Bev decided that she would work as hard as she could because she felt she must be doing something wrong. No matter how she tried to reinvent herself, the doctor was never satisfied. By the end of ten months, he was openly ridiculing her on a frequent basis. He went so far as to tell her what to do, and when she went to do it, the doctor would push her out of the way and do it himself. He used silence to confuse her and then berated her for not talking to him. He told her that she was "doing well" but her work was only at 90 percent and that "if she really tried, she could do better."

The final straw for Bev was a Friday afternoon. After being told to go to the doctor's office, the doctor told her she was causing him so much stress he had to see a doctor and that she should try to get along with him so he was not stressed.

Stunned and humiliated, Bev left the office in tears. During the weekend, she cried and blamed herself for her failure at work.

Bev was suffering from depression and was showing signs of PDSD. She consulted a therapist and was referred to her physician for an *evaluation for depression. She was placed on disability, began therapy, and started attending a women's group. Slowly she began to feel better about herself, but after two months, she received a letter from the doctor. To her surprise, the letter outlined all her faults, told her once again that she had injured the doctor, and informed her that she had "quit" and had been replaced.*

This cruel letter threw Bev back into a tailspin. She felt like she had been kicked in the stomach. This was followed by many days of crying and obsessing about her job. She continues therapy and her support group is helping her come to terms with what happened. At this time, she continues putting her life back together.

The more you obsess about the trauma, the more it becomes the focus of your life. This is where emotional numbing can take over. All your time is spent in organizing your life so that you can avoid the emotional feelings that accompany the memories of your trauma. However, when reminders of the trauma present themselves (driving by the worksite, seeing other workers, contacting those working on your disability claim), may trigger an emotional response just as intense. For you, this will be just as if the trauma has occurred again. Your body can revert back to the fight or flight response which is, in Michenbaum's words, "the wisdom of the body" taking over in a survival response, or, if you become too scared, your body will shut down because your very safety and security are threatened. This is a natural and important part of the process.

All trauma should heal with time as long as the Target acknowledges that she is not to blame and starts the road to recovery. Be aware that events and circumstances that prolong trauma and a return to pre-injury functioning include battling interfering physicians, dull lawyers, disbelieving colleagues, doubting family members, and defamatory references that find their way to the next employer.

Chapter Five:

The Irreconcilable Difference

. . . .

There is exploitation when an owner considers workers not as his associates or auxiliaries but as instruments from whom to obtain the most service at the least possible cost. The exploitation of man by man is slavery. —Antoine Frederic Ozanam

M any people who find themselves the target of a bully wonder why. Why is this happening to me? The foundation for all bullying is the concept of control. Whether you are a Target or a bully, you have to deal with control. The problem lies with the definition of "control." Bullies and Targets see control in two different ways. It is this difference which creates bullies who mistreat Targets.

We all start out at the same point. As babies, we exist in a world where we are under the complete control of our parents. We benefit from this control to learn how to talk, walk, and function in society. Our different experiences in life define whether or not we become Targets or bullies.

As briefly stated in Chapter 3, the need for control exists for many of us. For Targets and bullies, the issue of control is vastly different. The Target operates as if surrounded in a world full of examples of cooperation.

The bully is desperate to dominate. The bully feels powerless, she only values herself when she is in control. She works in a reality that says she is only in control when she controls others. She avoids feeling powerless by flexing her control muscles. The more "exercise" she gets for that muscle, the less secure she is feeling.

The Controller

The bully lives, eats, and sleeps to control others. She never really experiences life any other way. Living, for her, *is* to control others with power. The power, real or imagined, she has is both in title and her ability to generate fear and chaos in a work group.

The Campaign Survey Says . . .

89 percent of Bullies are Bosses

The bully never experienced the security of self-acceptance and cooperation in childhood that allows for adult cooperation. Because this was lacking, the bully was left insecure. With little self-acceptance, she developed intense feelings of powerlessness and worthlessness.

There is an Oz-like quality to a bully. Because of her inherent insecurity, she requires the smoke and mirrors presentation that the Wizard used in the Emerald palace of Oz. Remember the wizard's debunking? Toto pulled back a curtain that revealed a little shriveled-up man working the levers of his great-man illusion machine. Bullies are illusion artists. It's all appearance, no genuine substance.

Bullies are ignorant of their deficiencies. This comes either from a lack of insight or a denial of the consequences of her behavior. She denies abusing or attempting to control others. Instead, she prefers to fabricate a hokey story that the Target "provoked and deserved" a verbal tirade.

Bullies are:
- ❏ unpredictable
- ❏ angry
- ❏ intense
- ❏ sullen
- ❏ critical
- ❏ jealous
- ❏ manipulative
- ❏ explosive

Bullies have no intention of being in a "relationship" with their Targets. Normal relationships at work require give and take by both parties. The bully never admits to such humble interdependency. She may tell her Target that they are equal, but does this only to lull her into sharing secrets, habits, and other private information that can be turned against her during attacks.

To be equal suggests inferiority to a bully. Equals have the right to reject one another. The bully hides a vulnerability to rejection, something she fears very much. As we said in Chapter 4, a bully's anger, her raging public face, covers up pent-up fears from earlier times in her life.

Also in a relationship of equals, the bully would have to show feelings and ask for what she wanted. She would eventually ask of others a question that could be answered "no." She abhors being on a level playing field like that.

Finally, there is a rebound effect that fiercely independent Targets experience. When that type of Target pushes the bully, the bully escalates her cruelty because the challenge to her control is so threatening. Remember, resistance to the bully's control was the No. 1 reason Targets believed they were bullied.

The Cooperator

The Target unknowingly smacks right into the wall of power and control projected by the bully. The most important moment for the Target is when she begins to question the rightness of the bully's behavior towards her. Depending on the difference in styles, it may take the Target a long while to acknowledge to herself that "something just isn't right." By then, family and friends question her unwitting tolerance of the bully's disrespectful mistreatment.

The Target and bully have opposing perceptions about control. The difference can be traced to their respective families-of-origin.

The family-of-origin is the biological family you were born into. The combination of heredity and parenting style within the family determined to a great extent how we behave as adults. Parenting styles affect the child's disposition (whether we become passive, respectful, hostile, or assertive) and our ways of relating to the world.

There are two main parenting styles relevant to Targethood: passive and autocratic. Passive parents make few rules and tend to overprotect their children. Autocratic parents have strict and fast rules and allow little, if any, input from their children. Egalitarian parents, however, use a more democratic approach, combining rule-making with input from their children. This approach is the least likely to foster Targethood.

Children who grow up in passive and overprotective families exhibit the shyness, reticence, and quietness that makes for an anxious adult in social situations. These same qualities make the children from these families unsure of their abilities, and thus, easy prey for bullies. Parents who are overprotective keep their children socially naive because their overindulgent loving never allows their children to develop a realistic view of the world.

Autocratic parents never allow their children to behave in a way that differs from the parents. These children have an unrealistic view of the world, too. Because children of authoritative parents repeatedly are told what to do and how to do it, they become shy and quiet and show signs of withdrawal. These children also are less spontaneous and lack confidence in social situations. This sets them farther apart from other children and makes them susceptible to bullies.

One's family-of-origin affects the adult ability to solve problems. Through the daily routine of family life and the celebration of family events, the family is the place where we first learn to be social, to get along with others. If you are raised in a family where there is constant upheaval and there are no predictable rituals [such as meals or large family gatherings], you never develop the ability to have a normal interaction with others. The disruption of daily rituals in a child's life has profound impact because without the daily exposure to normal conversation, the child has little chance to begin learning the first steps of problem solving. Without the ability to problem solve, the child is easy prey.

Research from the area of addictions, gives another possible answer. It is clear that there are differences in children from alcoholic homes that allow some to grow up with more resilience than others. It is possible that this resilience is also what allows Targets to be able to learn to cooperate.

Targets as children are those who learn through the first two years of life that they don't have to use control to get what they need. Like the resilient children, they are given much attention, no prolonged separation from a parent or caregiver, and they experience no overt parental conflict. (They may have problems, but these problems do not overwhelm the rest of their lives.)

They learn to use cooperation in a way that doesn't require winners or losers. They don't need to control anyone. They live and function by collaboration. At work as an adult, they prefer an atmosphere that will foster teamwork, cooperation, and creativity.

Bullying is made possible by the failure of the Cooperator to realize the world is peopled by Controllers who do not have the Cooperator's best interest in mind.

The Target's naivete determines the size of the surprise when she finally realizes the bully's cutthroat nature.

Into the snakepit steps a Target who believes that colleagues at work will express freely their feelings and ideas and actively seek collaborative relationships. Because the job and good relationships define her work world, she assumes this is true for everyone else, including bullies. She loves her job, meaning the tasks that push her to employ her skills. Office politics are either ignored or considered of minimal importance.

Unfortunately, bullies see the workplace as a battlefield, a site to plunder others, home to the carnage that they consider unworthy adversaries who populate their work day and interfere with their divine right to unchallenged control over minions. Getting along is the farthest thing from a bully's mind. Politics is the sport of competitors. The spoils, literally the body count of those successfully dominated and devastated over the years, go to the bully.

The Inevitable Collision

It is disingenuous to characterize the clash between two such fundamentally different people a mere "personality conflict" or "miscommunication" or "misunderstanding." All those labels suggest that the Controller is willing to meet the Cooperator at least halfway. This is not true.

As long as the Target keeps functioning under the rules of cooperation, she may believe that she is doing something "wrong." She will continue to turn herself inside out to please the bully who never will be appeased. The Target's healing cannot begin until she realizes the relationship with her bully is not normal. Once she starts doubting the bully instead of herself, she takes a step toward health.

Our portrait of a bully is sad. It turns horrific when we look at the pathological dance with an unsuspecting Target. How could a Target fall into such a trap?

The answer is that Targets rarely see bullies coming. They simply see the world through a completely different lens.

> *Jill is a supervisor at a glass factory. She came to work at the factory after serving ten years in the Navy. She prides herself on running a "tight ship" and has received commendations for her work as a supervisor. Sandy decided in high school that she wanted to work as an artist. She started her job in the glass factory immediately after graduation. After three months working under Jill, Sandy is ready to quit and give up her dreams.*
>
> *What happened? Sandy walked right into a relationship with a Controller. The following is an example of the relationship between the two women.*
>
> *Jill comes walking into the break room and flops down in a chair at the same table with Sandy and casually says to her, "Boy, are you a troublemaker."*
>
> *Sandy, looking up, replies, "Why do you say that?" (Although she is surprised, she responds as though they are both operating under the same rules, a shared reality.)*
>
> *Jill is now ready to begin the battle for control. To her, Sandy needs to understand that Jill is the SUPERVISOR. "The boss just vetoed your crazy idea to simplify the paint line." Jill says this with a touch of anger and a discernible note of triumph.*

Sandy then feels she must defend herself. She says, "When I talked to you yesterday, I was just discussing some ideas that I thought might help us work faster."

"Well, I thought you wanted the boss to hear your idea. He did and he feels my way is better." In her mind, Jill has won. She has used her control over Sandy to attack Sandy's basic perception of her abilities and herself.

Sandy is hurt and confused. She cannot seem to get Jill to understand that she only wants to help in their department. She is frustrated and doesn't seem to understand what Jill expected of her. She doesn't perceive Jill's need for control at all—because Jill often tells her that new ideas are important, this to Sandy, means mutual empowerment, not the control over others.

If Sandy had said, "I feel hurt when you said I was a troublemaker," Jill, as a confirmed bully would have discounted her feeling by saying, "You're really blowing this out of proportion!" or (sarcastically), "Well, aren't you the poor thing."

Sandy would still be left feeling hurt and confused.

If Jill were in the reality of cooperation (Sandy's reality), she would have said, "Oh, I'm so sorry, I guess I should have talked more to you before I talked to the boss." In this case, Jill could be accused of being crabby but she would then acknowledge her irritability.

Although Sandy operates under the reality of cooperation, she has no idea that Jill will never consult her about anything. Sandy has no idea that Jill functions with an entirely different mind-set. Unfortunately, Sandy might never realize that Jill is not a Cooperator, but functions in a hostile world of control.

What's Yours Is Mine, Too

There is another way to represent the contrast between Controller and Cooperator. It is a way of describing relationships that involves keeping score for the things that matter most to people. It's a model of social exchange that turns into exploitation.

Consider the Cooperator's world view with respect to keeping score in a game. Do you remember Mark McGwire's stated wish during the 1998 baseball season as he and Sammy Sosa eclipsed the all-time home run record? McGwire said he wished they could end the season in a tie. That statement was rare coming from a professional athlete whose world is dominated by competitors. For a brief moment, the world watched as competitors at the highest level of sports chased the record as friends, each wishing the other the best.

The ideal outcome for a Cooperator is to achieve a 50/50 split of the "goodies" (resources) that employees play for at work. Some Cooperators have angelic souls and act the altruist. Altruists prefer to give to others. They would settle for giving the other person 100 percent of the resources, taking nothing for themselves. No one has spotted an altruist in the workplace in years. They are an endangered species in the competitive arena of business. Call if you spot one.

In the following diagram, the two end points on the horizontal line depict the altruist on the left, the Cooperator in the middle seeking common ground, and the Controller at the right end of the line seeking an absolute payoff.

A Cooperator's optimistic world of equality — 50/50 split

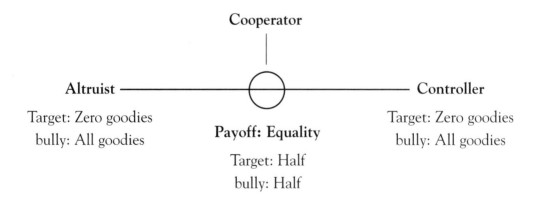

Cooperator

Altruist ——————◯—————— Controller

Target: Zero goodies
bully: All goodies

Payoff: Equality
Target: Half
bully: Half

Target: Zero goodies
bully: All goodies

Controllers are strict competitors, zero-sum game players. Their winnings come at the expense of others' losses. The ideal outcome for a Controller is 100 percent for herself and nothing for the Target. Their logic: what's mine is mine and what's yours is mine, too. Note how in the second diagram, the Controller cuts into the Cooperator's half of the "goodies."

Bully exploitation of the Target's split, on the way to domination

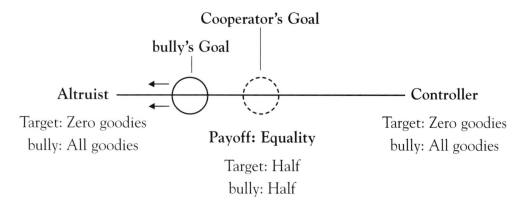

The Target-bully tango in this exchange-exploitation model is a struggle between the two where the goal should lie. The bully pushes from her side, trying to flatten the line, to achieve domination. The Target is pushing back (once she realizes the exploitation she is suffering) just to get the halfway mark. The Target does not think about pushing past the 50/50 boundary into the Controller's turf. If and when she did go beyond the restoration of self-respect, beyond getting back to neutral, she would then see herself as a bully.

Resources over which Controllers seek domination:

❑ Approval   ❑ Authority on the job
❑ Credit for accomplishment   ❑ Respect
❑ Time (hours worked, free time)   ❑ Reputation with co-workers
❑ Supplies to do the job   ❑ Target's competence

Chapter Six:

Bullying Paralysis

. . . .

You gain strength, courage, and confidence by every experience in which you really stop to look fear in the face....You must do the thing you think you cannot do.
— Eleanor Roosevelt

Targets are trapped by bullies in a deliberate web of lies. The gravest danger comes when self-doubt begins to overwhelm the good employee. Over time, even the strongest person is worn down by constant verbal assaults.

Some Targets are surprised that another person, supposedly a fellow human being, could treat them so cruelly. These are people just wanting to do their jobs. The shock of having to react constantly to the uncompromising bully drains a great deal of their energy. Exhausted and disbelieving, they are unlikely to assert their rights effectively and renounce the bully.

In a way, bullies have much of the work done for them by veteran Targets. After the initial bully assault plants the seeds of doubt, many Targets become their own worst enemies by staying wounded. The failure to mount a counteroffensive, to put the bully back in her place, sustains the suffering.

Procrastinating

Targets may be too shocked or surprised to respond at first, but eventually fear freezes them. They don't seem to be able to take action to protect themselves.

When friends and family ask why they are immobilized, several different reasons are offered, but fear explains them all.

- "I love my job. It's the manager I can't stand. I will just stay away from her."
- "I need major surgery in six months and have to have insurance benefits to pay for it."
- "Some days are better than others. I can make myself invisible for a couple of weeks at a time."
- "We are putting two kids through college and my wife doesn't work. I have to bring home a paycheck."
- "I can tough it out. At least he's not as bad as the supervisor who left."
- "No one in my family would understand my quitting. We've had only winners for generations. I can't quit."

Each of these people is more afraid of an unknown future in a different place, of doing different work than they are of the certain misery faced daily at the hands of their tormentor. If these people would draw two columns, labeled Personal Costs of Doing Nothing and Benefits of Doing Nothing, they would see that costs far outweigh the benefits. Unfortunately, like an alcoholic who has to hit bottom before finding the motivation to change, Targets wait an incredibly long time before taking steps to purge bullies from their lives.

Catastrophizing

Targets also freeze themselves by getting caught up in worst-case thinking. Targets play disaster movies in their heads. The script for this melancholy movie may feature:

- Target complaints are met with indifference or rejection.
- She feels no one listens to her or takes her seriously anymore.

- The bully is made a hero by the company for her toughness and squeezing every ounce of productivity out of her staff.
- Family and friends threaten to abandon the Target.
- The dog and cat sniff her and run, sensing a foul odor oozing from a day of clawing and fighting with the bully.
- The bully steals her husband in the ending scene, leaving the Target homeless, unemployed, and disabled with an appeal of a denied workers' comp stress claim pending as the sun sets. The End.

This type of thinking is an illustration of how deep inside a Target's life a bully can get. The Target is the star, but the bully is the film's director.

Action Is the Antidote

Whatever you do, you need courage. Whatever course you decide upon, there is always someone to tell you you are wrong. There are always difficulties arising which tempt you to believe that your critics are right. To map out a course of action and follow it to the end, requires some of the same courage which a soldier needs.

—Ralph Waldo Emerson

Ask yourself: how can it be any worse than it already is? You answer, "By being retaliated against by acting out." This is harassment heaped on top of harassment.

The point is that continued crap is guaranteed if nothing is done to stop the bully. Even if stopping the bully by complaining is unlikely, you cannot be certain of retaliation until you try. What have you got to lose?

How Real Is Risk?
Guaranteed Misery vs. a Chance for Peace of Mind

**When asked what they would have done differently,
veterans of bullying wars said, in their own words:**

- I would have challenged the bully more and stood up for my own beliefs instead of backing down.
- Take a stand and get the help you need to confront the bully because you wouldn't have a bully on your back if there were more people on your side.
- Fight back from the beginning.
- Realize that the bully is really a coward.

Why Team Members Do Not Help

The bully typically singles out one Target at a time. However, there are witnesses. Why do they watch and do nothing?

TO THRIVE, BULLIES REQUIRE
Secrecy • Shame • Silent Witnesses
You can stop them. Cut off their life support!

If groups (call them work teams) are powerful enough to bend individuals to their will, to get inside individuals' heads and make them doubt their own competence, to make them do things that hurt themselves, then logic would dictate that fellow workers who see a bully hurting someone would run to the rescue. Right? Wrong!

The strange tale of people acting in groups and influencing individuals now gets stranger. For many reasons, people witnessing the injustice of workplace bullying rarely act. They either will not act, by choice, or cannot act, for reasons often unknown to them and to the Target who could certainly use their help.

Let's take a look at five common things that affect co-workers and witnesses of bullying which discourage them to intervene or help.

Abilene Paradox

Social psychologist and noted author Jerry Harvey honored his Texas roots when he named this phenomenon. The group dynamic is perhaps the most relevant to understanding why bullies can be witnessed by so many people and still get away with it.

The Texas city is the namesake for the paradox. It refers to the retelling by Harvey of a lousy decision by his family. On a hot summer day, the family piled into a car without air conditioning and drove too many miles to Abilene to try a new diner. The heat was oppressive and the food was lousy. But no one dared to speak in those terms until later that night back home.

Finally, the matriarch of the family broke the silence by complaining about the food. Then everyone chimed in with their complaint—the car was hot, it was stupid to try an unknown restaurant. It turns out that no one wanted to go in the first place, but no one said so when it mattered. Eventually, they all blamed the father for suggesting the drive.

To Harvey, whenever a group is about to do the wrong thing, despite knowing it's the wrong thing, it is a group "on the road to Abilene."

Imagine a committee of bright people making a stupid decision. We know from talking with each person alone that each and every one of them thinks it's a stupid thing they are about to do. When the committee votes, however, they choose to do the stupid thing anyway! Later, usually much later, when the decision backfires, the committee tears itself apart in its search for a culprit. The group desperately needs someone or something to blame, long after the decision could easily have been prevented.

This describes a group in agreement, not in conflict. They all agree privately and individually about the true state of affairs. They do not communicate their feelings to one another, however. Then publicly, in the presence of each other, they all deny the agreement that they don't know exists among them.

The paradox is that both the private and public versions of reality coexist. In fact, this is the mismanagement of agreement, not disagreement. It is all made possible by a public silence regarding what each individual knows to be true. Sound like where you work?

Take a bullying example.

All the Target's co-workers know what is happening. If interviewed alone and free from retaliation, each would deplore the obvious pain the Target is experiencing. However, in group settings, even without the bully present, they don't do the right thing.

When together, they don't plan how to use their group power to overcome a lone bully. Instead, they ignore the rampant mistreatment by not communicating their positions or feelings publicly. If the Target later pursues legal action and investigators on her behalf interview the team that made up the hostile environment, the finger pointing begins.

Why does this happen? Harvey traces it to people's overblown negative fantasies. That is, they imagine the worst possible riskiest outcome from confronting the bully—they would lose their jobs, the bully would turn on them, they would have a heart attack, the bully would kill their children, and so on. We called this catastrophizing above. With a mind full of negative thoughts like these, mostly about events that will never occur, the individuals act very conservatively as a group. As a group, they want to take no risk. So, they do the wrong thing, all for lack of talking about it openly. They let bad things happen to the Target that they believe, as individuals, should not happen.

Sick? No, simply a natural human aversion to risk, thanks to an exaggerated imagination that limits thinking about possibilities.

Silent, inactive witnesses to the bullying of others is a group "on the road to Abilene."

Groupthink

Groupthink is the second group dynamic that inhibits witnesses of bullying to intervene or help Targets.

This also involves groups making poor decisions such as allowing the bully to hurt people in the work team. In groupthink, the wrong thing is done by the group, but they are not aware that the action is wrong, as they were in the Abilene paradox.

Groupthink is George Orwell's term from *1984*, the dark futuristic novel. Psychologists borrowed the term to describe a group incapable of critically assessing the pros and cons of decisions. Because the group members feel so tightly connected, so cohesive, they prefer to see only one side of an issue. They are easily led by a forceful leader and busy themselves by falling in line behind the boss and kissing up to stay in good favor. They become a mindless, overprotective clique when assembled as a group, putting the political goal of squashing dissent above all other matters.

Groupthink is relevant to bullying if we imagine a management committee on which the bully sits. She is in the club, so to speak. The Target tries to find an ally among the bully's peers. If and when the Target approaches group members, she will be given the cold shoulder. The management group will not be open to hearing complaints about one of their own. The bully is safe in her cocoon; the wagons are circled to protect a club member.

Little wonder that appeals for help to the bully's peers so frequently fail, from executive suite clubbies to shop-floor buddies. Groupthink is designed to protect club members from hearing anything that contradicts their comfortable view of the world. It's the wall that separates the in-group from all others. It carries with it a code of silence that plays into the bully's strategy.

Dissonance

Cognitive dissonance is the third dynamic that inhibits witnesses. Leon Festinger is the psychologist closely associated with cognitive dissonance theory.

Dissonance about cognitions, beliefs held by the potential helper, freeze the group members as individuals. Let's get inside Sally's head and try to understand her thought process.

> *Chris and Sally were Helen's best friends during her short stay in the department. All were psychotherapists. Sally was the first to offer her friendship. Sally spent many lunch hours telling Helen horror stories about Zoe, Helen's terrifying boss. Zoe had chased out a man from Helen's position a year before and he was rumored to not have recovered from the stress Zoe caused.*
>
> *Sally herself had transferred to another supervisor to escape Zoe's unpredictable rages and admired Helen's ability to get along with her. Chris had once held Zoe's position as boss, but gave it up after Zoe was hired as a staff therapist. Chris' life was made completely miserable trying to counter Zoe's political tricks and sabotage. So she abdicated and Zoe got her job, the one she wanted.*
>
> *Chris confided in Helen that she was terrified of Zoe and managed to avoid contact with her as much as possible. She even took to hiding in her office until Zoe passed so she wouldn't have to face her in the hall.*
>
> *Helen was later driven from the department by Zoe. Despite the similar experiences with Zoe by Chris and Sally, both refused to meet to comfort Helen after she left. Both left unanswered telephone messages left by Helen. Later, when Helen sued the corporation, Helen's attorneys interviewed Chris and Sally and concluded that their testimony would damage Helen's case as they both chose to support Zoe's position.*

The most common way to reduce dissonance after choosing sides is to exaggerate the positive aspects of the side chosen and the negatives associated with the side not chosen. For example, Sally could focus on the unfairness of Helen's banishment, but that could lead her to support Helen in court, risking good relations with Zoe, the tyrant.

However, Sally, like most people, chose the path of least resistance. She decided to downplay Helen's plight and conclude that where she works isn't so miserable after all. She rationalizes to herself that she would have to be stupid to stay in such a place and she is not stupid. Therefore, Zoe's world with Zoe in it must not be so bad; Helen was wrong.

As with all these phenomena, we're simply trying to explain why people do not help more. Dissonance is not about morality. Once people rationalize away internal conflicts to make themselves feel good, the likelihood of them taking the humane, but more difficult, action decreases.

You can probably see how dissonance is related to siding with the bully. Since the survivor and bully are both still there, the survivor engages in a mental calculus of sorts to justify staying. She concludes, like Sally, that Zoe is more important than Helen, who is gone anyway.

Co-Workers Side with the Bully

The fourth reason the team fails to use its power to stop a bully is that team members side with the bully. The origin of the principle of identification with the aggressor is in psychoanalysis, but let's not get Freudian here.

What's important is that this explains how the Target's best friend or the person who once stood as the Target's strongest ally can turn against her.

Most bullies want to torment the Target out of her job. Loyalty switching typically happens after the Target leaves. Without the painful daily reminders of the bully's devastating effect on the Target, her friends and co-workers are free in the aftermath to act as if the person were never there. They may buddy up to the bully more obviously to the observer, but without a personal awareness of what they are doing. The new-found loyalty to the bully may be borne out of fear to protect themselves, but to all observers, it looks like a choice made freely.

Sadly, after the Target is gone, former co-workers will dump on the Target, blaming her for her fate, for simply not understanding office politics, or for having a "personality clash" with the bully. This rationalization protects those left behind at the expense of the departed Target.

Winners Take All—Targets Are Losers

Without the book *Winner Take-All Society* by Robert Frank and Philip Cook, we would have called this explanation "Americans' love of competition." We revere winners and have no "mental shelf space" left for the losers.

It is a pervasive marketplace mindset that has invaded our social relationships. The vast majority of riches go to the privileged few at the top of any profession, sport, or hierarchy. In a way, the classic American competitive zeal encourages us to denigrate luckless Targets and elevate the bully. After all, if the workplace is war, the conqueror (even if she's a bully) gets the post-game interview while the vanquished retreats unnoticed and unloved.

> From the *San Francisco Business Times*, July 16, 1999:
> *"...a lawyer at San Francisco-based employment law firm Littler Mendleson, Tannebaum asserts...that bullying has its benefits. 'This country was built by mean, aggressive sons of bitches. Would Microsoft have made so many millionaires if Bill Gates hadn't been so aggressive?'...Tannebaum says that inappropriate bullying is in the eye of the beholder. Some people may need a little appropriate bullying in order to do a good job."*

Competition requires scarcity. There has to be a limited pool of possible rewards—monetary and social—over which workers have to fight. At work, social goodies can be as simple as civilized conversation, decent humane treatment, empathy for another's pain, and personal time given to someone who needs nothing more than the validation that companionship or an open mind can provide. These "resources" are not scarce. They are limitless.

Yet, the bully and her accomplices, by virtue of witnessing but taking no action, hoard them. By doling out praise and kindness in a miserly way, the bully controls the competition.

We naively refer to the "free market" competition as if the game is fair. In fact, the distribution of opportunities always tilts toward the powerful. In organizations, bullies control those who are opportunists, those whom they designate as Targets don't have a chance.

It is unthinkable that we treat bullies decently at work, while ignoring the deliberate harm they cause to others. What we score as success doesn't make sense either. We place a high value on the size of a person's workstation, type of chair, type of benefits for which she's eligible, window or interior cubicle, basement or penthouse office, day or graveyard shift, expense account or out of pocket, and so on.

Success is defined by relative standing rather than absolute performance. Companies blithely credit bullies with winning and treat Targets like losers. Hey, the game is rigged!

Chapter Seven:

The World Declares War on Bullies

. . . .

In the societies of the highly industrialized western world, the workplace is the only remaining battlefield where people can "kill" each other without running the risk of being taken to court. —Heinz Leymann, M.D.

Bullying may be running rampant through the United States, but it certainly doesn't stop at the borders. In fact, when it comes to acknowledging bullying's destructive effects on the workplace, America could stand to take a few notes from the rest of the world.

International Roots of the Anti-Bullying Movement

The European Pioneer

Heinz Leymann treated Swedish victims of workplace "mobbing," in the world's first clinic for those traumatized at work. He held the equivalent of two doctorates (M.D. and Ph.D.) which enabled him to not only work to heal victims but to conduct research at the same time. His scientific publications on the topic began in the 1980s. He defined mobbing, his term for workplace bullying as:

> *Psychological terror or mobbing in working life involves hostile and unethical communication which is directed in a systematic manner by one or more individuals, mainly toward one individual, who, due to*

> mobbing, is pushed into a helpless and defenseless position and held
> there by means of continuing mobbing activities. These actions occur
> on a very frequent basis (statistical definition: at least once a week)
> and over a long period of time (statistical definition: at least six
> months' duration). Because of the high frequency and long duration
> of hostile behavior, this maltreatment results in considerable mental,
> psychosomatic, and social misery.

Note that Dr. Leymann focused on the impact on the Target. He writes that the level of PTSD (post-traumatic stress disorder) suffered by mobbing victims is more intense and persistent than that felt by train operators who witnessed suicides by people leaping onto railroad tracks in front of them.

Leymann's concern was the set of medical stress consequences of bullying for the Target rather than with classifying personal types or re-engineering organizations.

Leymann also claimed that the chances of healing from acute trauma from bullying are reduced if the individual faces continuing threats. As long as the perpetrator goes unpunished, or the victim does not receive effective support, he or she can be torn to pieces again at any time.

The trauma is sustained by loss of income, spouses leaving due to discomfort in the marriage, pro-management Employee Assistance (EAP) counselors, uncooperative personnel department, insensitive managers, uncooperative co-workers, doubting union stewards, doctors in general practice, the company's insurance carrier, state disability agencies, and lawyers and the courts, if legal steps are pursued.

Leymann died of cancer in Spring 1999.

In the United Kingdom

British journalist Andrea Adams coined the phrase "workplace bullying" based on her 1988 investigation of the mistreatment of employees in a bank. She reported on bullying for BBC radio and wrote the first book in the United Kingdom on how to confront and overcome bullying in 1992.

In the U.K., unions have assumed the mantle of leadership. It is they who provide national awareness campaigns, telephone hotlines to report mistreating employers, and support. There are several individual pioneers and crusaders who also contribute much to the public movement—Andrew Ellis (who sits on an employment tribunal in judgment of cases brought by harassed and bullied employees and is a website host) and Tim Field (author and founder of the U.K. bullying hotline and website host).

Academic researchers in the United Kingdom, like Charlotte Rayner, Ph.D., of the Staffordshire University Business School, work collaboratively with unions to design and analyze workplace surveys. One such independent study was conducted by UNISON, a union representing workers in various public service organizations.

According to the 1996 UNISON survey:

- Sixty-six percent of the respondents either experienced or witnessed workplace bullying.
- Of those being repeatedly bullied, 74 percent said management knew about it.
- A whopping 94 percent thought the bullies could get away with it.
- Eighty-three percent of bullies were managers.
- Over 75 percent of the bullied reported some damage to their health—stress, depression, and lowered self-confidence were the most common psychological complaints.

In Australia

In 1994, four Australians—two business school professors, a psychiatrist, and a school psychologist—convened their country's first conference on bullying. The four founders of the Beyond Bullying Association had concluded that bullying was a major problem in schools, homes, and workplaces. The BBA works to create codes of conduct for schools, prisons, and workplaces and to develop guidelines for laws protecting individuals from harassment.

In Finland

Katri Kytöpuu tells of a Finnish association that supports Targets of bullying, both at school and in workplaces. In Finland, they use the term bullying to describe at-school mistreatment and the term psychological violence to describe workplace terror. Though Sweden is a neighbor, the word "mobbing" is not so familiar even though most of Finnish research is based on Leymann's work.

In Italy

Harald Ege, Ph.D., with a background in work and organizational psychology, is the president of PRIMA, the first Italian Association Against Mobbing and Psychosocial Stress. The organization, founded in January 1996, in Bologna, Italy, is a non-profit organization and was the first one in the Mediterranean area to speak about mobbing. Ege wrote several books in Italian on the topic.

In Germany

The KLIMA Association was founded in 1998 in Hamburg, Germany, to help victims of mobbing, to provide counseling, and to prevent mobbing in businesses, the state, and society. KLIMA operates independently of any employer, employee organization, or ethnics, political, and religious groups. Its members are chosen by a governing Board and Advisory Council. Its primary contact is Dr. Alfred Fleissner.

International Laws Against Bullying

Bullying at work is increasingly seen as an important issue throughout Europe. Scandinavian countries in particular have recognized bullying as a work environment or health and safety issue and have introduced measures to prevent it.

In Scandinavia

Norway recently improved its Work Environment Act to provide protection to employees against bullying at work.

In Sweden, an ordinance on measures against victimization at work came into force in March 1994. This defines victimization as "recurrent reprehensible or distinctly negative actions which are directed against individual employees in an offensive manner and can result in those employees being placed outside the workplace community."

The ordinance makes clear that this includes adult bullying, mental violence, social rejection, harassment, and offensive administrative sanctions. The ordinance requires employers to:

- Plan and organize work so as to prevent victimization.
- Make clear that victimization cannot be accepted.
- Provide routines for the early detection of, signs of, and the elimination of, such unsatisfactory working conditions, problems of work organization, or deficiencies of cooperation as can provide a basis for victimization.
- Implement countermeasures without delay if signs of victimization become apparent, including investigation of whether the way in which work is organized may be a cause.
- Have special routines to provide rapid help and support to employees who are subjected to victimization.

The Swedish legislation makes it clear that bullying is an organizational issue and that employers have a duty to organize work and the work environment so that it does not provide the sort of climate in which bullying is likely to occur.

In Britain

Laws in the United Kingdom indirectly prohibiting bullying invoke either Health and Safety or Employment Law codes.

Employers have general duties to protect employees' health and to consult safety representatives about health and safety matters. Furthermore, every employer has a legal duty to make a suitable and sufficient assessment of the risks to the health and safety of their employees while they are at work.

Although not explicitly stated, the employer's duty to protect employees' health should be taken as referring to both physical and mental health and the employer should assess the risks to both.

The British Health and Safety Executive (HSE) has published guidance for employers on preventing stress at work that makes it clear that bullying can be a cause of stress and that preventive measures must include action to eliminate bullying where it exists.

According to U.K. tort law, employers also have a general duty of care for their employees. It allows the victim to claim damages where the victim suffers some injury.

In certain circumstances, those in which bullying leads to a fundamental breach of the employment contract and is serious enough for the employee to terminate without notice, an employee may be able to pursue a claim of constructive dismissal. Contractual terms can be expressed in written form—as in a labor agreement—or implied. Typical examples of implied contract terms would be "mutual trust and confidence" or the statutory term to "provide a safe system of work." Employees can take their claims to employment tribunals.

Sometimes, the English judiciary can be far-reaching and imaginative when it comes to interpreting a statute. For instance, if an individual manager or a company is found responsible for causing psychological harm (a recognized psychiatric illness like PTSD, for instance), the mistreatment may constitute either Actual Bodily Harm (a violation of the Offences Against the Persons Act, punishable by up to five years imprisonment) or Grievous Bodily Harm if committed with intent. The latter offense qualifies the perpetrator for a life sentence, a sentence rarely imposed.

In Australia

The government of Queensland issued "An Employer's Guide to Workplace Bullying" that summarizes the status of state laws related to bullying.

Workplace bullying is defined as "the repeated less favorable treatment of a person by another or others in the workplace, which may be considered unreasonable and inappropriate workplace practice." It includes behavior that intimidates, offends, degrades, or humiliates a worker, possibly in front of co-workers, clients, or customers.

Employer obligations:

Under common law, an employer is under a duty to protect workers from workplace bullying. This duty exists:

- in tort; for example, negligence—failure to provide a safe workplace.
- as an implied term in the employment contract that the employer would not, without reasonable cause, destroy or seriously damage the relationship of trust and confidence between employer and worker.

Employers who do not take suitable precautions to protect workers from workplace bullying may be liable for any physical and psychological injury suffered by the victim. Recent cases at common law are setting precedents for workplace bullying to be dealt with under personal injury claims.

The Public Sector Ethics Act 1994 states five "ethics obligations," including "respect for persons." These obligations are intended to provide the basis for codes of conduct for public officials, to be developed by government departments and other public sector entities.

The WorkCover Queensland Act 1996 allows a worker to submit a claim for workers' compensation if an injury or disease is suffered as a result of workplace bullying.

The Workplace Relations Act 1997 entitles a worker to make a claim under the unfair dismissal provisions of the WRA when a worker is dismissed or is forced to resign as a result of workplace bullying.

According to the Anti-Discrimination Act 1991, where bullying involves acts of discrimination or sexual harassment, a complaint may be lodged and the employer may be held vicariously liable for the action of employees.

Chapter Eight:

America Enters the Fight

. . . .

Some way must be worked out by which employer and employee, each recognizing the proper sphere of the other, will each be free to work for his own and for the common good, and that powers of the individual employee may be developed to the utmost.
—Justice Louis Brandeis

T he U.S. is at least twenty years behind Sweden, which began exploring mobbing in 1979, ten years behind England, and four years behind Australia on focusing on workplace bullying. Thanks to the American media obsession with the mantras—"globalization," "competitiveness," and "productivity"—our attention gets diverted from the mistreatment of colleagues at work. We are bamboozled into mistaking the Dow Jones average for an index of the national mood, while ignoring completely personal accomplishments that feed our souls rather than our pocketbooks.

Let's recruit competition to do some good. The United States had better catch up with the rest of the world to stop bullying as a demonstration of America's parallel leadership in the arenas of economic dominance and compassion for those who do the work!

Another distraction is the widely popular comic strip *Dilbert* where many of the problems with the cubicled world of work are sketched. Scott Adams, the creator, populates the strip with idiot bosses, idiot co-workers, and names of the latest management fads foisted on unsuspecting workers. It's great to laugh.

Newspaper columnist Norman Solomon's book *The Trouble With Dilbert* takes the comic's popularity as proof that employees recognize that the way corporations currently operate has to change (we assume this would include stopping bullies). The tragedy, according to Solomon, is while fans vent their anger, they only symbolically thumb their nose at the boss or employee without taking any real steps to improve their workplace.

We interpret *Dilbert's* popularity as proof of the number of people facing frustrating problems at work. It's a problem of immense size.

U.S. Pioneers

To study the darker side of the world of work could jeopardize an academic's job security. Traditions within schools of business naturally promote management as a profession. It takes a rare individual to declare bullying-related phenomena as one's research specialty. To do so is to risk angering one's employers, government and foundation underwriters, or corporate executives at whose right hand most professors long to serve as highly paid consultants. The study of illegal violence and sexual/racial harassment are safer topics for academics. Some approach, then avoid the topic by exploring "incivilities," "workplace etiquette," or "job stress."

Here are the courageous few who study the bullying phenomenon in a direct, challenging way. All are scholars affiliated with the Campaign Against Workplace Bullying. Their work extends the meager knowledge base about the "Silent Epidemic."

Loraleigh Keashly, Ph.D., a professor of urban and labor studies at Wayne State University in Detroit, reviewed the collection of bullying-related research. For her 1998 report, she chose the label "emotional abuse" in the workplace. She defines it as the hostile verbal and nonverbal behaviors, independent of racial or sexual content, directed at a person to gain control over, even subservience from, that person.

Keashly and Karen Jagatic presented at the Workplace Bullying 2000 U.S. conference the strongest estimate of the prevalence of mistreatment in the U.S. workplace. The percentage of the stratified random sample of 1110 Michigan residents who reported being mistreated within the past twelve months and sufficiently bothered by it was 21 percent. This can be extrapolated to the nation, unless there is something peculiar about Michigan dwellers. Wow, a whopping one in five workers reports being bullied at work!

Joel Neuman, Ph.D., is a management professor at the State University of New York at New Paltz. He explores organizational conditions related to the frequency of workplace aggression and factors, both personal and workplace-related, that predict a bully's hostility. Many of his studies of aggression point to the increasing rate and extent of change facing employees and managers. His work bridges the gap between macro-economics and impact on individual lives.

Judith Richman, Ph.D., is a professor of psychiatry at the University of Illinois at Chicago. Her long, distinguished research career centers on the role substance abuse plays as an ineffective coping strategy for those harassed at work. Her most recent work compared sexual harassment to "generalized workplace abuse," which we call bullying.

David Yamada, J.D., professor at Suffolk University Law School in Boston, is also an academic affiliated with the Campaign. His very important work is summarized in the next section.

U.S. Courts Frown on Employees

The least helpful people on your side are judges and juries. Do not believe employer groups who warn their members that frivolous lawsuits brought by disgruntled employees will put owners out of business.

According to this type of disinformation propaganda, cases that bottleneck the courts are filed by fun-loving employees who suffered nothing more than irreparable "personality conflicts" with benevolent, but misunderstood, bosses. This is pure fiction, a mythology that unites business owners and large employers against employees.

Here are some facts that should buoy employer confidence in the court system. At the same time, it should scare the hell out of an employee like you who deserves legal redress for suffering at the hands of a workplace bully.

- There's been a steady decline in the number of class action suits against employers filed by the Equal Employment Opportunity Commission (EEOC, the federal agency responsible for ensuring that the federally protected classes of employees are not discriminated against). In 1976, 1,174 suits were filed. The anemic, understaffed EEOC had only sixty-eight class-action cases active in 1996.

- How about those costly accommodations for the disabled? The Americans with Disabilities Act (ADA) was supposed to drive many large companies out of business. On the contrary, it was found that Sears spent an average of only $45 per person to adjust the workplace to meet the needs of seventy-one workers. Not a budget buster, if done wisely!

- Sexual harassment is not the plague employers portray it to be. A recent study by the University of Illinois found that despite efforts by women's groups to educate the public, few women who are harassed, according to the legal definition, recognize it. So, fewer report it and fewer still file a claim.

- In 1994, the median jury award in a sexual harassment case was $100,500. The median award granted to those who claimed job discrimination in federal court was $100,000.

- The number of people who actually file a claim with the EEOC for discrimination of any kind is less than six in ten thousand employees.

- The 1991 Civil Rights Act made possible both jury trials and punitive damages for discrimination cases. For the dozen years prior to the act, just 24 percent of the cases went to a jury. Employees (plaintiffs) won 24 percent of the time. Between 1991 and 1995, the employee win rate crept to 30 percent despite a doubling of the percentage of cases heard by juries. Still, less than half the cases ever go to a jury!

Do the math. Employees 30, Employers 70. Who wins? A most unsettling comparison is made by Theodore Eisenberg, a Cornell University law professor stating that "job discrimination cases remain one of the single most unsuccessful classes of litigation for plaintiffs. They settle less and lose more than almost anything else." The only class of complaints with a lower success rate is the one filed by prisoners.

- Pre-trial settlements are not typically expensive for employers. True, the amounts paid by Texaco ($176 million), Publix Markets ($80 million), and Home Depot ($80+ million) grab headlines and fuel employer apprehension. The statistical reality is much different. A methodical analysis of wrongful termination cases in California courts during a recent seven-year period resulted in the following: 17 percent were dropped, costing employers on the average of less than $500, 40 percent were settled before a trial costing an average of $60,000 including attorneys' fees.

- As always, headlines are deceiving. Dramatic awards like $50 million to a single WalMart employee are often drastically reduced on appeal. In that 1995 case, $50 million became $385,000. Judges often set aside jury generosity.

A rare, true success story:

Carla was fresh out of graduate school and eager to launch a research career. She won a low-paying position at the massive, prestigious state university working for a scholar with an international reputation in her field. Carla loved research more than teaching; it was her calling. She planned on a decades-long career collecting data, authoring journal articles, writing books, giving symposia, the flurry of activities that announced that this academic had made a mark in her field.

Then, the highly esteemed scholar-boss asked Carla for her shoebox of raw data for a certain project. Not thinking twice, she handed it over.

There was some talk of publishing articles based on the data, but Carla began to feel left out of activities. The boss refused to return Carla's data when asked. When the scholar-boss' boss was told about the theft, he threatened to fire Carla if she continued to complain. She did and he fired her. For four years, Carla was without a full-time academic job to replace the one stolen from her. She taught courses on campus on a part-time basis, while simultaneously pleading with university administration to retrieve her data and give her job back.

At the end of the fifth year, she finally took the two supervising professors—the thief and the hatchet man—to court. A jury found them guilty of theft and illegal retaliation (see what can be done when a lawyer can see possibilities beyond the narrow scope of the law against discrimination). The initial jury award for damages was over $1.5 million. The university legal eagles dug in and appealed. It took a total of ten years from the date of the original bullying acts before the case ran its course through the appeals process. The university never gave up, nor did it ever acknowledge blame. The thief and hatchet man still work there. Carla has completely given up on the academe. But, she finally got her award...with interest!

Toward An American Legal Solution for Bullying

The law is attentive to harassment or discrimination when it relates to sex and race. Title VII of the 1964 (revised in 1991) Civil Rights Act created "protected classes" of individuals. Members of protected classes have a lower burden of proof than members of other groups when harassment or discrimination is claimed.

Many ostensibly "disadvantaged" individuals who harass others consider themselves immune to punishment for their deeds. Protected class members are often the worst bullies. Too often, they threaten lawsuits, based on race or gender, to scare away co-workers and employers who want them to stop harassing. The classic formula is for a woman or minority bully to shout discrimination as Targets or responsible employers begin countermeasures. Organizations then settle for cash with the bully, allowing her to stay on the job and force the Target to leave. The message is sent that the bully has the full backing of the organization, and gets paid for tyranny backed by U.S. federal law.

Recent U.S. Supreme Court Rulings

There is little reason for optimism that a federal prohibition of general harassment is forthcoming. In fact, in the 1998 season of rulings by the U.S. Supreme Court, there were three rulings relevant to bullying. All focused exclusively on pervasive, hostile workplaces created by sexual harassment.

On June 26, the Court ruled on two cases putting employers on notice that they can be held responsible for misconduct by supervisors even if they knew nothing about it. Legally speaking, these were rulings on the issue of "vicarious liability."

Buried deep in the legalese of the rulings was evidence about how the Court defines the employer-employee relationship. In both rulings, references were made to the employer as "master" and the employed harassing supervisor as the "servant who purported to act or speak on behalf of the principal and…reliance on apparent authority, or he was aided in accomplishing the tort (wrongdoing) by the existence of the agency relation." Master-servant terminology at the new millennium in the United States? This is a huge hurdle to overcome if the dreams for employee dignity of Justice Brandeis are ever to be realized.

The good news appears in the following excerpt from the Beth Ann Faragher decision. She was sexually harassed while working for the City of Boca Raton, Florida, as a lifeguard. The Court held the City "liable for the harassment of its supervisory employees because the harassment was pervasive enough to support an inference that the City had "knowledge, or constructive knowledge" of it; under traditional agency (that master-servant hierarchy reference again) principles…and a third supervisor had knowledge of the harassment and failed to report it to City officials."

Both rulings by the Court said employees have to first "take advantage of any preventive or corrective opportunities provided." This is exactly what we tell those who seek our advice to counter bullying. Comply, in a minimal way, with the frustrating internal procedures to protect all future claims—unfortunately, at this stage, complying with the system is a necessary evil. The worst thing a Target can do is to keep secret all that she is going through.

If a complaint is filed, thus providing "constructive knowledge," then the employer is liable for the mistreatment. Because of this, more credence is now being given to "hostile environment" cases (as long as it is outlawed by the Civil Rights Act). Much of the repeated mistreatment that characterizes bullying relies on a poisoned, sick workplace to permit and sustain the madness.

However, the Supreme Court's March 1998 decision dimmed hope that harassment's definition will ever be broadened by the Court. Justice Antonin Scalia, writing for the unanimous Court in the Oncale decision, explicitly stated the law "does not prohibit all verbal or physical harassment in the work-place....And there is another requirement that prevents Title VII from expanding into a general civility code...the statute does not reach genuine but innocuous differences in the ways men and women routinely interact.

"Common sense and an appropriate sensitivity to social context will enable courts and juries to distinguish between simple teasing or roughhousing...and conduct which a reasonable person in the plaintiff's position would find severely hostile or abusive."

This means the Court turned away from using discrimination law to enforce a general code of civility banning all workplace harassment. Looking from the top down, rather than through the eyes of a bullied Target, much harassment looks "innocuous," like mere personality conflicts.

A *Washington Post* newspaper editorial reaction to the Court's ruling saw the coupling of harassment to discrimination as missing the point. The *Post* called for Congress to write specific anti-harassment laws that do not require sex, race, or national origin protections, but instead require only that a work environment be sufficiently abusive. The editorial stated, "what bothers people about abusive workplace conduct, after all, is not the fact that it may be discriminatory but that it is abusive in the first place."

Employers see themselves as the "reasonable person" who can then define a harasser's conduct as hostile rather than the simple teasing of a Target who needs to have thicker skin. Stephen Bokat, spokesman for the National Chamber Litigation Center, the business defense arm for the U.S. Chamber of Commerce, believed the ruling would actually make it easier for employers to defend themselves. He felt that more complaints will be dismissed as boisterous horseplay or casual flirting.

Bokat trivialized workplace harassment and discrimination problems with a glib comment to the Associated Press, "I don't think it happens that often."

The Campaign Survey Says . . .

- ✓ Female Targets were bullied by women in 46 percent of the cases
- ✓ Male Targets were bullied by women in only 28 percent of the cases
- ✓ EEOC-complaint criteria (race or gender discrimination) applied in under 10 percent of the situations (Bullying is different than Title VII harassment)

The Need for a Change in Public Policy

Thanks to a Herculean research effort by David Yamada, Campaign-affiliated scholar and professor at Suffolk University Law School in Boston, we know that the favored legal basis for addressing emotionally abusive workplace mistreatment is to sue for Intentional Infliction of Emotional Distress (IIED). IIED cases seem the most applicable legal remedy to bullying as this book and the Campaign Against Workplace Bullying define it. If IIED cases brought by workers hurt by bullies are successful, then we already have a legal solution.

Professor Yamada reviewed the records of several hundred state court IIED decisions for the period from Summer 1995 through Summer 1998. The record of success is dismal.

The legal criterion used by several courts to define IIED is:

"One who by extreme and outrageous conduct intentionally or reck-lessly causes severe emotional distress to another is subject to liability for such emotional distress, and if bodily harm to the other results from it, for such bodily harm."

Which is translated into the requirements that the perpetrator's conduct must be intentional or reckless, outrageous, and intolerable (it offends standards of decency and morality), that conduct be shown to be the cause of the emotional distress, which in turn, must be severe.

Unfortunately, the rulings researched by Yamada proved that the threshold for holding the employer liable is very high, often unrealistically high as perceived by a rational layperson.

Here's one example from a 1996 Arkansas Supreme Court case that involved a female employee, Holloman, who worked for a male physician, Keadle, for two years. Holloman claimed that her boss "repeatedly cursed her and referred to her with offensive terms, such as 'white nigger,' 'slut,' 'whore,' and 'the ignorance of Glenwood, Arkansas.'" The physician repeatedly used profanity in front of his employees and patients, and he remarked that women working outside of the home were "whores and prostitutes." He told Holloman that "he had connections with the mob" and mentioned "that he carried a gun," allegedly to "intimidate her and to suggest that he would have her killed if she quit or caused trouble."

The bullied employee claimed that she suffered from "stomach problems, loss of sleep, loss of self-esteem, anxiety attacks, and embarrassment."

The Arkansas Supreme Court agreed with a summary judgment (dismissal without proceeding through the entire case) in favor of the doctor. The Court said the Target had failed to make the doctor "aware that she was 'not a person of ordinary temperament' or that she was 'peculiarly susceptible to emotional distress by reason of some physical or mental condition or peculiarity.'"

This then is the legal forum to which bullied individuals are expected to turn for relief from unbearable emotional, physical, and economic damage.

It is David Yamada's contention that new laws are necessary which extend the protection against hostile workplaces to all individuals, regardless of membership in a "protected class." The law would then be "status blind." The sad reality about IIED case decisions and the proposal for new policies comprise Yamada's article published by the *Georgetown Law Journal* in Spring 2000—"The Phenomenon of 'Workplace Bullying' and the Need for Status-Blind Hostile Work Environment Protection."

The Campaign is prepared to educate legislators and public policymakers about such status-blind protections when the legislative language is ready. These statutes will give lawyers the weaponry they need to combat harassing, destructive bullies at work.

Chapter Nine:

Getting Help
for Yourself

. . . .

Freedom is the will to be responsible to ourselves. —Friedrich Nietzsche

With understanding and the support of loved ones, the stress reactions of Targets usually pass more quickly. Occasionally, the traumatic event is so painful that professional help may be necessary. This does not mean the person is weak. It simply indicates that the particular traumatic event was just too powerful for that person or any reasonable person to manage alone. Isolation is the enemy. Asking for help is essential.

Listen patiently and carefully, spend time with the person, offer unsolicited help with daily tasks, reassure the person about being safe, don't take expressed anger personally, don't tell her that she is "lucky" it wasn't worse (say that you are sorry that the bullying ever occurred and that you want to understand and help).

As mentioned earlier, when Targets call for help, there is a good chance that much time has passed. Targets often wait too long to seek help, thinking the problems are their fault. It is extremely important that Targets are not isolated. They should rely on, not distance themselves, from friends and family during these stressful times. Caring friends can help. Here's how.

How Family and Friends Can Help

- Targets did not cause the bully to assault them.
  (If you think Targets invited harm from the bully,
  stop now. You will do more harm than good.
  Do NOT volunteer. You can't help!)
- "Bullying" is the name for what they experienced.
- They are not likely the only Target of that bully's
  unreasonable behavior (they are probably not alone).
- There are witnesses, perhaps silent at first, who may
  eventually help combat the bully.
- Shame and guilt are what the bully wants the Target
  to feel. Both are natural, but are useless. They delay
  recovery and healing.
- Their perceptions are valid and OK. Being kind, bright,
  or cooperative still matters most.
- They are not imposing on others by seeking help. People
  do want to right wrongs and help others.
- Bullying is common at work (25 percent to 85 percent
  according to surveys).
- The bully's way of viewing the work world is perverted,
  not the Target's.

Giving Support

➤ LISTEN without judging or evaluating

- Avoid criticism.
- Affirm, be positive.
- Avoid asking why the Target did what she reported. This
  puts the Target on the defensive and makes you seem an
  investigator, virtually an accomplice of the bully.
- Be patient. Let the Target talk at her own pace. Do not
  interrupt or fill silent time with your talk. Do not finish

sentences for the Target. Take a breath before you speak so you can be calm and deliberate. Put care into your voice. The floor belongs to the Target. You are to follow the lead.

➤ CONFIRM/VALIDATE the Target's reality

- Assume the Target's perspective completely. Do not try to be "balanced" by stating both sides of the conflict between the Target and bully.
- Use only as much information as necessary, based on a strict "need to know" basis. Sometimes simply putting a name to the experience is enough to start the healing process.

➤ SHOW EMPATHY

Empathy is the ability to walk in someone's shoes and to feel what they feel. See the situation from her perspective. If you have had similar feelings, say so. If you have not, don't lie. Simply try to understand what it must feel like and convey that understanding.

➤SHARE PERSONAL EXPERIENCES

When appropriate, without imposing, try to tell your story. Make sure you emphasize your success in moving on with your life. You have the chance to be a source of hope. Seize it.

➤ EDUCATE

- Be current on the topic. Turn to the Campaign and other sources for information.
- Suggest actions to take—call the labor commissioner, ask co-workers about their experiences, call the Campaign for an attorney referral, plan an internal tribunal to bust the bully, visit a physician to document impact on health. Be an idea generator for the Target.

Consumer Guide to "Helpers"

Therapist Selection

The ideal therapist can help you heal from work trauma but the key is in finding the right one. Make sure you ask the right questions of your therapist before you sit down in a session. A more complete guide to finding a qualified professional can be found in Chapter 19.

Employee Assistance Programs

EAP is a counseling program provided by employers in addition to health insurance coverage that may include counseling by a mental health professional.

EAPs were originally developed to treat employee alcoholism. In many medical plans, the broader scope of services now includes help for "job stress." Ideally, independent professional counselors are available off-site to visit on company time with no need for the employee to divulge to management the reason for the limited number of visits.

However, like every employer-provided benefit, EAPs come with strings attached. Here are some of the disturbing trends we have learned through direct experience and from visitors to our website who report the following EAP traps for the unsuspecting employee.

- Counselors are employees. When counselors are no longer independent contractors, they become accountable to management and fall under company control. They lose their neutrality and ability to see oppression in the workplace. With employee counselors, employees with troubles will be seen as causing problems and loss of money for the company. Loyalty is given to the company that issues the paycheck. Ask who your counselor works for.
- The company's preference for on-site locations. This means that someone seeking relief from a bully has to seek help in an office visible to co-workers and the raging boss on the

premises. Confidentiality is compromised. Furthermore, on-site counselors' time is subject to exploitation by managers seeking "tips" for dealing with troublesome employees. So, instead of teaching supervisors how to manage, they hang around counselors and nag them for advice.

- Supervisor referrals are given priority. Employees with problems should be able to refer themselves (self-referral) to counselors, when needed. However, supervisor referral, the most frequently used EAP service, demonstrates that management views counseling as punishment to "straighten out" the employee who doesn't agree to be subservient to a bad manager. Your job security may hinge on participating in mandatory counseling. This is an abuse of mental health services and undermines its effectiveness.

- Privacy invasions are on the rise. Supervisor-referred clients, just like those mandated to do EAP following a dirty drug test, have few protections of their counseling record. Notes taken during an ostensibly confidential session should be off limits to the management. Check to see exactly what information the company is entitled to require from your counselor. Ask your counselor. In court cases, the case notes can be dragged into public court. Even voluntary EAP clients risk invasions of privacy through increased access to records. The most horrific trend is for insurance company representatives to attend sessions and direct the therapist with respect to techniques used to reduce the number of sessions.

- Peer counselors with dubious qualifications. EAP began as alcoholism counseling done by recovering alcoholics who worked for the company. Some programs still favor peer counselors with less training and experience than outside, independent professionals. Of course, if your EAP counselor is an addictions specialist, he or she won't understand the impact sick workplaces will have, nor will they necessarily be sympathetic to the complex effects of bullying, such as PTSD and other effects of stress separate from chemical dependency. Ask your EAP counselor about credentials and experience with situations like yours.

Union Representatives

Unions, like employers, are organizations. They have agendas and goals that may or may not meet your needs. As incredible as this sounds, unions are not automatically good at giving unconditional employee support. Unions have appropriated the name "labor," but their influence extends to less than 15 percent of the American workforce today.

Excerpted cases from the Campaign files:

Clara was a Teamsters union member and schoolbus driver. Her boss was an old-fashioned sexual harasser who sabotaged her bus so that she lost her brakes with a load of children on board. Because the national union publishes guidelines clearly defining how the local union is supposed to defend harassed employee members, she called the union for help. But when she called, her rep called her a "fat, ugly broad not worth fighting for" and refused to see her.

Susan is the only female meat packer at a grocery store. She belongs to a union. Troubles with her immediate boss and the store manager led her to the union. In preparation, she wrote eighteen questions she wanted answered about the reprehensible behavior of both bosses. The union rep scheduled only thirty minutes to hear her complaint. Halfway through the meeting, after rolling his eyes in disbelief, he terminated the session. Susan protested so much that he scheduled a follow-up session the next day. Her husband accompanied her to that meeting. The rep was formally cordial and did start the formal grievance paperwork. When asked when they would get answers to Susan's eighteen questions, the rep yawned and said, "maybe never, there isn't time." Could they fax the list for him so he could find answers at his own pace, they queried. He refused. Only after Susan called the local union president, whose election she helped win, did the rep consent to read her questions.

Gary works for a steel mill with a local union. Recently, his company decided do away with all employee breaks, despite the fact that most employees work eight hours a day for a forty-hour week. The company says they are becoming a continuous operation, and not only have they extended the time worked, but they have removed people from Gary's department. Now, two people are expected to do the work of three people. Gary asked his union rep about laws that say an employer has to give breaks after an employee works so many hours. His union refuses to help. They are letting the company do what they want to do.

Tara was bullied by a sexual harasser. She ran to the union and simultaneously to an independent employment lawyer. Her legal claim was postponed until the union grievance procedure was completed. She expected it to be weeks. Her case was a clear-cut example of illegal sexual harassment. Once a month for a year, she called the union checking on the status of her grievance. They always put her off. Her lawyer could do nothing. Two years later, a union rep called Tara to announce her hearing had been scheduled the next week. But she had returned to college and could not attend at the scheduled time. The rep said this jeopardized her claim. She called the local union president at home explaining her dilemma. He assured her that a new time could be set taking into account her class times. He told her to fax him her schedule. She did so. Weeks passed with no word of a new time for the hearing. Then, nearly two months after she first contacted the president, he called

her to formally announce that her grievance had been dropped because
she failed to appear at the hearing two months ago! He denied receiving
her faxed schedule and the conversation they had about rescheduling.

It is a shame that young employees are ignorant of the positive role unions can play in improving working conditions. However, to reverse the rapid decline of unions' popularity, unions will have to improve service to existing members. There is no excuse for the only official employee advocates to be too busy to help employees who seek relief from horrendous workplaces.

Several corporate-sponsored foundations and groups have large fund reserves and pose as friends of employees. Most are imposters. One such group is the National Right To Work Legal Aid Foundation. In 1997, they had four hundred cases active in the courts to fight "union abuses" on behalf of employees. In reality, the only "abuses" they challenge are compulsory union dues of which a portion is earmarked for political action committees. The NRTW, a union-busting organization, is hardly the type of helper you need to get better service from your union.

If you feel that your union fails to protect your union rights for arbitrary, malicious, bad faith, or discriminatory reasons, you can sue under the National Labor Relations Act.

Chambers of Commerce: Employee Hazards

This national organization lobbies to forbid "frivolous" court action by mistreated and terminated employees while using the courts to stop OSHA from making America's most dangerous worksites safer for employees. Any contradiction here with "community service"?

As beltway insiders spun the Starr-Clinton-Jones-Lewinsky fiasco into an indecipherable mess, a stealth campaign likely to affect every hometown and every worker was underway. A wrecking crew had been silently amassing a fortune for a lobbying campaign to destroy the tattered remains of the few inadequate legal workplace protections American employees still have.

Who are the enemies of the working public? Its employers. Large corporations who spent nineteen times labor's $60 million 1996 campaign contributions got what they paid for. The subcommittees of the House Committee on Education and the Workforce began disassembling the EEOC and OSHA to get government off the backs of employers.

The death of federal worker protections is imminent. These initiatives are done on behalf of the "new" worker who needs to move freely among employers, selling his talents to the highest bidder, as a free agent does in professional sports.

Of course, the question about why there must be movement in the first place goes begging. This line of reasoning suggests that historical job security is imprisoning for workers who "deserve" to start anew every few years.

In every town, the local Chamber of Commerce, heavily populated by realtors and builders, acts as the unelected leadership who brings urban sprawl and traffic. Chamber membership is often the springboard to name recognition and increased electability. The Chamber portrays itself as a benign good citizen, making highly visible contributions to local organizations and contributing to local causes. But beneath this cover of community service beats a callous anti-employee heart. One formal 1998 initiative and one representative court action tell the true story about Chamber values.

Business is about competition for customers. Ironically, inter-member competition in the Chamber is downplayed. Every business is invited to join. So how is the competitive instinct of these capitalist owners manifested at the Chamber? Sadly, it's against their employees.

Employees, as the U.S. Chamber of Commerce sees it, file "frivolous" lawsuits against employers that prove costly to Chamber members. So, in 1998 the Chamber launched an attack on employees' rights to sue employers.

Since most Chamber members are small businesses, traditionally exempt from most state and federal regulations, employees who are mistreated or terminated seeking a remedy have only the court system. Going to court requires a lawyer.

In 1998, the U.S. Chamber of Commerce declared war on the Association of Trial Lawyers of America (ATLA) whose members represent employees accusing employers of harassment, defamation, abuse, discrimination, and wrongful termination. Never mind that only a fraction of complaints ever turn into lawsuits. Additionally, fewer than half of all employee-initiated lawsuits make it to trial. And the whining employers win 75.5 percent of the trial decisions. How dare they cry foul!

The war is a lobbying war between the ATLA and the U.S. Chamber of Commerce in state legislatures. It is about dueling trade association fundraising to pay lobbyists, their conduit to influence over elected officials. Make no mistake, though, the Chamber embarked on an anti-employee campaign. It called upon two hundred thousand members to provide the dollars to fuel the distortion campaign.

Larry Kraus, a Chamber senior VP, believes that 75 percent of lawsuits faced by Chamber members involve charges of bias by employees. So, conditions for filing a suit will be curtailed in this drive for so-called "tort reform." In addition, the Chamber is pushing for "loser pays" legislation. The loser in a civil action would have to pay the legal bills for both sides. This slap action is sure to discourage already tormented employees from exercising their only route to redress from a bullying employer.

Legal action is portrayed as "frivolous" when an employee sues. In mid-February 1998, a federal appellate court granted the delay of an OSHA initiative as requested by the U.S. Chamber of Commerce. Through legal action, OSHA was stopped from giving the 12,250 worst workplace safety offending employers an incentive to reduce the likelihood of safety and health inspections. Targeted companies faced a certain annual inspection because of their documented failure to protect employee safety, but OSHA had a plan.

OSHA had tested and perfected a program for employers that was proven to reduce workplace injuries and illnesses. The under-funded, under-attack safety watchdog agency promised to the most dangerous companies that adopted the safety program a reduction of inspections from 100 percent to 30 percent. That was promoted as getting government off their backs.

In court, the Chamber called the incentive plan "coercive" to its members who ignored the federal mandate, and the moral obligation, to provide a safe workplace for employees. The court agreed to suspend OSHA's ability to give the dangerous companies a choice.

The Chamber is not the employee's friend. Its claim of community service at the local level is hypocritical. Lest we forget, the community is comprised of employees. Employees are the target of the Chamber's assault on civil rights and safety in workplaces owned by Chamber members.

Lawyers for Employees Only

If you are the target of harassment, in most situations, the bully will not have broken the law. That is part of what is so frustrating about workplace bullying.

Federal laws dictate under what limited circumstances you are protected. We are not lawyers and cannot interpret the law for you. The National Employee Rights Institute published *Job Rights and Survival Strategies* by attorneys Paul Tobias and Susan Sauter. The following brief summary of the anti-discrimination acts was taken from that book.

Title VII of the Civil Rights Act protects employees from workplace discrimination if they are members of one of the "protected classes": according to race, color, religion, national origin, or sex—this includes discrimination based on pregnancy.

Employees are protected from age discrimination under the Age Discrimination in Employment Act (ADEA) for workers age forty years or older. However, beginning in 1997, the courts have begun to allow employers to claim "economic reasons" to cut loose older workers who just happen to earn the higher salaries, thus eroding federal safeguards.

It is also against federal law to discriminate based on disability (defined as a physical or mental condition that substantially limits a person in a major life function or functions). Only permanent, chronic, or long-term conditions apply, according to the Americans With Disabilities Act (ADA).

In nearly every other instance of workplace bullying, whether or not your complaint has legal merit will depend on the ingenuity of the legal counsel you contract. We recommend calling the National Employment Lawyers Association

(NELA) national office (415-227-4655) for a recommendation to an employment attorney in your area. Remember, you want a labor or plaintiff-only attorney. Plaintiffs are employees who complain against employers, abusing individuals, or unions. Attorneys who represent both sides may have a conflict of interest as well as hidden biases that could affect your case.

As we said, we are frustrated with lawyers. We're not sure whether to blame them for their helplessness or to fault the steady erosion of employee protection laws by heavily financed corporate interests.

The U.S. Chamber of Commerce also has declared war on trial attorneys who represent employees, vowing to fight an employee's right to bring cases against employers. The Chamber wants to chill lawsuits, and they will accomplish this by requiring that the loser in court pays the winner's legal fees.

So, lawyers who represent plaintiffs are the good guys, but they are rarely the crusader atop the white steed that you might imagine. Ideally, they want fees paid up front—a retainer. However, contingency contracts are becoming more common (up to 40 percent of damages won plus expenses). There is consensus among those in our network that lawyers working on contingency are less focused and feel less urgency than attorneys paid a retainer.

Attorneys with expertise in employment law, unless they are NELA members or restrict their practices to plaintiffs, probably represent both employers and employees. Who do you imagine provides the greater revenue? Of course, the attorney is obligated to tell you if she or he has a conflict of interest in your particular case. A partner in the same firm might represent the employer in other cases. When this happens, the attorney should disqualify herself.

Screening Lawyers

Here's our condensed guide to what to look for when selecting an employment lawyer. Ask direct questions if the attorney does not offer this information during the initial telephone call. No attorney is likely to answer all questions or demonstrate all the desired principles, but you are the customer and you have the right to know.

Desired principles:
- a fighting spirit
- an ability to be empathetic
- wisdom based on direct experience in court
- the realism to tell you whether or not your situation has legal standing
- the ability to clearly explain the law so you know it's not the attorney's fault if no remedy exists

Ask for:
- telephone numbers of satisfied clients.
- experience with similar cases brought against similar defendants.
- record (or fear) of going up against your employer.
- how and when you will be prepared for your deposition.
- an assessment of time available for your case, given the current caseload.
- their victory percentage.
- their average monetary award won for clients with similar cases.
- willingness to accept case on contingency (court costs paid by firm or by you) versus retainer and fees as you go.
- a recommendation of another attorney if any of the questions are not answered to your satisfaction or if the attorney doesn't want you as a client.

It's not fair for you to expect your attorney to be your therapist also. You must have a support network in place to help you maintain balance.

Even the lawyer blessed with the most empathic ability cannot manufacture a law. She is stuck with what the legislatures have written and court interpretations. That is, limits in the law most often account for the abrupt refusal to take your case, though the rejection may feel like another personal attack. It's just that it is more important that we work to create laws that give even the least skilled attorney a fighting chance to win your case.

Screen several lawyers until you sense a comfortable fit. Then, lower your expectations for riches and justice.

Your Best Advocate Is You

Let institutionalized helpers help, but be aware of their limitations. Optimize their usefulness to you by knowing their shortcomings. For most of us, we have to weigh carefully the decision to rely on institutionalized helpers for anything. Engaging co-workers can be helpful for your bully-busting campaign. Right now, they either can't or won't help.

Confronting your bully is the least expensive—in terms of money and emotion—and quickest way to regain personal dignity. Your fate is often best managed in your hands.

Section Two

. . . .

BullyProof Yourself
to Stop the Hurt

Chapter Ten:

Assess the Bully's Impact

. . . .

*A scientist heated a pan of water to a high temperature. Then, she tried
to put a live frog into it. The frog jumped out immediately. A second
frog was put in a pan of cold water that was gradually heated to boiling.
That frog never tried to jump. It was boiled to death.* —A parable

When exposed to a bully, most people go through three stages of emotions.
1) You are excited about your job and consider it a positive experience.
2) The bullying starts and you bend over backwards to please the bully. Your
efforts are unsuccessful but you continue to appease the bully. 3) Finally, you can
no longer ignore your frustrations and you explode at the bully, leaving you feeling even more terrible than before.

The phases go something like this. You get a new job and you are eager to go
to work. You are ready to do all you can do, not only for yourself, but for your boss
and your company. You come to work ready to move mountains. No task is impossible. Usually, this over-enthusiasm fades within the first month, and you settle
down to producing the best work you can.

You become aware that something is wrong. You don't seem to be able to do
anything right. Though you continue to do the same good job as before, your good
ideas are not recognized. Soon, you are questioning whether or not you have the
capability to do your work at all. The more you try and improve, the more your
boss or co-worker gets angry at you.

You have run into a bully. Instead of questioning, you imagine that you are not doing something you should do. You then decide you must change in some way. But, regardless of any change you make, the bully still continues to find fault with you or your work. This, in turn, makes you even more determined to find a way to please someone who will never be pleased.

When you have exhausted every avenue (and then some) and you still are not doing it right, you become frustrated. You have done everything to please, why can't the bully understand? Why can't she see how hard you are trying? Why isn't your best effort good enough?

Then comes the explosion. One day when you have been harassed and shamed once too often, you look the bully straight in the eye and you say, "Leave me alone. I'm doing the best I can. Just leave me alone."

Your explosion does not make you feel better, it only makes you feel worse. You begin to think, "What if she's right? What if my work is inferior?" Now you've really done it, you've alienated the one person you need to keep your job.

Sound familiar? That is the reaction most people have when they are faced with continuous bullying. You feel your best just isn't good enough. You are full of self-doubt. Finally, you begin to see the pattern in this sick cycle. You question why this is happening. You decide it is really not you. Now it is time to stop the bully, once and for all.

Getting to the step at which you know it's time to stop the noise, the lies, the venom from the bully is made more complicated because you are immersed in hurt. It's easy to lose track of how deep your troubles are.

Adaptation to a toxic environment carries a price. Only much later, sometimes too late, do people realize the price they have paid for going along with someone else's hurtful plan for their future.

Assessing Impact Before It's Too Late

We present two exercises to help you when the bully attempts to control. It is important that you control the definitions of who you are.

For each exercise, A and B, there are two sets of questions to ask.

Exercise A

You have seen how to recognize bullying. The first exercise is designed to help you counter the bully's false accusations so you can remind yourself of just how competent you are.

There are four areas that will help you begin your recovery from bullying. These are the areas or aspects about yourself that you, friends, family, and co-workers (if any can be trusted) will evaluate.

The four areas are:

- *How I Relate to Others*
  Descriptions of strengths and weaknesses in relationships with friends and co-workers.

- *How Other People See Me*
  Do you get along well with others? Are you seen as angry? Helpful to others? Shy?

- *My Performance at Work*
  Describe the way you handle job assignments. Are you on time? A procrastinator? A "neatnick"?

- *My Ability to Reason and Solve Problems*
  Do you like the freedom to improvise? Are you a quick learner? Do you have special knowledge in certain areas?

Now take some time to write down as many phrases as you can on the following page to describe yourself. Be candid with yourself. Don't be shy or humble.

Note: As with all exercises, we suggest that you create lists and fill in boxes on separate pages so that parts of this book may be shared with friends without the risk of revealing information you'd prefer to keep to yourself.

How I Relate to Others:

How Other People See Me:

My Performance at Work:

My Ability to Solve Problems:

Now, make two blank copies of the series of questions. Give one to a trusted friend or co-worker, and one to a supportive family member. Ask them to jot down how they feel you do in each of the four areas (these are to be shared only with you).

When the sheets are returned, lay them side-by-side. Do you see similarities? What are your strengths. Do you judge yourself too harshly?

Exercise B

This exercise is another way to evaluate how BullyProof you are in the following three areas. Add any dimensions or aspects that are important to you.

- *Quality of Relationships with Others:* This is an indirect indicator of whether or not the bully has poisoned the good relationships you have with others. First, evaluate how you see the quality of your relationships with family and friends. Then, have family members rate the relationship they each have with you. Repeat for friends (as before, co-workers may be included if they are trustworthy). The pattern that emerges can send a warning signal of pending trouble.

    We have noticed that many couples are severely strained when one person is bullied. Split-ups and divorces are common. The worst-case scenario is when the bullied Target loses track of the decline in quality and the partner waits too long to tell her how he is impacted.

- *Confidence in Personal Competence:* This area taps resilience under duress, the ability to focus on "the work" in a storm, and the firmness of your belief in yourself as being right and not deserving the mistreatment received. All bullies, regardless of the particular tactics used, aim to erode the Target's belief in herself. The erosion of this confidence is perhaps the most devastating effect bullies can have. It is among the toughest setbacks from which Targets have to recover.

- *Emotional Effectiveness:* Bullies play on Targets' emotions heavily in order to push them out of control. Too much or too little emotion can be problematic. Make a special note to see who among the list of evaluators believes that you have no right to be hurt or mad.

Of course, you should add any aspects of your life that the bully has tried to dominate to this short list. Then, complete the four-step process described on the following pages for each aspect or dimension.

First set of questions

Turn a critical eye toward yourself. As honestly as you can, state what you *Do Well* and what you *Could Do Better* in a two-column table like the one below. Record observations about yourself, as you see yourself. Answer the question for yourself, strictly from your personal point of view.

After you fill in your answers, you can compare both the quantity and quality of responses. You are not necessarily immune from the bully's attempts to control and influence you just because the list under *Do Well* is longer than under *Could Do Better*. Only you can know if the items in one column are more important than items in the other.

Example

Let's demonstrate how the exercise works for the first worklife area—Quality of Relationships with Others. You will rate that quality, as you define it, strictly *from your point of view*. If the good news (*Do Well*) outweighs the bad (*Could Do Better*), then it's safe to say that you feel your relationships with others have remained relatively immune from damage.

Quality of My Relationships with Others

	Do Well	*Could Do Better*
Rating Myself		

Second set of questions

Ask trustworthy friends and family to rate, *in their opinion,* your contribution to the quality of the relationship they have with you. In other words, you will ask them to say what you *Do Well* and how you *Could Do Better,* strictly from *their point of view.* Each person answers for her- or himself only.

Quality of Your Relationship With Me

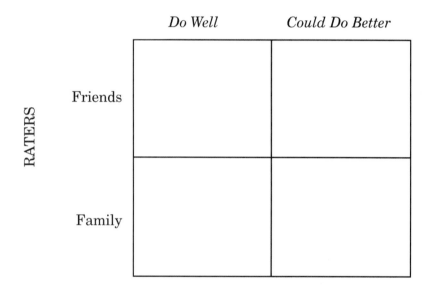

There's no need for raters to see the comments of others. Encourage brutal frankness. This tool works only if raters are honest and forthcoming. When raters are truthful, you will discover problems that you did not, nor could not, see for yourself.

On the other hand, if raters prefer to tell you what they think *you* want to hear (and minimize the bad news), you and they might stay in denial. Without candor, no changes are possible.

Next, assemble an Impact Table summarizing the observations that you and the others noted.

Impact Table
Quality of Relationships

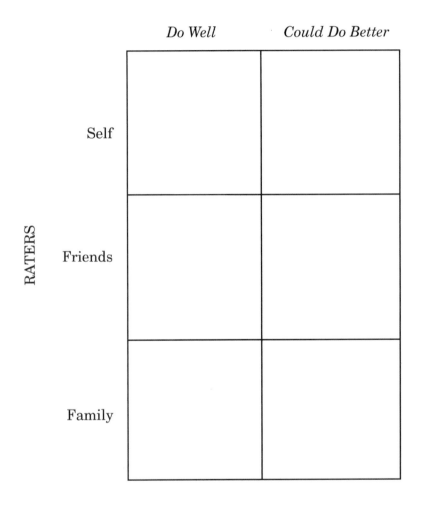

	Do Well	*Could Do Better*
Self		
Friends		
Family		

RATERS

Interpret the Impact Table

Make the comparisons between columns of opinions that others provided. Compare the rows. Look for patterns.

Who thinks you are relatively BullyProof?

Regarding what aspects?

In what areas are you blind, and therefore, vulnerable?

Who sees the effects of the bullying experience as you do?

Are they right or are those who disagree with you right?

How are the differences in observations related to the different
    levels of support you receive?

On whom can you count for a reality check when needed?

Have you lost your sense of perspective? Are you the frog
in boiling water?

Repeat this four-step process for each relevant aspect of your worklife.

1. Do your self-rating.
2. Ask others to rate you.
3. Summarize the observations in an Impact Table.
4. Interpret patterns for meaning. Regain perspective.

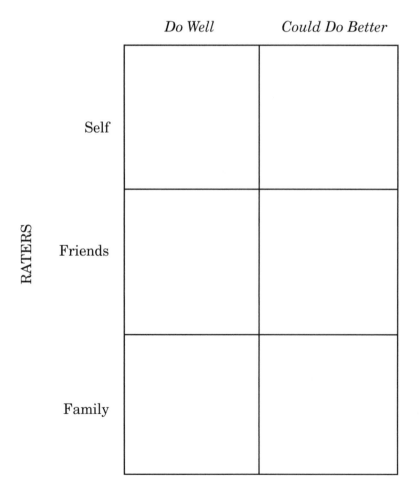

Confidence in Personal Competence

	Do Well	*Could Do Better*
Self		
Friends		
Family		

RATERS

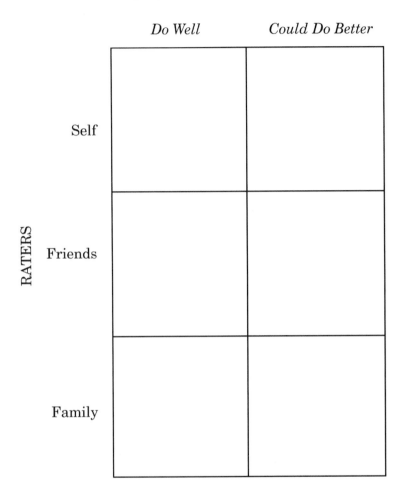

Emotional Effectiveness

	Do Well	*Could Do Better*
Self		
Friends		
Family		

RATERS

Changing Your Perspective

After you have decided what things you can do to change the way you act and feel at work, there is a simple tool to help you when you encounter bullying behaviors.

The way you look at situations with the bully will dramatically affect your attitude. Practice dissociating yourself from unpleasant memories. By mentally stepping away from an unpleasant event or a bully, you can adjust your point of view.

Remember, you can never change the behaviors of the bully, you can only make changes in yourself.

Try using the following three steps to re-evaluate your situation with a bully.

Step 1.

Compare your bully problems to a catastrophic event. Does this compare to losing a leg or a loved one? Do you need a different perspective on this situation?

Step 2.

Mentally edit the memory of your encounter with the bully as if you were editing a film. As you replay your last encounter, view it as if it came from another camera angle. Turn the camera so you can try looking at it in different ways. Go over the memory with a friend to try and get a new perspective on the situation.

Step 3.

Reframe the problem and change the meaning of the experience. Try to look at the experience as a positive event rather than an attack on you. Are there any ways the bullying experience could be positive?

Chapter Eleven:

Establish and Protect Boundaries

. . . .

No one can make you feel inferior without your consent. —Eleanor Roosevelt

Boundaries are central to separating who you are from who the bully wants you to believe you are. Much of what applies to understanding boundaries carries over into other areas that influence Targets.

Much of a person's identity and self-confidence comes from having appropriate boundaries in place for protection against assaults by bullies who seek only to control and hurt their Target.

Boundary Characteristics

Two boundary characteristics that affect, and are affected by bullying are:

- your personally chosen and defined boundaries, established so you can live your life the way you seek and want
- your boundaries' susceptibility to invasion by a bully

In its simplest definition, a boundary is an unseen, unmeasurable limit or barrier that simultaneously creates an inside and an outside. It is an invisible wall with two sides. Inside each individual boundary resides an identity—personal, family, or group. Challenges to those identities are launched by invading bullies from the outside who want to dictate the terms of a Target's identity.

Except for skin, boundaries are psychological. For our purposes here, we speak of psychological boundaries. They can be identified by gauging your tolerance for having them invaded. Invasions of personal boundaries by others causes discomfort and anxiety. When uncomfortable enough, we typically take steps to stop the invader that caused the pain.

People have different thresholds. Some have a higher tolerance for letting others meddle in their lives; some tolerate little to no meddling. Meddling ranges from suggestions about how you should live your life (typically tolerated from close friends) to full-scale verbal assaults by bullies repeatedly telling you how incompetent and worthless you are.

The greatest danger a Target faces in the working world is to have loose or non-existent boundaries. That person becomes an unprotected Target for all who love to hurt others.

One way to repel invasions by bullies is to use verbal commands to stop the bullying behavior, to announce that a line has been crossed, that you have a policy of zero tolerance for such unacceptable actions and that it will be enforced. This is "tit for tat." Most bully invasions are done with words. Most Target's have little practice dealing with these intrusions.

INVASION → DISCOMFORT → REPEL INVASION

Below are categories of boundaries ordered by an orientation toward others. This list builds from the primary boundary of personal identity and widens to include one's social world.

Identity Boundaries
- Physical/Personal Space
- Emotions
- The Self

Family Boundaries
- Unit Solidarity
- Empathy
- Work and Family

Work/Social Boundaries
- Jobs
- Friends, Co-Workers, Supporters

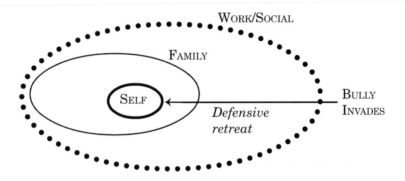

Depiction of a bully invasion piercing protective boundaries in stages, with the Self serving as the Target's last stand.

Identity Boundaries

Skin, Touch, and Space

The knowledge of separateness from the world begins in the crib. Just connecting the act of swinging your little baby foot with moving the mobile begins the journey to Selfhood. Your developing infant brain gets and implants the message that you are *not* your environment. Though your mind cannot yet fathom philosophy, you know that there is an "out there." Miraculously, you've taken the first step toward an "internal you." The assembly of an Individual begins that early.

For humans, our skin literally becomes the physical boundary between us and the external world. It is through that skin that so much brain and neural development takes place. Touch stimulates and comforts. It is the language of love, nurturing, and acceptance. The absence of touch sets the stage for needy, love-starved adults.

The rules about who you allow to touch your skin develop in childhood. Nearly everyone touches an infant.

As you grow older, based on cultural mores and family tradition, strangers will be forbidden to share the intimate zone of touching skin. When the unwritten rule is violated, you automatically get anxious and take evasive action. That's why inappropriate contact by strangers is a hostile gesture. More will be said about the use of personal space when we discuss traps in nonverbal communication.

Emotions

Emotions are also learned in childhood and follow family- and peer-specific unwritten norms and rules. Those values learned early in life are:

- expressivity: emotions are publicly displayed, and
- labeling: names given to internal feelings in response to events.

There are entire textbooks written about the healthy development of human emotions. Growing up with few inhibitions about expressing feelings tends to create adults who readily show their feelings. It's good to grow up free from much of the anxiety that seems to burden those who live scripted lives. An uninhibited spirit is less likely to suffer from stress.

The point most relevant to workplace bullying is that people who naturally show emotions will generally be seen as more vulnerable than those with a closed style.

You have the right to call your emotions what you want. Gut feelings are ambiguous. They are normal reactions to potential stressors in your life. The emotional label you choose determines whether the feeling is positive or negative.

The Impact of Feelings

Imagine the gut-wrenching, sweaty-palms feeling as you're about to turn in a project you've worked on for six months. If the person you're giving it to is the office tyrant, your sworn enemy, you're likely to call that swirling feeling nausea in anticipation of the undeserved verbal tirade you've come to expect. You're literally sick, knowing that she will bark about how "stupid and incompetent" you are. You condition yourself to recognize the symptoms as those of impending shame. No one should have the right to inflict shame on you or be able to trigger it through fearful anticipation!

On the other hand, if you're submitting the project to the person who promised a promotion and raise when it was done, those are harmless butterflies in anticipation of a new phase of your career. You're dizzy with anticipation of spending the extra money and all the recognition a new job brings.

Same stomach, different names for the feeling that goes with physiological symptoms. Research has shown that we're all somewhat susceptible to labeling of our emotions by others when the feelings are unclear. However, it's dangerous when you are ready to experience a positive emotion and an outsider barges in and defines the feeling for you. In anxious times, we are more susceptible to an invasion of our emotional boundaries.

The Self—Putting It All Together

All the "firsts" in your life begin in early infancy with parental relationships. Besides meeting your needs for food and shelter, parents influence and impact whether we develop into strong or weak selves. When old enough to interact with others besides parents, the Self is further developed by peers who shape you into what you are and will become. The final product called "you" continues to develop through a lifetime. The core—your fundamental approach to how you deal with what life throws you—is predominantly determined at a young age.

With a well-developed Self in place, you can resist all attempts by others to define your identity, to invade your personal space without permission, to excercise control over you, and to define feelings for you. A poorly developed Self seems to doom adults to search outside themselves for answers to inner questions. This renders them more vulnerable to influence by others. It is not a question of goodness or badness, but rather a matter of dependency on others for definitions. This dependency puts such people in the bully's direct line of fire.

The Self is the safe place to which you can retreat when under attack. It is the one boundary that should never be compromised, invaded, or traded away to get along with another person. Think of it as the last box inside several other boxes, each inside the other. You and you alone control access to it. And the re-programming of the lifetime of scripts stored there will be undertaken only by you, on your terms. Changes are yours to make.

Let's not get bogged down in psychobabble here. Simply put, never discount the importance of selfhood. All feelings of adult worthiness, entitlement to certain "rights," pride, and competence flow from experiences, many of which were too early to recall.

Family Boundaries

Family-of-Origin Factors

Our first social group is our family-of-origin, a group of manageable size. The family-of-origin is the place to rehearse behaviors for the larger world of strangers in which we don't always get our way. Families teach us to be social beings, capable of respecting or disregarding others. In a healthy family, a child is taught to develop a self-concept separate and different from other family members.

Healthy families also provide unconditional support for us as blossoming little people. Ideally, parents and older siblings foster independence by teaching us to fend for ourselves while tolerating dependence on the family for comfort in the toughest of times.

Family Interactions and Targethood

Unfortunately, there are families that live with sick "enmeshed patterns," better described as smothering rather than helpful. One for all and all for one sounds like teamwork until the identities of all the children and usually one parent are sacrificed. Distinct personalities rarely emerge from such families. Enmeshed families squash the human need to become an individual, to matter, to be special in some unique way.

"Disengaged" families are equally defeating. They are families where members have little contact with each other and little to no love. Children grow up believing they are worthless, needing to justify in their own minds the neglect they experience.

Adults who grew up with either of these disturbed arrangements are likely to rely too heavily on people at work for support, validation and even for an identity. Bullies smell neediness and exploit it to their advantage.

Healthy Families

Healthy families form a protective boundary behind which adults and children can retreat to safety when and if necessary. It's a much looser boundary, woven more by solidarity among family members, than the shell around the Self.

A bully is a person who denies her emotions (low expressivity). She operates from rigid boundaries. In her disengaged family-of-origin, she was not connected with her parents. Because of this, her feelings were not developed or brought to the surface. More importantly, when any feelings do surface for her, she easily becomes overwhelmed and withdraws from all contact with others.

Empathy

Another gift taught in healthy families is empathy. Empathy is the human capacity to understand, intellectually, what another person is going through when things go poorly and to recognize the emotional state of that person because you've gone through it. Sympathy is cold—that's why pity serves no purpose. Empathy is sympathy with emotions included. It is the basis of compassion. Families are the first teachers of compassion.

Empathy requires the loosening of rigid, personal protective boundaries. It involves letting in the experiences of others. Empathy is always considered one of humankind's higher level traits. Unfortunately, the openness and compassion that characterize empathy render you vulnerable to assaults from a bully who despises positive traits. As a witness to the bullying of another person, it is empathy that will compel you to take action to alleviate the Target's suffering.

In general, bullies are thwarted by independent Targets and don't bother with them. Research in workplace aggression found that bullies are essentially lazy. They prefer easier-to-control, vulnerable Targets.

Work and Family

When you're the adult and parent, you face the issues of allocating your energy and time across family and work activities. The critical boundary question is how much intrusion by work into your private time will be tolerated. The answer is necessarily personal. Some advisers sketch pie charts slicing an ideal life into several domains: income-generating, physical health, learning, love, and spiritual, to name a few. Their concern is balance.

For BullyProofing yourself, the concern is whether or not you can fight work's intrusive effect on the rest of your life. Targets under fire from bullies may try to keep the torment a secret from everyone at home. However, the strain takes its toll in small, unavoidable ways. There may be loss of sleep, increased moodiness, a shorter fuse for getting angry, and general depression. Astute family members cannot help but notice, but may say nothing until you, the Target, share the cause of your grief or ask for help.

The thing to remember during bullying is that the separation of the work-family boundary fools no one. The family cannot help but be affected by trouble at work. Trying to will away the negative impact of bullying on the family with words ("I won't discuss at home what happens in that hellhole") or the shutting down of discussion about it during family time prevents Targets from getting the support and love they so desperately need to offset the lies and isolation that has become work. Also, the family, as a unit, can brainstorm together what can be done to bust the bully, to turn off the source of the pain. Attempting to go it alone while feigning a calm, collected exterior is foolhardy.

Well-intentioned Targets want to spare their families the hurt, but they are wasting too much energy by covering up. It's better to recruit the family's help right from the start. Isolated Targets are weakened. Targets, backed with a family's love, can shorten the period of vulnerability. Supported Targets can move forward quicker and re-establish a normal work-family barrier when work is more normal.

Work/Social Boundaries

Social boundaries are looser and less permanent because so many people share in their development and maintenance. Nothing is as personal, nor should be as inviolate, as a person's identity.

The Job

Based on the figure depicting family and personal boundaries embedded with the work/social boundaries, you can see how far from a personal identity the job should lie. That is, your identity was formed long ago and is very distinct from what you do for a living, for economic necessity. At least that's true for the majority of folks. There are a few among us whose work and soul are deliberately fused and inseparable (usually artists).

For the rest of us mere mortals, and nearly everyone who gets bullied, it is critical to separate your identity from the job. Jobs are frequently snatched away without warning, without care for the consequences you and your family face. If every time you change jobs, you had to change the person you are, you'd be exhausted from the task of restructuring a life several times (five to seven changes, according to recent surveys).

Jobs pass and are shared by hundreds, if not thousands, of others. Your identity has to remain relatively permanent to lend stability and purpose to your life. When you can no longer count on a job, you still must be able to count on the uniqueness that is you.

Here is the critical point about job boundaries. Assaults on boundaries force the Target into a defensive position. The question you have to ask yourself is whether or not a job is worth defending—"I have to have this job, there are no others for me," "I can't do anything else," "I have to hold onto this job that tortures me daily because it's easier to get a job when you have a job." It's especially maddening when The Work Doctor hears advice seekers defend holding onto a job (thus showing a strong job boundary) immediately after describing the incredible destruction it has brought to their lives.

With this perverted logic, Targets elevate the importance of keeping that specific job at the expense of their self-worth as if they deserve no better (thus yielding to invasions of their identity boundary). This rationalization and compromise make little sense. There will be another job. However, if this job kills you, you won't be around to work it.

Friends, Co-Workers, Supporters

This boundary captures the widest group of non-related people in your world. It is not of a uniform size, thickness, or permeability. It is in a constant state of flux. Essentially, this boundary separates those in your "in-group" from those not within your inner circle. In broad societal terms, common grouping variables are profession, race, age, gender, etc. These are broad group identities that may be invoked when you and your peers gather together for breaks and social events.

At work, the co-worker boundary is a good example of how a temporary, constantly changing group identity can hurt Targets of bullying. One day, the group is commiserating about the bully's torment. They may even share stories of misery while they themselves were the bully's Targets. As a reasonable person, you might assume that you will all stand together to fight the bully in front of her boss.

However, the next day, you, as the Target, may suddenly and inexplicably find yourself out of the group and left to fend for yourself. You stand alone with your plight. It's as if the frank griping sessions never happened. The many reasons for this turnaround are based on fear.

The feelings of abandonment by a group that originally supported you compounds the pain. When a group turns on you, it is easy to doubt that you are right and the bully is wrong. The speed with which a group forms, disbands, and re-forms should send a warning that groups deserve the least trust.

Unions are also a group to which you may belong, whose ostensible purpose is to defend your rights. However, they, too are prone to abandon you for various reasons driven by the group's survival priorities rather than the merits of your case. They satisfy their contractual obligation by starting the grievance process, but that is long, tortuous, and inefficient for dealing with daily bullying. The courage of a special individual in the group willing to take risks on your behalf is more important than any group identity.

Boundaries and Defenses

When facing assaults from a bully and retreating to a defensive position, it's natural to first seek validation from your work group for the perception that you're not crazy. If it's a team of turncoats, you will get no support. The response to this rejection is to focus entirely on your job. Targets try to "stick to the job" and ignore all the madness manufactured by the bully, thus, going it alone at work.

Then, when intense concentration to your job fails to serve as a distraction from bullying, the next possible source of comfort is the family. Sadly, even families can tire of the steady stream of workplace horror stories. We wish it were not true, but it is a rare family that gives unconditional support from the beginning to the absolute end of a bully's campaign.

This leaves the final source of comfort as the Self. It's the box within the boxes, the innermost circle, the one thing you have to count on—faith in your identity.

Of course, this model of levels or layers of boundaries that one after another fail to ward off the bully is the worst-case scenario. In the best of all possible worlds (though rarely occurring), your work group stands solidly with you so that you have multiple sources of support, with family and identity providing additional support. With all boundaries intact, a bully has no chance to overcome a Target.

Boundary Rights
Cats and Dogs

The writer Mary Bly compares boundaries with cats and dogs. "Dogs," she writes, "come when they are called; cats take a message and get back to you."

Dogs always want to be close to people. They will jump on our laps (no matter what their size), or come on the bed, always trying to get as close as possible. Their boundaries are very close and they expect all other animals to have the same boundaries.

Cats, on the other hand, have very distinct boundaries. They come and go when they want and if they want. When they want to be close, they determine when, how, and where. They are aware of the humans in the room, but human movements do not interrupt what they are doing. Their boundaries are very different from dogs. Cats need more space and their boundaries are more rigid.

Like cats and dogs we all grow up with different boundaries. We learn and tend to practice the boundaries we were taught as children. We tend to see them in black and white and rarely even question them. What we fail to see is that boundaries are not only black and white, but also come in shades of gray.

Avoiding Spineless Flexibility

The contrast to rigid boundaries is when boundaries are so flexible they can't hold shape. When you encounter someone with loose boundaries you will see that they are like chameleons.

> Lisa is a chameleon. At work she will agree with a co-worker that their boss is unreasonable. Ten minutes later when someone else states that she feels their boss is a great and understanding fellow, Lisa will agree with her. She is unable to let the phone ring at lunch and at the end of the day, for fear she will miss something important and get into trouble. Thus, she misses many lunches and spends many hours working after 5 P.M., just to finish the work that was interrupted by phone calls.
>
> Because Lisa's boundaries are too flexible, she often feels overwhelmed with balancing life and work. Each new demand distracts her. She has difficulty setting priorities and following them. She gets started on one task only to get sidetracked by something else. She may appear disorganized.

Maintaining Your Boundaries in the Face of Power

Certain roles carry rank or power—parent, supervisor, boss, teacher, coach, doctor, policeman. It is important, however, to know that no matter what power a person has in relation to you, there are still boundaries they should not violate.

No matter how understanding your boss seems, you are not her priority. A supervisor who invites confidences, who treats you as a peer, or who leans on you for support is violating a boundary. Your supervisor is not your peer. No matter how much she cares for you and your job, her own job is most important to her. If she has to sacrifice you to keep her position, she will!

Your supervisor's job is to support you as a worker. It is not your job to listen to her problems. If this happens, you become her sympathetic ear and your own loyalty becomes divided. Your energy then is diverted from your actual work and a bond is created between you and your supervisor that causes confusion between loyalty to yourself and to the company.

Good boundaries between workers and supervisors and bosses is like good parenting. It allows for safe communication, security in risking, appropriate meeting of needs, attention to role requirements, and support of subordinates. The goal in any business should be the maximum and finest development of the worker.

There's much talk about "flat organizations," "boss-free workplaces," and "egalitarian management." We'd love to believe it, but our experiences with the dark underbelly of the work world has taught us to doubt. Better to err with cynicism and be safe than to let down your guard and be eaten alive.

If you doubt that power differences truly exist, ask who has the power to terminate your livelihood based on a false rumor, vague concept such as "competitiveness," or a whim. Whoever has that clout is NOT your equal. Remember that fact when you are encouraged to "let down your guard, to just be friends." Friends outside; acquaintances inside.

Recognizing Unhealthy Work Boundaries

It is a fact of life that some bosses and supervisors (and even some co-workers) are very unhealthy and abuse their power to get their needs met. If your boss is unhealthy, bullying behavior will echo throughout your organization. If bullying is part of your organization, you have a choice. You can try to develop a healthy base with your co-workers and promote a healthy relationship with your supervisor or boss. If this is possible, you might find that as you become more healthy, the people around you will become more healthy.

However, if you are asked to cross a boundary that violates your personal space, you will need to assess whether or not this is a healthy place for you to work. You need to ask if you should take yourself out of a work situation where you are being violated. You should do this as soon as you can. If it is with co-workers, you can practice and use the skills you need to preserve your dignity. If it is with a supervisor or boss, decide whether you can repair the damage to your boundaries. If you can't, you need to look for a new position.

Your Personal Boundary Rights

You have a right to privacy. You have the right to choose what questions you answer. You don't have to tell anyone your thoughts or feelings. You are not overly sensitive if you decline to answer a thoughtless question.

If a boss, supervisor, or co-worker seems nosy and asks inappropriate questions, you can practice these answers: "I don't feel like talking about it." "I want to keep that to myself." "That's my business." "I'm surprised you think you have a right to that information." "Whoops! That's private."

Chapter Twelve

Avoid Unattainable Standards

. . . .

Face your deficiencies and acknowledge them, but do not let them master you. Let them teach you patience, sweetness, insight....When we do the best we can, we never know what miracle is wrought in our life, or in the life of another. —Helen Keller

The internal compass that governs much of our lives is a set of privately held beliefs and values. There are other forces exerting their influence over what we do and say on a daily basis (a bully is an example of an obnoxious external factor). However, the legacy of our parents is the presence or absence of beliefs that are as broad as a philosophy toward life or that can be as narrow as obsessing over uncrossed handwritten letter "t's."

The Shoulds In Our Lives

A "should" is an internal, private expectation about how the world ought to be. It is our personal standard, the ideal, to which reality is compared. Everything and everyone we encounter is compared to the standard in our head. After a lifetime of judging, the scrutiny is done without deliberate thought. It is automatic.

The teaching of values and beliefs began in infancy. Attention to our cries was an early sign of respect for us as human beings. Attentiveness rather than neglect molded one of the most primitive attitudes toward others. We progressed into learning how to handle anger, mistakes, and pain. We learned rules about what is acceptable conversation. Even life goals and the manner in which we treat others were modeled for us or informally introduced by parents and older siblings.

For most of us, parental evaluation of our behavior played a large part in determining confidence or worthlessness. In turn, our values developed from that scrutiny. Values like commitment, honesty, generosity, dignity, intelligence, and a strong work ethic are the parental legacy that ripples through our adult lives.

Kind and ambitious parents were the types to find ways to keep their children inspired. Here's one such inspiring quote.

> *Aim at the sun and you may not reach it, but your arrow will fly*
> *farther than if you had aimed at an object on a level with yourself.*

Your childhood experience determines whether you read that statement as a challenge to do even better (with the understanding that you always do well, keep striving to do more) or that your history is one of always taking the easy way out (aiming at a low level) therefore you should take a wild shot at the big prize, though you most certainly won't win.

If evaluations meant anxiety-plagued scrutiny, devastating criticism, and a steady tearing down by your parents, it is no surprise that you, the adult, are paralyzed by fear.

Unfortunately, the world is not populated just by caring, loving parents. In dysfunctional families, children were taught to distrust, to attack rather than cooperate, or to lie constantly to cover up family problems.

Deep-seated beliefs can convey a sense of security when they conjure up sweet memories of the time when they were first introduced. Not only are the values important, but the legend of how they were introduced reinforces the security.

On the other hand, if chaos is what the child lived with while growing up, there can be little safety in adulthood.

With luck, we acquired a realistic set of expectations about how the world should treat us. We learned to strike a balance between giddy over-optimism and perpetual gloom and doom.

The last point we make about the parental role in establishing expectations is that most expectations have a moral tone to them. That is, if you should or ought to be doing something one way, then you had better feel guilty if that is not what you are doing.

The shoulds are also the product of:

1) The need to feel part of a group and to have the approval of others. The group has tremendous clout over the individual. When a group of co-workers uniformly turns on you, they put your version of who you are in direct conflict with the one they want you to believe. Most people yield to the group, as incredible as that sounds.

2) Our status in life or our role at work. People internalize hierarchies. Different views accompany different levels of organizations in our lives. Husband status activates one set of expectations and wife status creates another.

We take the values and beliefs we learn from our parents to our jobs. If we learned to be overcritical in our family-of-origin, then those critical values are the values we take with us to work.

> *Linda was recently fired from her job as an account representative. She tells her family and friends that she was stupid to ever consider, much less take, this job. She reports to her mother that the job was "demeaning, boring, and unchallenging. I've never met anyone in that line," she says, "who wasn't uneducated and stupid." She vows never to take another job like this. Her opinions are a rationalization created by her need to maintain her self-esteem. She must devalue her job and employer or see herself as a failure.*

> *Shellie works hard at her job, often spending six to eight hours of overtime per week to ensure that her work is done. She is very vocal in*

her opinion that one must be completely committed to every job. She states she hates the smallest sign of laziness. However, another way to look at her actions are to consider that she works so hard to only show others that she doesn't need help from anyone. She needs to feel confident and safe and avoid the criticism of others. She stays in control by drowning herself in a pile of work.

In these examples, both Linda and Shellie use their critical beliefs and values to judge themselves in their business lives. Their goals are unattainable, impossibly high with regards to their need for love, safety, and feeling good about themselves. When this happens, Targets need to be more realistic. Often the values that they have been taught have little to do with reality.

Consider Sally. She has graduated from a college that strongly espouses that women are entitled to fulfill themselves personally and through their work. However, she has three strong needs that generate her beliefs about work. The first is the need to win the love of her father who is very critical of what she does for a living. Her second need is to be able to work and give enough time to her family while she works. A third need is to set an example for her children that both women and men can find fulfillment in work and family. Unfortunately, her needs are in conflict.

Sally has encountered the "tyranny of the shoulds." She operates under the belief that she should be able to be all things to all people (her father and her family), and the unforgiving sense of what is right (she should be able to please everyone) and wrong (if she doesn't, she is a bad person).

Why do we do this? We sometimes torture ourselves with guilt and self-blame over things we cannot change. This is why we become paralyzed when we are forced to choose between unbending rules (unattainable or unsustainable expectations) and genuine desire.

Self-Defeating Shoulds

I should:

- be able to give to everyone all the time.
- never make a mistake.
- be the perfect partner, co-worker, team member.
- never feel hurt.
- always see the bright, positive side of situations.
- always keep my negative emotions under control.
- always be totally self-reliant, never depend on others.
- be a complete, multi-faceted life partner.
- anticipate my child's every need all the time.
- never complain about being tired or sick.
- never let the emotions—anger or jealousy—show.
- be respectful and polite to everyone.
- make no enemies.
- never believe I'm good, but wait until others say so.
- always put the needs of others before my own needs.
- never be afraid.
- never make a mistake.

The Tyranny of Totality Is Self-Defeating.

Think about it. We all torture ourselves with guilt and self-blame when we are unable to live up to standards that may be too high. We see ourselves as failures. The gap between the way we think the world "should be" for us and our perception of "what is" can generate a sense of worthlessness.

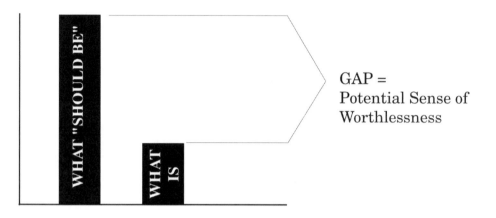

GAP =
Potential Sense of
Worthlessness

Bullying and Standards

The bully's irrational, unrealistic hammering may be reminiscent of tyrannical parents who imposed and enforced martial law while growing up. The emotional cruelty was sufficiently evil. But the longer-lasting legacy is the deeply imbedded belief that you are never quite good enough, that you are always falling short.

Now that there is a bully at work, the parental voices resonate in your mind. It is as if it were yesterday—getting yelled at over trivial matters that "justified" a verbal assault. The bully is the bad parent come home again. As if you needed reminding that you are not a complete individual. The bully thinks her job is to police you so you don't miss an error or shortcoming. This is an outrageous intrusion into your life.

Chapter Thirteen:

Counter Your
Inner Critic

. . . .

Face your deficiencies and acknowledge them; but do not let them master you.
Let them teach you patience, sweetness, insight... —Helen Keller

The inner critic is born during parental teaching of right and wrong. Later in life, it's that personal, negative, nagging little judge whose attacks only you hear in your head. Everyone has a critical inner voice. Some voices are more strident and demanding than others.

Your critic:

- blames you for things that go wrong
- compares you to others, especially achievements and abilities others have but you want
- sets impossible standards of perfection
- beats you up if you are not perfect
- sticks to a script that describes how you should live
- screams that you are wrong or bad if your needs drive you to violate its rules
- tells you to be the best, and if you're not the best, it tells you that you're nothing
- calls you names, leading you to believe they are true

- reads your friends' minds to prove to you that they are bored, turned off, disappointed, or disgusted by you
- exaggerates your weaknesses by insisting that you "always say stupid things," or "always screw up on the job," or, "never finish anything on time"

In other words, the inner critic is busy undermining everything you do. If you listen carefully, you might recognize the voice as that of your mother, father, or yourself.

The most important thing you need to know about your very special critic is that no matter how distorted or false the attacks may be, *you always believe what is said*. In almost every situation, the critic is there to find fault, blaming and judging you harshly in the process. The critic also reminds you of past failures, connecting them to the present, forever limiting your ability to start anew or to soar with newfound wings.

Our inner critic can be compared with Freud's superego. The superego is the internalized parent, the moral authority that develops supposedly to hold the pleasure-driven "id" in check. It's the self-righteous, pontificating, boorish part of our personalities.

The critic examines everything we do and puts its own spin on it. The critic is always there, whether tearing you down or helping you solve problems and meet basic needs.

Yes, there is a benefit to having an inner critic.

Its Purpose

The need to do right: We all have our own values and morals that we learned in childhood. These serve to create an ethical framework for all activities in your life by defining how to act with family members, authority figures, co-workers, and friends. The critic helps you distinguish right from wrong. The critic also tells you how wrong or bad you are when you are tempted to act beyond your own ethical standard.

The need to achieve: The critic helps you achieve goals by whipping you like a race horse. It pushes you along—constantly telling you that what you thought was good is not good enough. It gives you the encouragement to reach goals others might feel are out of your reach.

The need to feel right: Even while the critic tells you you're no good, it helps you by evaluating how you stack up against others. Although it usually finds you lacking, once in a while it will confirm that you are stronger, more attractive, and smarter than others. Because this occurs rarely, it reinforces the critic by encouraging you to keep trying to reach unreachable goals.

Your inner critic can both hurt you and help you. The good news is that with practice you can learn to recognize, analyze, and refute the negative destructive criticism while keeping and using what is useful and helpful.

Countering the Critic

You need to be realistic. Face the fact that the most painful criticism of your work might be coming from your own inner critic. Most people spend a good portion of every workday bombarding themselves with unrealistically high expectations, while bombarding you with harsh criticisms of the things you don't do well. It is a recipe for feeling like a failure. If you combine this with the critical statements and lies from a bully, you cannot help but feel like you are a failure.

You can improve the way you handle your own inner critic. Use the following questions to examine your attitudes toward yourself.

- When you make an error or an oversight at work, do you criticize yourself in a harsh manner?
- Before important meetings, job interviews, or work assignments, are your thoughts negative—do you focus on all that might go wrong?
- When you are running late, do you bombard yourself with harsh criticism, even before anyone else notices you are late?
- Do you worry you will be found out and others will discover you're not really able to do what is expected of you?

- Do you lie awake at night criticizing yourself for anything that went wrong during the day, even though you didn't have much control over what happened?
- Have you ever said or thought to yourself that you are your own worst critic?

If you answer yes to even *one* of these statements, your inner critic is working overtime.

If You Invalidate Your Own Hard Work, Stop the Self-Destruction Immediately!

Instead of attacking yourself with criticism, take a moment to stop and catch yourself. Ask, "Is this self-criticism necessary and should I spend any time or effort on it?" or, "Would my time be better spent getting support and ideas for solutions," or, "Does my supervisor's critical nature amplify my own doubts and leave me feeling doubly bad?"

Do not lose sight of all the good work you've done right on a project just because something has gone wrong. Ask yourself if you could address the problem without calling on your own critic. It is also important to keep in mind that you have done a lot of good work that got you this far.

Remind yourself each day or evening of
three good things you did that day.

Don't remember only the things that go wrong. Avoid focusing only on the things that you can't fix or control. Be good to yourself! At least once a day or at night when you are unwinding from work, take a few moments to acknowledge to yourself (or with a trusted friend) the hard work and worthwhile efforts you did that day. Even on projects that did not turn out as well as you planned, you need to take stock of the valuable planning, thinking, and actions that you've taken that day or that week.

Make sure you don't talk to
yourself in a critical manner.

If you notice you tend to talk badly to yourself, stop and say to yourself, "I don't need to be so mean to myself or anyone else. I don't need to listen to the negative remarks from the bully, I'm doing a good job."

Be aware of an increased susceptibility to be destructively self-critical in certain circumstances. You might try a "thought-stopping" technique to disrupt your train of self-defeating thinking. One way is to wear a rubber band on your wrist (hidden under your blouse or shirt sleeve, if you're self-conscious). When the "stinking thinking" starts, simply snap the band. Mindfully switch to another thought. Deliberately get yourself off the negative track. With sufficient practice, you can switch mental gears at will. Then, you can do without the rubber band prop.

Know that the inner critic thrives in situations like these:
- ✓ Meeting new people
- ✓ When you have made a mistake—public or private
- ✓ At the start of a new job, project, or task
- ✓ When you feel criticized and defensive
- ✓ During interactions with management
- ✓ When you feel hurt
- ✓ When someone gets angry with you

Chapter Fourteen:

Control Destructive Mind Games

. . . .

Whatever you do, you need courage. Whatever course you decide upon, there is always someone to tell you you are wrong. There are always difficulties arising which tempt you to believe that your critics are right. —Ralph Waldo Emerson

Initial reactions to a bully's misconduct are typically emotional. Scientists and philosophers have been speculating for years about what causes bad moods. Certainly there are stories about dysfunctional families and people who suffer from child abuse. However, the Greek philosopher, Epictetus, first observed that, "Men are not disturbed by things, but by the views they take of them."

The view that our thoughts, rather than the actual events themselves, create our moods has gained acceptance by psychologists, too. According to this view, emotions have two components: 1) arousal (physical sensations—gut churning, butterflies, dizziness, profuse sweating, etc.), and 2) a label so the mind knows what to call it.

Those who subscribe to this line of thinking believe that we become upset because of the way we *think* about these events. We have the ability to distort meanings related to dramatic events. This ability then helps define our emotional experiences—good and bad.

The distortions, or mind games, weave a protective net around ourselves that twists and colors our feelings according to what we think.

Self-defeating labeling forms the prison walls from which you yearn to break out. The bully brought the bricks and mortar. Through mind games, the Target is responsible for the prison's upkeep.

Here's another metaphor. Everyone looks at herself through a telescope. If your telescope is in good repair, you see yourself as important and clearly focused. Unfortunately, most people look through a telescope that is not clearly focused, or it's smudged, or slightly cracked. This blocks the way you see yourself in your life and work and actually can distort your impression of a critical situation.

These distorted thinking styles can make you judgmental, can cause you to automatically apply labels to people and events before you get a chance to evaluate them. These distorted labels give you only one side of any situation and cause you to base your decisions on an emotional rather than a rational basis.

You are the only person in this world who can make you feel depressed, worried, or angry. Similarly, you are the only one who can elect to not have these feelings–you can choose to be happy.

If you lose your job, you may feel sad, angry at yourself, or self-critical. Your inner critic starts to whisper in your ear. Your thinking becomes distorted and you may tell yourself that you're no good, that there is something wrong with you. It would be less self-defeating to tell yourself that life is unfair, but for too many Targets, the choice of a label is mindless. It is an automatic process honed over years of practice.

These are mind games and they are very natural. When you *choose* to change the way you think, you turn negative, distorted thoughts into useful concepts.

Take a few moments to scan the following list of mind games we all play.

1. *Overgeneralization.* From one isolated event you make a general, universal rule. If you failed once, you'll always fail.
2. *Global labeling.* You automatically use pejorative labels to describe yourself, rather than accurately describing your qualities.
3. *Filtering.* You selectively pay attention to the negative and disregard the positive.

4. *Polarized thinking*. You lump things into absolute, black-and-white categories, with no middle ground. You have to be perfect or you are left feeling worthless.

5. *Catastrophizing*. Worst-case scenario thinking. The danger is that expecting the worst helps it become a self-fulfilling prophecy.

6. *Personalization*. You assume that everything has something to do with you, and you negatively compare yourself to everyone else.

7. *Mind reading*. You assume that others don't like you, are angry with you, don't care about you, and so on, without any real evidence that your assumptions are correct.

8. *Illusion of control*. You feel that your have total responsibility for everybody and everything, or feel that you have no control, that you're a helpless victim.

9. *Emotional reasoning*. You assume that things are the way you feel them to be. Others are assumed to have the same feelings as you.

Chris was laid off of work with several other employees from the company because of a business slowdown. She felt rejected, worried, angry, and guilty. Her mind game distorted the layoff as a situation in which she had failed, that the layoff was directly due to her inability to do her work.

Using the mind games list, let's analyze Chris' feelings that she is a loser.

- *Polarized thinking:* She's looking at herself in black-and-white categories because she sees herself as a loser.
- *Overgeneralization:* She lost her job, but she is generalizing to her entire life.

- *Filtering:* She is dwelling on her job loss and letting it color her entire view of life. Her choice of husbands is now clearly seen as a poor one.
- *Personalization:* She blames herself for the layoff, rather than the fact that business was slow.

We may say mind games are distorting as compared to the perceptions others might have of the same event. However, it is important to remember that there need not be an objective "true" reality. Everyone has their own agenda, perspective, and eyes and ears.

Targets may fall into the trap of undermining themselves with destructive, mental distortions that can slow down or block recovery from the bullying.

Reversing the Distortions

Inside the Target's head

With workplace bullying in mind, note some of the internal monologues you typically hear.

Now, counter the echo of the bully's words with positive, balanced statements in rebuttal.

Try to identify the Distortions, Mind Games.

Self-Statement	Distortion	Rebuttal
She's right. Nothing I do is ever accurate. I hate to agree with her, but the job I did on the project was not as good as before.		She's not right! She's just mean. It pleases her to tear into me. Wait a minute. The caliber of my work exceeded that of others then AND now. It may not be perfect, but it is better than this company has ever had.

Overgeneralization

Filtering

An internal rebuttal like the one above helps defeat the irrational thinking that plays into the hands of the bully.

Chapter Fifteen:

Escape the Trap
of Self-Blame

. . . .

The people who get on in this world are the people who get up and look
for the circumstances they want, and, if they can't find them, make them.
—George Bernard Shaw

When you are a Target, there is no doubt that the bully initiated the campaign to disgrace, defame, and demoralize you. There is certainty; it is an absolute fact. When you tell friends and family, they believe you and stand by you up to a point.

However, witnesses, co-workers, the bully's allies, "institutional helpers" (human resources, personnel, employee assistance, legal, ombudsmen, mediators), senior managers, and lawyers are either less certain or call you a liar outright.

Yes, it is true that this wildly different version of reality stems from defensiveness, workplace politics, fear, timidity, lack of conscience, group dynamics explored elsewhere, and sometimes evil. As strange as it sounds, in their eyes, it makes more sense to see you, the Target, as the cause of your misery rather than the menacing bully.

The lack of support resulting from myriad personal biases further undermines your sanity, increasing the self-doubt you did not deserve in the first place. Heinz Leymann credits this "secondary mobbing" for extending the bad times and postponing recovery from bullying and your ability to move on with your life.

Power of Perspective

We also think it is important for you to understand another factor that explains the madness of blaming the recipient of direct, hateful assaults—perspective. The perspective we describe is a visual, physical vantage point, not a philosophical one. The determination of who caused what depends a great deal on where one sits.

It's this simple: there are two players in the destructive workplace bullying game—the bully and the Target. If I, as a witness, observe a nasty encounter between the two and am asked who caused it to turn out the way it did, I have three options: 1) the bully caused it, 2) the Target caused it, or 3) they jointly caused it to happen.

We know from psychological research that the choice of explanations for events depends on a person's vantage point. The phenomenon is called causal attribution. The term attribution refers to the assignment of responsibility to the person, event, process, or thing that *caused* the behavior to happen.

Imagine two people seated across from each other in a TV studio. Position three cameras as follows: two peering over the shoulder of each person and aimed directly at the other person (call them bully-cam and Target-cam) and the third recording the situation from the side with both "actors" given equal amount of space in the picture.

We know from research experiments using such a video set up, as presented in the *Journal of Personality and Social Psychology*, that observers watching the encounter from the bully-cam tend to hold responsible the person they see, the Target in our example. These observers have no pre-existing biases, or interest in the taped session and still take the side of the bully in blaming the Target.

To prove the power of visual perspective, other observers, also without bias, hold the bully responsible when watching the encounter from the Target-cam. They literally see the situation through the Target's eyes.

Guess who is held responsible for controlling the direction of the interaction by a third group watching from the side camera? Yes, each person was responsible. In all fairness the researchers dealt with benign conversations, not emotional altercations more likely in the bully-Target duo. So, an equal split of responsibility would probably not happen. However, the research finding is so strong that we can safely predict some sort of shared responsibility.

Bias Begets Blame

Attributional biases are normal for humans. A person has to mindfully and deliberately fight the power of perspective to be fair. In the bully-Target situation, holding the Target even partly responsible when she did nothing to provoke the bully sounds fair to most observers. But it is unfair to the Target. Calling for "balance," as mediators do, underestimates the bully's role and discriminates against Targets who are the unwilling recipients of indefensible assaults.

As a society, we've had this discussion before. It was about rape victims. Is it fair to fault victims for dressing "provocatively" in the name of balance? That would be the equivalent of seeing the crime from the rapist-cam rather than from the victim-cam. Fortunately, reason prevailed and we have decided to fault the criminal rather than the victim (though the courts and defense attorneys have been dragged slowly to that conclusion). Blaming or denigrating the victim (she was "flirtatious") is showing a compassionless, attributional bias.

So, too, we should stop blaming Targets for their own plight which no one would voluntarily choose.

Avoid the Trap of Self-Blame

As the targets of most severe bullying tell us, the experience can be as destructive as the complete shattering of one's personality. The Target comes to believe the bully's false story about her. This can happen because the personal attacks are *cumulative*. Regardless of her initial strength, the Target gets worn down.

This is the beginning of the end of self-confidence in one's competence. It's her personal faith in her competence that enables her to confront the bully. When the inner strength is chipped away, the Target is most vulnerable.

Let's extend what we learned about attribution of responsibility to get a peek at how self-destruction happens and what can be done to avoid it.

As far as the delusional bully is concerned, the Target is the reason for the bullying, and those are the words the Target hears from the bully. "You, you, you." (Can't you just see the finger wagging?)

Now, switch sides and see the world from the Target's perspective, at least as it should be seen. The bully, operating in a workplace supporting the bully's misconduct, is rightfully seen as the cause of trouble. This is the way attributions normally work. Targets would be biased to blame bullies and the workplace culture that grows them. Bullies would be biased to blame Targets. It's a matter of perspective, depending on the angle from which the situation is viewed.

Targets exposed to verbal battering over time, however, mistakenly commit a sort of "reverse empathy." Normally, empathy is a valuable human trait to have—the ability to see the world from the other person's perspective and to share the emotions. In this sick case, it is the Target who sees herself as a defective unit in agreement with the bully.

Siding with the bully actually makes the bully's task easier. The Target inadvertently becomes an accomplice in the tearing apart of her own personality. Too many Targets come to accept the Bully's lies as fact. The campaign of destruction is made easier by the Target's paradoxical cooperation.

Family, friends, and co-workers witnessing this self-destruction find it hard to believe as they watch the individual spiral down. There's no objective reason for it, but the process is real. The pain the Target suffers while doing it can be severe. Extensive self-blame may require professional help from a counselor to correct.

A Target's explanatory style of assigning responsibility is related to mental health. For the sake of the remainder of this discussion, non-Targets will be referred to as "Self-Promoters." They tend to use an attributional bias that keeps them healthy. Call it hubris, vain self-glory, or confidence, they interpret causes of interpersonal behavior differently than do Targets.

Explaining Success and Failure

When explaining their own success (taking a test, winning a job), Self-Promoters generally take credit. They point to either their talent or the effort put into preparation to make the success happen. That is, people usually see success as a result of something about them or some action they took. These causes are *internal*. To credit internal factors means to take *personal responsibility*.

Core internal factors are unchangeable personal characteristics that define who we are. Talent, ability, and personality are all internal relatively constant explanations for events. Crediting personality as the reason for success provides quite an ego boost. Change in personality is very hard to accomplish as you know if you've ever tried a major self-improvement campaign. (Changing someone else's personality is a recipe for misery—yours.) Your personality's stability, its constancy, is crucial to living an organized, chaos-free life.

Effort fluctuates with circumstances. Sometimes you prepare or rehearse hard, sometimes you do not. With each opportunity comes the chance to do it differently. Effort is internal, but changing.

	CONSTANT	CHANGING
INTERNAL	Intelligence, Talent	Good Effort, Motivation

Of the two internal sources of success, intelligence is preferred by most people because internal, stable causes are more predictable. Better to do well because you're smart than to have put forth a good effort.

When it comes to explaining failure, Self-Promoters prefer *external* factors. External causes include the difficulty of a task. Why did the Self-Promoter fail the test or not get the job? She may reason, it "did not test for the important things;" "they hired only 1 percent and they all had friends on the inside." If no plausible explanations come readily to mind, the Self-Promoter points to bad luck, "It just wasn't my day."

Applying the same categories of constancy and changeability to external factors, the range of possible explanations (attributions) for events is complete.

	CONSTANT	CHANGING	
INTERNAL	Intelligence, Talent	Good Effort, Motivation	◄ Preferred for Success
EXTERNAL	Difficulty/ Ease of Task	Fate, Bad Luck	◄ Preferred for Failure

To blame external factors for failure is technically ducking personal responsibility.

Attribution theory and the therapeutic approach that evolved from it are more about mental health and wellness than finding fault or fixing blame as a moralist would dictate. Moralists have a political agenda. Don't confuse the information they disseminate in a public arena with solid advice that has helped people recover from life-damaging events like bullying.

The Positive Mental Health Bias

Success: Take Personal Credit
Failure: Blame Something 'Out There'

Unnecessarily Taking Blame

It is instructive to study depressed individuals and their explanations for why things happen. Bullied Targets often are depressed. Their pattern of explaining events is exactly the reverse of normals. Failure is blamed on internal factors. One can beat oneself up for not trying hard enough (the internal effort explanation), but even the depressed person can be made to see that there will be other chances to try harder in the future.

However, when a person sees her personality as hopelessly flawed or defective, it is the strongest type of self-inflicted attack possible. That is what depressed people do. Their self-loathing somehow seems justified in their mind. All negative thoughts and lost confidence begin with the assumption that the person is irreversibly screwed up. It's not easy to escape from a pit like that.

In the same self-defeating manner, success is discounted by crediting external forces—"I passed only because it was an easy test." "I got the job because the interviewer was unskilled." "I was lucky."

"Cognitive therapy" with depressed people attempts to reverse self-defeating attributions. Restoring self-confidence requires the person to see that the core of her being has a solid, positive foundation. In addition, the person has to be taught to look for environmental factors that can account for, even if only partially, personal behavior.

Here's how the table of explanations works for self-defeating Targets. The rows are swapped with the Self-Promoters' preferences. That is, success is discounted and minimized. Failure is taken on the chin, which is an unnecessarily harsh disrespectful approach.

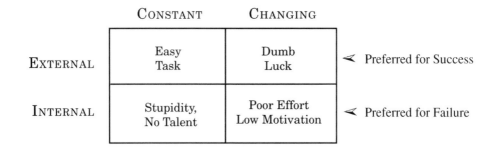

	CONSTANT	CHANGING	
EXTERNAL	Easy Task	Dumb Luck	◁ Preferred for Success
INTERNAL	Stupidity, No Talent	Poor Effort Low Motivation	◁ Preferred for Failure

Now relate this to being an unwitting Target of a series of bullying verbal assaults. The heart of the attacks is the lie that the Target is a worthless human being. This is not true and the Self-Promoting person knows this. Over time, doubt can creep into the minds of even the strongest. If the bully is shrewd (and most bullies are), she will use subtle lies that are offensive only in their repetition. This wears through the Target's defenses.

Part of the bully's effectiveness in disrupting the lives of other people is her ability to create chaos. Making statements that run counter to the reality everyone shares in a workplace certainly is the manufacture of madness. If the bully gets away with keeping everyone off balance so that no one can predict the next assault's timing or content, the bully achieves the control she desperately seeks.

Working in a chaotic, assaultive place can wear down the defenses of the "strongest" people. It is difficult for Targets to be close-minded, even when it comes to hearing the bully's pathological view of the world.

By somehow justifying the fit between lies and reality, the Target begins to let the bully define a darker reality for her. The actual person gets lost in the translation. [If you want to fundamentally change who you are, don't let the bully define your goals for you.]

Bullies Win When Targets Accept Personal Criticism As If It Has a "Kernel of Truth" in It.

Finally, we witnesses see evidence that the self-blame process has taken hold. Successes are discounted or explained away. Setbacks are internalized, with a disproportionate amount of responsibility taken for events that were completely out of the Target's control.

In other words, the bully can goad the Target into adopting a depressed person's perspective. Then, shortly thereafter, genuine depression sets in.

Suggested Interventions

Targets and their loving family and friends need to be aware of how attribution works. By recognizing the shift to explaining success outside themselves while blaming themselves as the sole source of failure, others can intervene to stop a Target's downward spiral into depression.

If it is you who is experiencing the mental and emotional shift, get help from a counselor now. Your awareness about how this happens will speed your recovery. Keep a written record of your thoughts, explanations, and feelings after events. The pattern of self-blame should become evident. You will have to deliberately re-train yourself to take credit for success and let failure roll off your back in order to get strong again. This may sound vain, but recovering from trauma requires dramatic corrective steps.

Ignore instructions from others about taking "personal responsibility." You did nothing to bring on the assault from the bully. Take responsibility for shutting out the bully's lies; ignore others who side with the bully. Their advice is not good for your mental health, for your survival. The bully wants to steal your dignity at work. Appropriately explaining your actions is a first step toward reclaiming that dignity.

If it is someone you love who is going through the early stages of self-destruction, avoid at all costs agreeing with the dysfunctional explanations you hear her utter. You have to counter the person when she says she is defective, no good, a total loser, etc. It sounds easy, doesn't it? How could you not resist the lies yourself?

Over time, the bully can penetrate the psyche of the strongest, most optimistic person alive in an attempt to "convince" her that she is wrong. Eventually, dealing with wounded Targets challenges the staunchest supporters. Do not listen to lies; be a constant booster of the person's competence. Give specific examples. Don't simply say "you are a good person." Say specifically that "volunteering to tutor immigrants in English is worthwhile and the students love you for it, they say so."

Finally, let a professional counselor help you help the Target if either of you gets in too deep.

Chapter Sixteen:

Satisfy Your
Needs and Wants

. . . .

The vision must be followed by the venture. It is not enough to
stare up the steps—We must step up the stairs. —Vance Havner

After working through the preceding chapters, you now have the tools for minimizing emotional devastation by the bully. Now, we will help you define your own needs and wants, so you can articulate what it is you deserve to have from others. Yes, you have the right to have certain basic needs met and you deserve a whole lot more. Your Targethood has convinced you that somehow you are less worthy than others. That kind of thinking has to stop. You are worthy. At some point, you will have to confront the bully, to make it clear that her unacceptable, inappropriate conduct must stop. You need to have it stop; you deserve to work free of trauma. In this chapter, we cover how you can stake your claim in a dignified, respectful, and assertive way.

The Target's Declaration of Needs and
Wants Signals the End of Targethood
to All Past and Future Bullies!

Fundamental, Basic Needs

We all have legitimate needs—environmental conditions, activities, and experiences important for physical and psychological health.

Targets often forget that they are entitled to having certain basic needs met. Needs are absolute rights to which every human being is entitled. During bullying episodes, when the bully's lies convince Targets that they are worthless, needs are ignored. Some Targets come to believe that they must relinquish their needs.

The following list has examples to remind you about what you need in life. Feel free to add or omit the needs you decide are important to you.

Physical needs
- clean air to breathe
- clean water to drink
- nutritious food to eat
- clothing and shelter
- rest and enough sleep
- exercise
- physical safety, freedom from harm

Emotional needs
- to love and be loved
- to have companionship
- to feel respected
- sympathy and compassion from others
- to reciprocate that sympathy and compassion
- when you do well—recognition and appreciation
- when errors are made—forgiveness and understanding

Intellectual needs
- information
- stimulation

- challenge of solvable problems
- variety
- time for recreation and play
- space to grow and to change
- freedom to honestly express your thoughts
- authentic, consistent responses from others

Social needs

- to interact with others
- to be by yourself
- work, not necessarily a "job"
- a role in society that helps define an identity through which you make a positive contribution to others
- to feel that you belong to a group
- to not have confidences broken by group members

Workplace needs

- employer-provided resources to do the work
- accomplishment of tasks free from interference
- consistent application of internal rules and policies
- compliance with governmental regulations
- work environment free from health hazards
- freedom from retaliation if civil rights are exercised
- a psychologically stable workplace culture
- privacy with respect to matters unrelated to work

Spiritual, moral, and ethical needs

- to seek meaning in your life
- a way of putting a value into your life
- compliance with a higher moral code

My Fundamental Basic Needs

Using the following worksheet to list your private needs.

Physical Needs:

Emotional Needs:

Intellectual Needs:

Social Needs:

Workplace Needs:

Spiritual, Moral, Ethical Needs:

Other Important Needs:

Needs vs. Wants

The important distinction between needs and wants is that needs are the basics for living. Quality of life depends on going above and beyond fundamental needs. Wants reflect wishes.

For many Targets, it is hard enough to ensure that others honor and satisfy needs. One shouldn't have to beg for the basics. Bullies who violate a Target's rights also are interfering with the satisfaction of basic needs. When feeling passive, vulnerable, and assaulted, it is almost unthinkable for a Target to believe she also deserves to have her wants satisfied.

Ask yourself: Do you ignore your less vital needs and wants if they conflict with someone else's? Do you often identify essential needs as "extras" and neglect them? If you do, then you forego your own comfort. Would others do the same?

You have a right to have your needs met. At the same time, you need to recognize that you deserve to have wants met as much as anyone else. You do not need to be stoic or a martyr. You are just as important as anyone else.

Sometimes you might absolutely *need* to talk to a co-worker about an aspect of your job. At other times, the job problem might seem less pressing and you *want* to discuss it, but you can postpone working on it until later.

You are the one, the only one, who can judge the importance of your needs and wants. If it is important to you, *you* have a right to ask for it. No matter what anyone else thinks!

The following inventory exercise can help you identify wants that you desire, but are afraid to ask for. They are divided into three parts: 1) what you want, 2) who can help satisfy your wants, and 3) situations in which you would ask for what you want.

Wants Inventory

Go through the list twice.

First pass: place a check beside all items that apply

Second pass: rate the checked items on a three-point scale

    1 = Mildly Uncomfortable

    2 = Moderately Uncomfortable

    3 = Extremely Uncomfortable

WHAT

I have trouble asking *FOR:*

- approval for _____
- help with certain tasks
- someone to listen and understand
- work evaluations
- promotions or raises
- respect
- time by myself
- answers to my questions
- permission to make my own choices
- acceptance of who I am by others
- acceptance of my mistakes
- other: _____

WHO

I have trouble asking for what I want FROM:

- my husband/wife
- fellow workers
- clients
- strangers
- friends

- my boss at work
- sales people and clerks
- authority figures
- a group of more than two or three people
- a person of the opposite sex
- other: _____

WHEN

I have trouble asking for what I want WHEN:
- I want help
- I ask for service
- I need a favor
- I ask for information
- I want to propose an idea
- I feel guilty
- I feel selfish
- I ask for cooperation
- I negotiate from a one-down position
- a lot of people are listening
- others' tempers are high
- I'm afraid of looking stupid
- I'm afraid the answer will be "no"
- I might look weak
- other: _____

What Your Inventory Says

Look over the inventory. Notice the things you want the most, the people from whom you want them, and when it is most difficult for you to ask for what you want. Look at the patterns that emerge. These are most likely the people and situations in which you need to acknowledge you feel less confident. List the problem areas in order of their rating and their importance to you.

Clarifying What You Want

After you have identified the wants important to you, formulate an assertive request. If asking for things is hard for you, prepare your requests in advance. By preparing an assertive request ahead of time, you can get the facts clear in your mind and be better able to relate them to others clearly. The clearer you are, the more certain you will be that you are not misunderstood. Instead, it's the bully who is distorting what you are saying.

Use the following guide to prepare your requests.

*From*_____

Write the name of the person who can give you what you want. If there are several people from whom you want the same thing, write out separate requests for each of them.

I Want _____

Spell out what you want the other person to do. Avoid abstractions like "show respect" or "be honest." Don't ask others to change their attitude, instead, specify an exact behavior: "I want an equal vote in deciding the new overtime policy."

*When*_____

Specify a deadline for getting what you want. Give the exact time of day you want someone to do something, or the frequency with which you want something—use any aspect of time that will provide you a time table and won't allow for any misunderstanding. For example: "I would like to have my review the Friday following the day my three-month probation ends."

*Where*_____

Write down the places where you want something: "Please give me one half hour alone at my desk in the morning to organize my day."

*With*_____

Specify any people involved with your request: "I would like to meet with you (the supervisor) and Sue (the coworker) when you decide what shifts we will have next month."

Rules for Requests

1. Try to get the other person to agree on a convenient time and place for your discussion.
2. Keep your requests small to avoid resistance from the bully.
3. Keep your request simple, one or two items will be harder for the bully to claim forgetfulness.
4. Don't attack the other person. Use firm "I messages" so you can stick to your thoughts and feelings. Remember to be objective and stick to the facts. Keep your tone of voice moderate.

For example: "I think the department looks unprofessional when customers witness all the screaming and berating you do." "I know that the company's Respect Policy is violated when you deny my request for the paid time off to which I'm entitled according to personnel policy." "I'm certain the reporter who called about the 'misplaced funds' would be interested in comparing the last three accounting periods and I plan to return her call in light of the mandate from the federal Fraud, Waste, and Abuse program." "I consider it disgraceful that you have driven out twelve good people in the last six months. I will share those feelings with the consultant this afternoon."

5. Be specific. Don't hedge when you give exact times and figures for what you want. Focus on asking for behaviors, not a change in feelings or attitude.
6. Use assertive words and high-esteem body language. Maintain eye contact, sit or stand straight, uncross your legs

and arms, and make sure you speak clearly, audibly, and firmly.

7. Practice, practice, practice! Stand in front of the mirror to observe how you look when you request what you need. This will allow you to correct poor posture and to practice confident facial expressions. Remember, you are practicing the truth. The poor bully has to rehearse lying. Your job is ethical, thus easier.

Once you have determined what you want to say and how you will say it, you will be ready to face the bully at work. Start with a small request. Build one success upon another. Work slowly through your list of wants.

You need to work on your requests until they are as clear and direct as you can make them. Remember, the satisfaction of your needs and wants does not come at the expense of others. You are asking for no favors, you are simply taking back that which is your right.

Slowly but surely you will chip away at the mountain of lies built by the bully who trampled your rights all along. Through one assertive request, which cumulatively become a demand, you reclaim your stolen dignity.

Clarify What You Want

FROM…

I WANT…

WHEN…

WHERE…

WITH…

Chapter Seventeen:

Anger and Shame: Emotions of Bullying

. . . .

Pain nourishes courage. You can't be brave if you've only had wonderful things happen to you. —Mary Tyler Moore

Bullying brings strong feelings. If you are like the majority of Targets, your feelings are expressed as anger. But the problem is not about anger.

Anger, the Mask

Anger is always the cover for another emotion. Lurking beneath the surface, waiting to be "outed" and confronted, is the real issue. It could be hurt, disappointment, jealousy, fear, shame, frustration, guilt, or some other emotion.

Anger is the wrong label. To stomp away in a rage from an encounter with the bully serves only to postpone a confrontation by the Target about the resentment felt. If the Target stays angry and never confronts, the golden opportunity to reclaim her dignity and self-respect vanishes in a cloud of unnecessary emotion. The bully fears most being held accountable for her illogical cruelty. An angry Target allows the bully to duck responsibility.

A Gallup poll conducted in the summer of 1998 for the Marlin Co. found that 42 percent of the eight hundred workers surveyed felt at least a little anger at work. The scale ran from not at all angry to extremely angry.

As Targets know, bullies are sources of stress and anger. We lobby against anger because it postpones a Target's healing.

Anger is an index of the toxicity of a poisoned workplace. We have to quit blaming individuals entirely. Instead of searching for the perfect personality test to predict which individuals are most likely to be angry, those who care about workplace health should search everywhere at the company for people who enrage others and set off anger for their personal viewing delight. Bullies "burn people." Like arsonists, they love to watch conflagrations of their making.

Investigators and reporters see workplace anger as a malady inherent in disloyal, crazed employees from whom prissy senior management (a.k.a. "leaders") must be protected.

The obvious alternative is to eliminate anger by eliminating the source of the devastating emotions that the workplace creates, which drive people to hide the pain beneath a mask of anger.

Anger Is the Target's Enemy.

The following indicate that you could be angry:
- flushed skin
- shallow breathing
- clammy skin
- rapid breathing
- tearfulness
- loud voice (if normally quiet)
- jitters
- light-headedness
- tensed muscles
- loss of concentration
- bulging veins

Anger can be turned inward and become self-destructive.

- Do you overeat?
- Overdrink?
- Overwork?
- Have you allowed yourself to become so stressed that you have trouble working and functioning adequately at home?
- Do you blame yourself for everything that goes on around you?
- Do you rage at your partner or children?

Sadness and feelings of loss often lie beneath anger. This happens when people are afraid of showing emotions of vulnerability. Anger, the more "socially acceptable" emotion masks sadness. Some stereotypes are invoked. Men should not show emotion; women show too much "soft emotion." Anger is the great equalizer.

People are afraid of anger itself, too. Unresolved anger causes the bearer pain. Many people carry their anger for years but are not aware of it.

Some people are afraid of any intense emotions; anger scares them the most. They worry about consequences if they express their anger. Sometimes anger erupts with disastrous results—harming not only those who hold the anger, but their co-workers, partners, and children. The violent expression of anger is destructive, nonproductive, and essentially ineffective. Violence hurts—it does not heal.

The perception of anger as destructive comes from childhood. Many children, faced with their parents' anger, feel that the anger is directed at them. These children feel helpless and overwhelmed. They want to disappear.

To them, the parents are angry and raise their voices because of something the child did. Whether or not this is true or logical, it is how the child feels. This fosters the idea that somehow the child is at fault. It is taken as a personal attack, even if not intended that way. Anger destroys the beginnings of self-esteem and feelings of self-worth. If the parents don't make a special effort to clarify why they were angry, the child could anticipate the worst. She assumes responsibility for the parents' emotions.

As an adult, this former child feels that if she disagrees with someone, if she needs to say "no" to someone, if she raises her voice in anger, that anger will hurt someone just as she was hurt by her parents.

This perception needs to be corrected. We all have times when we raise our voices. We all need to say "no" once in a while. We need to disagree. However, these incidents do not need to be a destructive. Certainly no one should dread disagreement or being different.

Anger also can be a very constructive energy. To be constructive, it needs to be worked through and released. The goal is to let go of the anger, not to collect and hold it. The first step in letting go of your anger is to own it, to acknowledge that anger is the best name for what is felt inside. Unresolved anger accumulates over time and eventually eats away at your soul.

Although no two people are exactly alike in dealing with their anger, experts on anger have defined five general ways anger is managed. These are: (1) with suppression, (2) with open aggression, (3) with passive aggression, (4) with assertiveness, or (5) by dropping the anger. The first three tend to perpetuate anger; the last two can lead to calm.

Suppressing Anger

Because so many Targets have witnessed the destructive effects of anger, they hesitate to admit their own anger. They vow not to be lowered to emotions that seem overbearing or crude. They never want to appear rattled or weak, so they maintain a cool exterior of being above all problems associated with anger. When confronted with anger, they want to appear emotionless and pretend to feel no tension. They express surprise that anyone would assume they might be angry.

Most Targets who suppress their anger believe that anger is bad, that expressing it will cause them to be seen in a negative light. Holding in anger is the only way they feel they can interact with others. Unfortunately, there are serious heart health risks associated with the angry, hostile personality.

Check the lines that apply to see if you hold in your anger.

  __ I am afraid I will look bad if I let others know my problems.

  __ I tend to become resentful of others although I don't want
    others to know.

  __ If I am flustered, I tend to keep it to myself.

  __ If a co-worker upsets me, I tend to let days go by
    without mentioning it.

  __ Sometimes I am frozen when faced with an unwanted
    situation.

  __ I avoid mentioning conversations about sensitive topics.

  __ I frequently suffer from headaches and stomach upsets.

If you checked three or more of these statements, you are very good at suppressing your anger.

Targets have been trained to think that anger is not normal. They have been invalidated when their perceptions are different than others. They fear retaliation if they express disagreement with others. However, suppression of anger only causes feelings of failure and personal defeat.

Open Aggression

For many people, anger brings a mental picture of open aggression. They picture anger as taking a stand for personal worth and needs that comes at the expense of someone else. This anger brings images of explosive rage, intimidation, and blame. However, it is not limited to such violent pictures. It also includes bickering, criticism, and sarcasm. This type of anger springs from a focus on personal needs rather than sensitivity to the needs of others. Open, overt aggression is publicly displayed.

Check the lines that apply to see if you practice open aggression.

  __ I can be blunt and forceful when someone does something
    to frustrate me.

  __ As I speak my convictions, my voice becomes much louder.

__ When someone confronts me about a problem, I am likely
     to offer a ready rebuttal.

__ No one has to guess my opinion—it is known by everyone.

__ I overlook others' feelings because I focus so sharply on
     fixing the problem.

__ I am likely to argue with my family members.

__ When in an argument with someone, I tend to
     repeat myself.

__ If I think someone else is wrong, everyone knows.

__ I give advice, even when it is not solicited.

If you checked five or more of these statements, you probably have a pattern of open aggression.

Passive Aggression

Targets who vow not to rage when they are angry recognize that open aggression creates a hostile environment. They refuse to explode loudly or get into a debate with a bully. They feel it is destructive to disagree. It is to be avoided at all costs. This leads to passive aggression which involves expressing anger in a manner that preserves personal convictions at someone else's expense. The passive-aggressive person is being dishonest to others and to herself.

The following list has examples of passive aggressive anger. Check the items that apply to you.

__ I use silence to let others know when I am frustrated.

__ I tend to sulk and pout.

__ I procrastinate when I do not want to complete a project.

__ I will never admit if I am frustrated, instead I will lie and
     pretend everything is fine.

__ Sometimes I avoid others so they won't bother me.

__ Sometimes I will deliberately ignore others when they
     try to talk to me.

__ I avoid face-to face conversations.

__ Sometimes I do things behind others' backs.

__ Sometimes I do things to others to irritate them.

If you check five or more items, you show the tendency to express your anger in such a way that you succeed in putting limits on your anger. But, you are only communicating the anger in such a way that will cause everyone tension and stress at a later time.

Assertive Anger

Anger defined as preserving personal worth and personal needs while also considering the needs and feelings of others represents a form of anger that truly helps relationships to grow. It shows maturity and personal stability.

It is important to distinguish between assertiveness and aggressiveness. In the past, assertiveness was often confused with pushy and abrasive behavior.

Assertiveness is not mean and is not meant to harm others. It allows a Target to address personal concerns about self-worth, personal needs. It leaves the door open to conversations about differences between the Target and the bully.

The following are examples of anger expressed in a non-hostile assertive way.

- When overworked, you can firmly and politely say "no" when asked to do more projects.
- As a supervisor, you can state project goals without resorting to harassment or being bossy.
- When overwhelmed by work, you can request help from co-workers without threatening retaliation if told "no."
- You can tell your boss or co-workers that you will take your lunch break and not answer the phone or solve any problems during that time.
- With co-workers, you can talk about differences and offer advice without raising your voice or altering your tone of voice.

To learn how to express assertive anger, remember two main points:

1. Make sure you expend your emotional energy on subjects that matter and concentrate your attention on matters that are not trivial.
2. Learn how to distinguish when you use tone of voice to convey your anger.

Remember, assertiveness is not always the easiest thing to learn. It takes time and practice to be able to manage your anger.

Dropping Anger

The hardest decision to make is the choice of letting go of your anger. There are times when you hope to communicate without anger and you use your best assertive voice, but you still become locked in an angry debate with a bully. At this point, you have the option to choose to drop your anger.

Dropping your anger means you recognize your personal limits. You accept the inability to communicate with the bully. This choice allows you to walk away from the frustration and hurt that the bully has created.

Dropping your anger also indicates that you have accepted the fact that your anger control does not depend on someone else. However, you must remember that dropping your anger is not suppressing it. Suppressing your anger is only an exercise that will leave you with unresolved feelings of hurt and bitterness.

Most bullies bent on controlling the emotional climate at work will provoke Targets to rage. Consciously choosing to disengage from the angry, raging bully will probably anger the bully. Walking away is the Target's victory. Denying the bully what she wants is a positive step toward humanizing the workplace again.

Final Thoughts About Anger

Reasonable responses to situations that cause anger are responses that help you maintain your cool and put the situation into your control, not to yield control to the bully.

Here are some ways to release anger:
- Re-establish your boundaries.
- Use active listening to communicate your willingness to understand any problem.
- Calmly tell the person that she is the source of your anger.
- Exercise by running, walking, working out, or swimming.
- Throw back your shoulders and arms as you say, "Get off my back."
- Talk to friends, family, a professional, or all of them to sort out your feelings.

When you take responsibility for your feelings and emotions, you are released from the bond that ties you to the bully and the ongoing feeling of inadequacy. You choose to take care of yourself, rather than use the bully's actions to dictate the destructive pattern of mistreatment.

Shame

If you have been bullied, you will experience shame. The shame might be slight, but in many cases it is overwhelming.

It is important for a Target to understand that shame is not guilt.

Guilt Is What You Feel When You Make a Mistake.

Shame Is Felt When You Believe You Are the Mistake.

Shame is a very painful feeling, the result of the incorrect, internal assumption that there is something inherently wrong with who you are. Shame is the gut-wrenching feeling that you are bad, inadequate, or defective.

After three years as a personal assistant to the vice president of her company, Pat lost her job. Her boss, Mary, always had been critical of Pat's work. Pat had tried her best to please Mary, working overtime and redoing projects when Mary complained that they weren't up to company standards.

After months of her boss's torment, Pat lost her temper and screamed at Mary. The result was a corrective interview and Pat was fired three weeks later.

Pat felt shame when she lost her job. She told herself, "I'm no good. I'm worthless. I'll never get another job."

For Pat, the pain of her harassment dominated all her thinking. Shame came over her in waves. Her sense of unworthiness became so strong that no matter what others said, she was convinced she was flawed.

Many families use shame to control others. Parents continually make statements such as: "All you ever do is lay around." "You're going to be a bum, just like your father." "You'll never get a job; you have no skills." "Oh, Susie, you'll never get in a college, your grades are not good enough."

Targets raised in families with shame carry that shame from childhood. When you are raised in a shame-based family, you don't know any other way to act. It's easy to understand how Pat might think, "I can't find another job, I'm just no good." Shelly, unemployed for ten months, truly believes she is a failure and reminds herself of this every morning as she looks into the mirror. These two women have retained the shameful messages of childhood and continue to reinforce them.

To Heal from Shame

Feelings of shame are natural consequences of bullying. Healing from shame involves breaking the silence of pain. When you encounter a bully and you recognize that you feel shame:

- Contact past co-workers and ask them to remind you of
  your past good work with them.
- As you listen to the positive feedback you get, take time
  to let in the message that you are a good and competent
  worker.
- Identify the shaming messages you have internalized and
  the hurtful events you have experienced.
- Separate what is unreasonable and untrue from who you are.

Hurtful events and messages that have been internalized need to be challenged. You need to be able to say, "That's not about me! It's not about my worth or identity. It hurt me terribly, and it has caused pain in my life, but it's not about me. Shame is not my identity, I am a good and worthy person."

As you put your feelings about shame into words, as you identify how bad you feel, you will be able to let go of the shame and move on with your life. The more you talk with others you trust, the easier it will be to let go of the bad feelings. The more you acknowledge that the bullying isn't really about you, the closer you will be to leaving the bully behind.

. . . .

BullyBusting to Topple the Tyrant

Chapter Eighteen:

Getting Ready to Confront

. . . .

It is better to die on your feet than to live on your knees. —Dolores Ibarruri

We have found that the effects of bullying on Targets follows a very predictable pattern. There are ups and downs and lots of switching directions in mood and energy.

There are two reasons for being aware of the emotional cycle you're likely to experience. The first advantage is that you will be less surprised. In a Target's chaotic world, any predictability is useful. Let's review the stages before talking about the second benefit.

Stage 1: Victimhood

The immediate pain of harassment dominates all thinking. Too easily forgotten are the twenty years experience you brought to the job. We guess that the harassing manager was new to the job or your unit. "How could this have happened to me?" you think. It's easy to feel beaten as you research your options and learn the destructiveness of the effects of bullying. People without the experience are incredibly naive about rights and procedures. The adversarial employer offers no information that gives you an advantage. Oddly, those who have gone before you rarely offer advice, somehow thinking it best for you to discover everything by yourself.

Cure: Know it is the system that creates or sustains a creepy, malicious person like the abusive bully. You were not singled out based on any real flaw or weakness. That means you're a nice person. Attackers prefer less combative, more cooperative victims.

Stage 2: Power Surge

Help is found! The workers' compensation/disability/EEO-complaint systems are discovered. Tales of favorable jury awards or large settlements in cases like yours suddenly appear. Attorneys are identified, though not carefully screened (you will be able to write a book about this topic within a year). With friends and advocates, you actually feel sorry for the wrongdoing employer. You are all-powerful. Sure, you hear warnings about how long justice takes, but at this early stage, the future looks rosy.

Cure: Hold onto these feelings. You'll need the strength. As you repeatedly hear the merits of your case and how much you deserve to win, let the rationale sink in. You'll need to hear the echo to get you through stages three and four.

Stage 3: Vulnerability

The counterattack begins by the employer. Their deep pockets become apparent as their legal spinmeisters paint you as a fraudulent, greedy, professional lout. Their resources are limitless compared to your puny contingency-based lawyer's office. Your lawyer stops returning your calls because, after all, she has *paying* clients. There is a steady stream of interrogatories (questions from the company counsel) leading up to the dreaded deposition. If your case goes that far, your lawyer's percentage also rises.

Depositions are institutionalized assassinations. You're never quite ready for the experience. Just remember corporate lawyers believe in a "scorched earth, no survivors" strategy. Your lawyer probably didn't have the time to rehearse you for the inquisition. To listen to the employer's defense arguments, you begin to feel like you should apologize for working for twenty years and hampering their productivity for so long.

Of course, if you are not suing in a court of law, the bureaucrat in charge of minimizing workers' compensation claims for the employer—someone you probably knew as an acquaintance while working there—becomes the enemy. Your needs directly conflict with her job security. These auditing types have few friends at work because distrusting others ("they all file fraudulent claims") is central to doing their job well. Yucky people. They staff the typical personnel, human resources (HR) department.

It finally dawns on you that HR works for management. Because you have an injury, you begin to learn firsthand how much access employers have to your medical records. They review your prescriptions. Had a temporary depression after your father's death? They've got records that will be misconstrued to impale you. They'll spin their records to show that you are a worthless piece of dung and hooked on doctors and drugs. Pain? You'll be labeled a "chronic pain patient"— code for illegitimate pain. Now the descriptions by physicians come to be used against you: spinal disk enlargement, not uncommon for a person your age, soft tissue damage is undetectable, pain is subjective, no treatment exists, you'll just have to work through it, and surgery is not advised. Stress is a mental fiction. Stress is for wimps. Stress builds character. And the daily torment the employer exposed you to was applied for motivation's sake.

Cure: Keep telling yourself it is the other side's job to fight back. Keep your mind on the justice you seek. Watch legal shows on television to see how adept defense lawyers are at rationalizing what they do on behalf of corporations. Also, you might get an idea or two for your lawyer on strategy. Read Ralph Nader's *No Contest* to validate your fight. Your cause is noble, but the courts don't recognize it.

Stage 4: Isolation and Abandonment

Now you feel alone. The other side has shown its muscle; it is scary. Your white knight attorney now seems weak and fades into the background. Colleagues from work, former friends, find it hard to keep in contact. They fear being in your place someday and treat you like you have the plague. It is ironic that it was they who encouraged you so strongly to stand up against the cruel bully. Of course, they did not take their own advice. You imagine them on the stand testifying against you at a trial.

Cure: Refuse to be alone. Force friends to maintain contact. Take the initiative. Join or start a support group for bullied Targets (ask the Campaign for tips). Stay involved with life outside your case. Volunteer to help a group do something you've always wanted to do. Start the at-home business you've longed for. Be your own boss. Don't let the dispute become your life's defining moment—shove it into the background. Don't lose the passion for your case, simply throw your day-to-day energy into constructive activity. Build or make something. Get involved with something or someone.

Don't let all your family discussions drift toward progress, or lack thereof, in your case.

Tell your story to a reporter. Renew old relationships with friends who knew you before this fiasco and who did not work with you. You deserve validation that you indeed had a life before. The current dispute does not define who you are as a person. Write the case details down and your feelings. Get therapy to deal with the downside of challenging a big bad employer.

Stage 5: Anger

It is usually aimed at everyone, primarily yourself, but even at supporters. Partly because you are no longer in your regular work routine, with time on your hands and isolated, the vengeful arguments directed at you from the other side erode your confidence. This is very dangerous. Don't let the "kernel of truth" in. Self-doubt feeds on itself, relying on the script written by your enemies.

Cure: Re-read the "Anger and Shame" chapter in this book. Read books about how to defuse anger. It is too destructive to turn it inward. It is antisocial to rage at others. Trust your sense of self defined by those who love you rather than to focus on garbage slung by opponents in a legal fight.

Stage 6: Resolution

You find a way to move on. In victory, you can become a forgiver of enemies more quickly than in defeat. At the end, partly to make sense of the stressful process just endured, you could become a Crusader. You fought for a cause and find that many others have the same plight. You want to help. There may not be a business in it for you, but you feel fulfilled doing meaningful work. You forget that you ever worked for that crummy employer.

Cure: Moving on while allowing resentment to fade is the most certain path to your positive mental health and feelings of self-worth. Winning a lawsuit does not necessarily give the sense of closure on the dark chapter in your life. What seems to matter most is registering your disgust at the bully's conduct and letting her, the company, the world know that you found it outrageous and intolerable.

One woman who suffered under a bully for years decided to complain, to fight Goliath. She passed through all the phases. Her very private resolution was the delight she felt the day she waved goodbye to her tormenter as the bully left work forever, preferring to take early retirement rather than stay and fight. No head-lines, just a long-postponed quiet victorious moment as the bully was banished.

South African writers Susan Marais-Steinman and Magriet Herman, authors of *Corporate Hyenas At Work*, wrote about the wisdom they had gleaned from surviving retrenchment (reorganization, downsizing) and its accompanying trauma-tization. Like us, they saw a multi-step process of an indeterminate length for Targets to fully and finally resolve the dilemmas in their lives that bullies create. Similarly, they describe stages that look like endings but prove to only be part of the middle.

Their Road to Recovery phases are:

1. Bewilderment—disbelief, a sense of unreality
2. Akuna Zinkinga (Zulu term for "there is no trouble")— the first window of relief
3. Moment of Truth—time for realistic assessment of personal strengths and weaknesses and planning to regain control over your destiny—perhaps the longest phase

4. Mourning—facing the reality of loss
5. Turning Point—choosing to either withdraw from life or to rejoin life
6. New Life—on balance, the positives outweigh the negatives—you feel Hyenawise (BullyProof in our terms)—empowerment—won't be fooled again
7. Free At Last—no longer can anyone steal the potential with which you are born

Your Readiness to Confront

The second advantage you get from knowing that your moods will cycle over time is that you can more accurately determine your "readiness to confront." When you do finally decide to stop the rationalization (for whatever reason—perhaps at the insistence of your heart doctor), it is critical that you have enough stamina to see the fight through to the end.

If you commit too early, at the early Power Surge stage, you will come crashing down, relatively unprotected, while your case languishes over time.

Little children cannot be potty-trained until their biological clock says all the organs are ready. In a similar fashion, no confrontation should be undertaken until you are psychologically stable. Because self-doubt plays such a major role in bullying, it is important to be genuinely confident that there is nothing wrong with you before you begin the fight.

You can't effectively fight alone, nor be motivated to win unless you are angry. Anger is on the other side of hurt. Stop the hurt first. Then, fight if you want to.

Being ready to confront this means you're ready for either a legal fight or the informal campaign detailed in Chapter 19's BullyBusting strategies.

Should You Fight Back?

First consider: Should you fight back? Fighting back through internal complaint channels and through our suggested informal system without reliance on lawyers both carry a low chance of success. It is an uphill battle; it is your choice.

Reasons to Not Fight Back

The disadvantages all revolve around the price martyrs pay when challenging institutions that can outgun, outlast, delay, lie, distort, and outlast any lone individual's campaign for the truth to come out. They include (a) costs to your health, (b) the toll vicious defensive employers can impose, and (c) economic losses.

Health Costs

You know that Targets pay for being bullied with their personal health—emotional and physical. They also pay a social toll. They are excluded and isolated at work by once loyal co-workers who now cower in fear about being associated with the "troublemaker." Worse yet is when the abandonment becomes betrayal, that they now side with and aid the terrorizing tyrant against the Target. Though this is somehow understandable through the lens of an intellectual, high-brow, dispassionate analysis, it sickens us all to witness when it happens. It's enough to drive a sane person to look like a raving paranoid lunatic. And this is in fact what the employers do.

PTSD (post-traumatic stress disorder) is common among Targets traumatized at work by cumulative assaults on their competence, confidence, self-image, and job security. Work-induced PTSD is recognized by experts as complicated and it doesn't go away easily or quickly. A prolonged fight through the endless steps of internal grievances and appeals or through the legal system with years of delays built in, ensures that the anxieties, listlessness, nightmares, and phobias that comprise PTSD will linger. It also can be re-lived at each meeting, retelling of the story, or receipt of mailed determination letters. Fighting back prolongs the agony. Your opponent knows how to exploit your vulnerability.

Defensive Employers Exact a Toll

It is the nature of the workers' compensation system (misnamed for suggesting that it benefits injured workers at all) and all internal complaint systems that the Target (the complainant) be treated as a fraud, a malingerer, and a thief trying to get something for nothing. Complaining threatens the appearance of organizational calm. Corporations revere their image. People and processes that uncover bullying face incredible pressure to silence them.

When an employer responds to your complaint, denial begins. Several people, departments, and institutions both inside and out get involved. Denial occurs in two ways: (1) ridiculous official pronouncements that the company has no problem with bullies, and (2) justification for the cruelty because it leads to something positive for the employer (productivity, meeting deadlines, "motivating" staff with toughness).

When faced with such bold lies and illogical excuse making, Targets initially get "perception shock." They can't believe what is being said to and about them. Because they have strong beliefs in equity and justice, they think the lies will eventually wither when contrasted with the truth they are prepared to tell. Don't believe it. Getting the truth to a public, safe and impartial forum on the employer's turf is nearly impossible. Even when you do, there is no guarantee that truth will triumph. Courts tend to be hostile by defining employers as masters and employees as servants. The assumption is that servants should be grateful for their paycheck.

The truth is that the Target has been placed in harm's way by the employer. It is the workplace that enabled the unwitting Target to expose herself to a cruel, control-driven bully. All the resources at the employer's disposal will be used to dodge responsibility at the highest level and accountability by the bully. They will try to paint you, the Target, as the problem.

When Targets dare to fight back, the bully's allies materialize out of thin air. Co-workers take sides against you. The personnel department role of bully and employer-protector becomes clear.

If you dare to actually file a lawsuit, the employer goes berserk. Its defense attorneys pull your medical records searching for a clue to convince the court that you were always crazy. This defense strategy drives them to discover or invent personality flaws. (If you also claim sexual harassment, they accuse you of being a slut—the "nuts 'n sluts" defense.) According to plaintiff Targets whose cases move to the deposition stage, the process feels like an "intellectual rape." Depositions and other steps in the battle can re-traumatize you. Before filing suit, Targets should ask their attorneys to explain every ugly activity they could face. Target lawsuits should be undertaken only by the emotionally strong. The risks of prolonged traumatization and postponed healing are great.

Economic Losses

Once a Target's health is compromised and her social support network torn apart, what more could go wrong? Economic devastation, that's what! After sick leave, vacation pay, and other paid time off days are exhausted, Targets are pressured by employers to take unpaid time off under the FMLA (Family Medical Leave Act). In the short-run, a physician's off-work order for job stress and disability pay are a better alternative to unpaid time off. If your fight is not resolved quickly (which it never is), long-term disability pays only a fraction of normal pay. Workers' compensation claims, if successful, also replace only a portion of your full pay. Employers have their physicians and insurers ready to deny your claim of suffering psychological injury at the hands of a harassing bully. You will have to fight long and hard to win an award. You suffer financially while the fight drags on.

The ultimate deathblow is termination. When a bully zeroes in on a Target, her job security is lost. The Campaign survey found that 75 percent of Targets said the only way they could stop the bullying was to leave, voluntarily or involuntary. Appeasing the bully never makes the Target's job more secure.

Staying under the bully's thumb only increases risks. Risk of declining health, self-defeat, and abandonment. Appeasement backfires. It did for Europe trying to postpone Hitler; it works similarly between a Target and the bully.

Getting out on one's own terms should be a goal of every Target.

A sad consequence of bullying is that the great paying, challenging work that you once enjoyed can be stolen from you. Remarkably, some bullies are not satisfied driving the Target out. They hound the banished person into the next job, killing chances with a defamatory job reference or actually contacting management at the next place to poison the impression they have of the newly hired Target. This is illegal. There are ways to combat both practices. A reference-checking firm can help stop the first type of attack and a lawyer familiar with defamation cases can address the latter.

Without a job, while living on savings, Targets turn to lawyers to seek justice on their behalf and they are told to pay a several thousand dollar retainer on good faith with no promises of results. In a short time, if the Target was the sole wage earner, the home has to be sold. The familiar saying that middle-class American families are two paychecks away from homelessness becomes a reality.

Our legal system, the alternative to an internal complaint mechanism for Targets, rarely does the right thing. Law professor David Yamada reviewed three years of Federal Court rulings in Intentional Infliction of Emotional Distress cases. IIED most closely parallels bullying. The Courts sided with distressed Targets in only about 10 percent of the cases. Sounds like justice for the injured rarely makes an appearance in the federal courthouse.

To summarize the case against BullyBusting, it can prolong health problems, costs friends, and is expensive. It is little wonder that Targets stay in horrific, destructive workplaces because they "have to have" their paychecks. No one has the right to blame them for making what appears to outsiders as a self-destructive choice.

Why You Should Fight Back

Fighting back cannot be undertaken until the Target is BullyProof. At some stage, the Target gets over being hurt and gets mad. That's the signal that BullyBusting can begin. Two major reasons to fight back, despite all the potential setbacks, are: (a) to satisfy your need for fairness and doing the right thing, and (b) being able to move on with your personal dignity intact.

Equity and Justice for All

BullyBusting also depends on how violated the Target feels. Targets believe the world should be fair. Payoffs and outcomes should be proportional to effort and skill invested in work. That would dictate greatest rewards for the most competent among us. Reality rarely meets this idealistic standard, however. Incompetent boobs who dominate their more competent peers thanks to organizational politics, utter the familiar refrain: "Life is not fair. Live with it."

Feelings of inequity and injustice seem to drive most BullyBusting, even though the odds are stacked against bullied Targets. Whistleblowers are extreme examples of bullied Targets who risk everything to fight back. They do so because they cannot imagine accepting what was done to them. They live according to a higher level of moral decision making than most of us who play the political game, deluding ourselves that we have to "pick the right fight worth fighting for." Then, we let others chip away at our integrity in small doses over long periods of time. Before we know it, we've lost sense of what, if anything, we stand for. If we dare to fight then our opponents can rightly claim that we have little reason to fight back now when so many earlier compromises went unchallenged.

Whistleblowers claim the moral high ground early and often, shaming the rest of us who are too cowardly to demand equity and justice. It is sad when bold American principles are dismissed as "idealistic" or "radical" when discussion turns to the workplace. We salute whistleblowers and other principled Targets for demonstrating the courage the rest of us should admire and emulate.

Inequity and injustice disgust Targets; they want to do something to right the wrong. Some Targets fight back because they know no other way.

Moving On With Dignity

The other reason to go BullyBusting is to close a dark episode in the Target's life. Naive co-workers, family, and friends admonish Targets for not "just moving on" with their lives. Bullying is not so easily put aside. Bullying is an invasion of the Target's sanctuary of how she sees herself. The damage to the psyche and the confidence to move on is more harmful than physical abuse.

In Campaign surveys, Targets repeatedly told us that their greatest regret was to leave without confronting the bully, without telling the employer what was done behind closed doors, or without letting everyone know how they were driven out. In the absence of identifying the bully as culprit, staff are frequently told that the departed Target left for "personal reasons," or for bad performance, which allows employers to blame Targets and never be held accountable for the bullying. When the Target does not provide information about the bullying, the bully and employer spin the story in a way that serves to cover up the dirty deeds.

By fighting back, word soon spreads through the grapevine that the Target was harassed by the bully and key people in the company caved in to the bully's demands and supported the wrong person. For the purposes of BullyBusting, we care less about the impact of knowledge on the bully and employer than the restorative effect it has for the Target.

BullyBusting restores self-respect and lost dignity. You owe it to yourself to go out on your own terms.

Despite the odds against success because the employer and bully collaborate to serve as prosecutor, judge, jury, and executioner, BullyBusting sends a message to witnesses that at least one Target did not accept the lies, distortions, and career-threatening tactics intended to humiliate her. She serves as a model of courage. With luck, witnesses and future Targets will stand firm and defeat the bully, shaming the employer who supports the perpetrator of psychological violence.

Advice from Veterans of the Bullying Wars

Here is wisdom, in their own words, from survey respondents who were asked to say what would they have done differently when bullied:

- *Take a stand and get the help you need to confront the bully, because you wouldn't have a bully on your back if there were more people on your side.*
- *Fight back from the beginning.*
- *Realize that the bully is really a coward. Also realize that you should not back down, but don't become a bully yourself.*
- *Tell others that you trust what is happening. Build support and get ready to confront. It is not OK! Reflect on your past work experiences and realize that this is related to the bully and not a truth about you. Constantly do reality checks with others.*

- *Don't take any kind of crap from anybody. Stand up to them.*
- *I think I did the best thing by confronting him. I also provided support to others who were being annoyed by his behaviors and encouraging them to speak up. I also informed my senior colleagues of his behavior and its effects on me...that was a tremendous help...they had been putting up with it and sloughing it off...when they realized that he was hurting me and [they] even heard some of the comments and thought them "stupid," they intervened by giving friendly advice to him.*
- *I would have challenged the bully more and stood up for my own beliefs instead of backing down.*
- *I would have confronted the situation earlier, taken legal action, and been less passive and forgiving.*
- *I would have gone to the operations of our corporate office or the district manager with my complaint instead of our immediate manager.*
- *I would have kept a better record of bullying incidents.*

As you can see, the message from those who have been there is to confront rather than to face certain ongoing humiliation.

Do Not Attempt BullyBusting Unless and Until You Are BullyProof.

Chapter Nineteen:

BullyBusting Strategies: 8 Steps to Topple Tyrants

. . . .

What counts is not necessarily the size of the dog in the fight,
but the size of the fight in the dog. —Dwight D. Eisenhower

N ow that you've decided to fight back, to go BullyBusting, these are the steps
we advise. Re-read the preceding chapter if doubts linger. Our suggestions
are for information purposes only—the authors assume no responsibility for
the outcome. Customize your strategy to best address your situation. Be fore-
warned that the fight is uphill. Few successfully mount a challenge and enjoy a
satisfactory result because powerful and vast forces can be mobilized against you.

There are three BullyBusting approaches:

1. Trust the internal grievance procedures and comply with
   union requirements, if present. These processes were not
   written to advance employee rights. They are full of hurdles,
   delays, and double standards, combining to make you more
   vulnerable to subsequent attacks.
2. Hire an attorney to fight.
3. Mount an internal, informal campaign to go to the top,
   outside normal channels, seeking justice.

We now outline the eight steps that define the third approach.

Warning: Read all of the steps to grasp the obstacles lying in wait before attempting to accomplish any single step.

Step One: Solicit Support from Family and Friends

Sounds easy, right? Yet, most people wait days, weeks, or months before telling their intimate partners what is happening at work. The less secretive you are, the less the burden you must bear alone. Share the information. Many stress-related diseases gain their destructive power from people bottling up emotions, fighting the natural need to express them.

Asking for support is not a sign of weakness. Don't buy the garbage about trying to "tough it out." Proponents of that message also say that bullies are needed to make the nation great, to provide a kind of "tough love" that weak people resent, but actually need in order to become better. That's absurd! Cruelty has no place in motivation or striving toward excellence. Bullying is only a destructive force and not "good" for anyone.

Explicitly define "support" for family and friends. Lighten their obligation. They are not required to solve the problem for you. State clearly that you need them to only listen without criticism as you pour out your unfiltered feelings of shock, surprise, disgust, shame, and humiliation. You need a safe harbor. Ask for the time now—offer to return the service in kind when she or he goes through a traumatizing series of events.

With family and friends, it is important that they keep you grounded. That can be done by reminding you of your pre-bully days of competence and skill. They can help you hold onto your definition of who you are. Resist accepting the bully's definition of who she wants you to believe you are. People who knew you before can show how much the bully lies.

Another reason for telling friends is that they may know about attractive job opportunities for you. If they don't know you are suffering and need to get out, they wouldn't even think about telling you. Start the job search the moment you decide to fight back, long before you actually take any action. Retaliation is so predictable, nearly guaranteed, once the organization sees that you have decided to resist the humiliating bullying assaults. It is much easier to fight back when you are already working at your next job.

Though your sense of justice makes you resist finding new work ("I did nothing. Why should I be the one to transfer or leave? Make the bully leave!"), it is useful to have options as you proceed through the BullyBusting strategies. You give yourself power when you have the freedom to walk away with minimal economic and health damage.

BullyBusting is about the regaining or retention of *your* control over your own life. The bully tried to steal it away. You are reclaiming it. If you deprive the bully of ways to hurt you, you win.

BullyBusting Is for Targets to Reclaim Dignity and Self-Respect.

Step Two: Consult an Outside Physician or Therapist

This a health preservation step. First, it is important to not ignore physical and emotional cues that the bully is affecting your health. Targets have a habit of thinking that it is a sign of toughness to shut out concerns about sleeplessness, anxiety, loss of appetite, lack of focus, or decreased sex drive. These are your body's warning signs that it is responding to stressors in your life. A harassing bully is about the biggest stressor a person can experience.

Stress is a biological process. The ability to respond to threats is a remnant of our animal kingdom legacy. It happens at the lower, more primitive brain level. Your body responds to stress even when you try to trick it into thinking that nothing is wrong. This is a disservice to your health. Pay attention to the alarm reaction your body is having. Seek medical or psychological help or both. Don't wait. Bodily harm results from prolonged exposure to stress. Stress kills!

When your safety and health at work are compromised by a tyrant, you are in real danger. The only way to end the stress is to remove the stressor—the bully in your life. Only by attacking the source will the pain stop.

Seek advice and possible relief from medical practitioners using your health plan. Get outside the employer's grasp. Company-employed doctors and therapists have a track record of forgetting their professional training and principles when it comes to diagnosing and treating employees who complain about workplace stress. Medical knowledge is thrown out the window as they reliably and faithfully serve their master, the one who pays for their service. Elsewhere, we've described in detail why internal counselors in the Employee Assistance Program are suspect. Run to outside help for the sake of your mental health.

We have heard about hundreds of wonderful physicians who insist that Targets take time off work because of the harm the doctors see in their exam rooms. It is important to tell your physician what is happening at work and how it makes you feel. Internal and family medicine physicians prescribe more anti-depressant medication than do psychiatrists. They are the gatekeepers in HMO plans and the ones to whom most Targets first turn. If your physician wants to write you an "off work order" for stress, comply with her or his request. Something about you is changing. She or he can see it, even if you can't. Accept the help. And with respect to future BullyBusting actions, it is important to establish a record with health professionals about the damage work has caused you.

Please remember that when you are later asked to sign a general release of your medical records by your employer, you can limit the search through your files to specific appointments with specific doctors and their notes concerning only job stress-related matters that were discussed at appointments like the ones described here. Never sign an open-book, general release unless advised by your attorney. Also, do not automatically file a workers' compensation claim until you have sought legal advice. Some states forbid lawsuits if this is sought.

Outside mental health help better protects your rights. However, the smart consumer of psychotherapy and psychiatry first learns all she can about therapist selection.

The ideal therapist who can help you heal from Work Trauma:

- will tell you exactly what information in your record is protected from the employer and courts and what is not.
- is interactive, directive, solutions-focused, and questions you about your situation (just doesn't sit there only listening without providing input) to help you think of solutions.
- understands that problems can be caused by the work environment. (Therapists bad for you do not accept this. They will beat you up with "personal responsibility" and "the bully is not the issue" rhetoric.)
- understands the role inequity and injustice play in your situation and any solution and is therefore tolerant of your obsessiveness and helps you stop it.
- has worked for a living before and understands the workplace and its pressures.
- speaks in terms of PTSD (post-traumatic stress disorder) and traumatization.
- feels "right" and safe to you in the first meeting. Trust your gut instinct. Avoid those with a personal agenda or who seem to want to hurt you more.
- if a not a psychiatrist (M.D.), then a therapist who has an association with one so that you can receive medications, when appropriate (only M.D.s can prescribe).
- is open to calling the Campaign as a resource to help her or him help you without violating confidentiality (you can sign a release for them to talk to the Campaign).

Step Three: Solicit Witness Statements

Elsewhere, we describe how paralyzed groups of witnesses fail to help, even when they know better or, as individuals, may want to help. However, do not be surprised when your former best friends appear to abandon you.

The importance of step three is to get a witness record of bully actions to avoid being put in the position of having only your word alone against the bully's.

According to Campaign surveys, approximately 50 percent of all bullying is done in front of witnesses. Bullies seek to humiliate Targets in front of co-workers. It's bully theater. The remaining torture occurs behind closed doors. One-quarter of bullying is meant to be overheard, and one-quarter is truly done in secret. However, closed-door bullying is witnessed, too. Berating and belittling is obvious to others when you emerge from the session. Caring co-workers ask what was done to make you look so defeated. Co-workers with empathy will ask what was said to you. Tell them exactly what the tyrant did and said, even if not asked.

Tell co-workers about the bullying for two reasons:

1. To establish an undeniable record corroborated by truth-telling witnesses.
2. To encourage them to share their experiences with the same bully.

Chances are that others once fell into the bully's path and suffered in silence, too. Who knows, your experience may prove liberating to all those who suffer or suffered. This will make group confrontation easier.

To capture witnesses on record, ask them to prepare a simple written statement. Ask them to avoid personal interpretations because it is safer for them to avoid taking a position to protect their own behinds in the future. Make it as safe for them to commit the "dangerous" act of political support for you.

In a statement, ask only for the following:

- designate the memo "To All Interested Parties;"
- date, time and place actions were witnessed;
- names of other known witnesses;
- a description of the actions, with specific quotes from both Target and bully, if possible (instruct them to strip away adjectives that hint of interpretation); and
- signature and date (the closer to the event, the better).

If the bullying was only indirectly observed, then the statement repeats what you told the witness when you first emerged from a behind-closed-doors session. With multiple witnesses, your account stands verified and is second only to witnessing a public display.

Since bullying involves repeated assaults, get a separate statement for each episode, directly or indirectly observed, from as many witnesses as possible. A pile of specific accounts is preferable to summarized witness statements that are prone to eroded or falsified memories.

If the co-workers who witness your bullying feel strongly about the mistreatment observed, ask them if they would be willing to deliver their testimony in person at a future hearing. This is very difficult for most people. Do not be disappointed that few, if any, take up this request. And they may agree to testify when you ask, then lose courage as the hearing or meeting date nears.

Though we've spoken only of co-workers as witnesses, often there are other witnesses. Customers (in person or over the telephone), the bully's peers, and higher-level management can all be asked for a statement or willingness to testify. Often, it is customers who are most angered at the mistreatment of their company contact person (you). Outsiders are completely free from retaliation for supporting you. Furthermore, they can state that injuring you has damaged the company's reputation with them and they either will cease to be a customer because of it or they will tell other customers. This supports your argument that bullying is bad business.

Step Four: Confront the Bully

This is a difficult, optional BullyBusting strategy. If confronting the bully alone were so easy, you wouldn't be a Target. The fact that about one in four people are Targets tells us that 75 percent of the workforce are not Targets. For non-Targets, confrontation comes more easily. Being non-confrontational is one of the defining traits that makes Targets out of kind, competent, and productive people. It is nearly impossible to expect you to suddenly become a different person just to have a showdown with the bully.

Common Mistakes

Sometimes, Targets do muster their strength (after a night of throwing up as preparation) to face the bully. However, two mistakes are common: (1) the bully is not blamed, and (2) it is assumed that the bully cares about pleas for emotional calm.

First, they prepare a script based on the conflict resolution strategy of not accusing the other person. They hold the bully blameless. Perhaps the bully is going through a divorce. You, the well-meaning, empathic Target, might open a session by saying, "I know you are having trouble at home and that may shorten your temper with me..." The bully is most likely to resent this "invasion" into her personal life. She will retaliate with a new tirade about "honoring her privacy."

Following this peacemaking logic, it is the Target herself who will be held responsible for her fate. This flies in the face of facts. The bully launched a unilateral series of cruel, verbal assaults on her own timetable. She attacked when she sensed the Target most vulnerable. She did not bother to ask the Target if now was a good time. She fulfilled her need for control, trampling the needs and rights of the Target.

Lone Targets who confront without fixing blame for unacceptable misconduct will be as successful with this appeasement strategy as were pre-World War II Europe and English diplomats who timidly offered up one country after another to Hitler in the foolish hope that a man hell-bent on world domination would be satisfied. Immoral action has to be called exactly what it is, whether in war or at work. Pussy-footing around allowed the bully to sink in her claws—it cannot be an effective strategy to then get that same bully to back off.

The second major error made by lone Targets who decide to confront is to rely on the language of feelings. Targets are superior readers of emotional states, both theirs and the bully's. When they "confront," they expose their jugular vein to their assailant, falsely believing the bully will stop once she realizes how hurtful her mistreatment has become. This is typically delivered in "I" statements like this: "When you call me incompetent in front of Suzy and Harry, I feel embarrassed and ashamed." In the unlikely event that she doubted her success at gain-ing control over you through humiliation, you just confirmed that she is getting through. She is beaming broadly inside, if not outwardly, at proof that her control campaign has been successful.

Rent the video of the 1995 movie *Swimming with Sharks* starring Kevin Spacey. In it, Spacey is the ultimate bully. Particularly relevant here is the scene in which the targeted assistant asks the boss to stop yelling at him because it makes him look bad in front of office visitors. The Target does not accuse, he simply asks the boss for empathy. The boss mocks the "psychobabble" request and rips into a new tirade. This is a realistic depiction of what actually can occur.

The second mistake is a misunderstanding of the conflict in values. Targets prize fairness and feelings. Bullies only respect power and control.

We suggest two methods for confronting your bully that might work better when you have a little help from friends.

Modest Suggestions to Confront

The first method is to confront the bully behind closed doors but with a silent witness and a tape recorder. The witness must be your faithful ally and least likely to turn against you or to snitch. Rehearse a rather stern speech about the "unprofessional, unacceptable, unthinkable" pattern of misconduct the bully has displayed. Fire both barrels at her. The session could attempt to humiliate the bully by threatening legal action (only if you have consulted an attorney and the misconduct is actionable) or exposing her incompetence to higher-ups.

Use your people-reading skill to exploit her vulnerability. If she values her relationship with the Vice President, threaten telling the VP how ignorant the bully is. Chances are good that the bully has already tainted your record with higher-ups as part of her defamation of you. The point is to let her know you know her weaknesses. Then, clearly make your demands—"and don't stand in the way of my transfer (or next job) or I'll bring you down."

This tough-talk approach accomplishes several things. It reminds you about the personal strength and confidence you had before the bully stole them. It forces the bully to weigh the disadvantages versus the advantages of keeping you as her

Target. Research indicates that workplace aggressors compute an effort/benefit ratio in their heads when selecting Targets. Targets who resist prove too difficult for bullies who want an easy mark. Most bullies are lazy. By announcing that certain Targets now will be "difficult" to push around, bullies have been known to retreat. They simply search for easier prey. Also, it does your soul good to reclaim dignity, declaring your life off limits to the tyrant. The irony is that some bullies state that "now (they) have a new-found respect for" their Target. Words like these and the cessation of brutality are proof that the bully is off your back.

A second method is to confront as a group. After all, it was the group's silent cooperation and failure to stand with you that enabled the bully to gain dominance. Despite all the reasons groups don't intervene, there is strength in numbers. The strength comes from a shared responsibility to decide how and what to say. Further, though the bully may rant about firing "all of you," this would prove much more difficult to defend to higher-ups than selectively eliminating only you, a "known troublemaker." In other words, the entire group cannot as easily be mischaracterized as "trouble" for the company.

Groups rarely recognize the power they have over weak people like bullies. Bullying easily could be stopped by an assertive group standing together. A shining example is the "Code Pink" technique used by surgical nurses. These highly skilled professionals are often berated and belittled by pompous surgeons, both male and female. In some hospitals, whenever a bullying surgeon steps over the line into mistreatment, "Code Pink" is called by the targeted nurse. Immediately, supportive nurses form a circle around the physician. Together, they declare their unwillingness to assist that person with current and future patients, if an apology is not given with a promise to behave in a civil manner. The interdependent nature of surgery makes the surgeon powerless without the help of the team in the operating room. All work stops and the physician is accountable for her or his bullying. It is the physician who is responsible for the patient's life. "Code Pink" is the group displaying its power to the bully, demanding cooperation instead of controlling games. According to reports to the Campaign, every bullying surgeon confronted in this way yields to the group. The nonsense can be stopped!

We know that if a Target opened the door to the bully's office when attacked and called for all colleagues to join her, the bully could be confronted with her cruelty, unable later to convince the group to join her side in a manufactured, unjustified "war" on the Target. Bullies thrive on lies, secrecy, and imagined fear, stopping good people from doing the right thing. Displays of fearless, public solidarity deprive the bully of all her weapons and would solve the bullying crisis informally, quickly, and at no cost. In the absence of such action, however, be aware that irrational fears settle in with time passing. The group becomes less likely to confront just as the individual Target is frozen into inaction after early opportunities pass.

Step Five: File the Internal Complaint

The U.S. Supreme Court held employers liable for their supervisor's misconduct in two sexual harassment case rulings in the summer of 1998. Employer accountability was contingent on both the presence of an internal complaint system and the complaining employee's compliance with its requirements. That is, you have to file an internal complaint. This step is a no-win, requisite process for Targets.

Filing can be hazardous to your career. The bully will know what you have done, probably before you have time to get back to your workstation. The call from the HR lackey begins the immediately after you file the complaint and leave. From our experience, filing escalates the bullying. Retaliation toward the Target closely follows filing.

Sadly, HR knows which bullies have long rap sheets and long histories of cruelty. You'll never see that record. Most bullies demonstrate a pattern, but the internal system blocks that information from you. Instead, for some strange reason, the HR person feels compelled to support the bully. The branding of you, the complainant, as "troublemaker" begins.

Employers are complaint takers, investigators, jury, judge, and executioner. They own the process. All internal complaint systems, except the most extraordinary pro-employee ones, exist to protect the employer.

Close scrutiny of internal complaint systems reveals several anti-employee assumptions. They include beliefs that:

- complainants are liars, intent on defrauding the company for personal gain.
- complainants are whiners, they deserve their fate.
- harassment is not practiced here, therefore our managers are not harassers.
- the process will give the employer power of discovery (of facts like your medical history) while depriving the complainant of similar powers (psychological testing of the bully is taboo).
- complainants rarely have legal representation without filing a lawsuit or paying expensive attorneys.
- employers have access to staff legal counsel or defense firms as a routine matter.
- deadlines are a double standard, inflexible and not to be missed by complainants, but nonexistent in the case of the Federal government.
- bullies have the right to free speech, but Targets do not. Whistleblowing is considered anarchy and therefore suppressible.
- systems are based on the limited legal remedies available in the courts, namely Title VII of the Civil Rights Act violations and nothing else.
- employers mount vicious defensive attacks against complainants (the "Target-is-nuts" defense), deflecting responsibility to respond to allegations and to sanction the bully/assailant.

Clearly, filing a complaint creates an adversarial relationship between you, the Target, and the employer, mirroring the sour relationship with your aggressive, destructive bully. The complaint system is not your friend. Approach it with skepticism and caution. They are the enemy. HR is not your friend—the department serves management, not you. HR, EEO, and EAP are not impartial truth seekers. They have a job to do which does not include representing your best interests. It is not the fault of the individuals in those roles. Your job is to protect your rights and dignity. You are your own best advocate, unless and until you are represented by an attorney.

Regrettably, too many Targets report to us that their union fails them. Either the steward is a bully herself and hates the Target or the steward fails to see any need to defend the Target in the absence of collective bargaining agreement (contract) language. Similarly, unenlightened EEO staffers frequently resist helping Targets if the harassment is not explicitly illegal discrimination.

Our advice is to file a complaint immediately after the first deplorable incident. Waiting too long can be used against you, taken as evidence that either the bully's conduct was not as outrageous as you claim or that the impact on your health could not have been severe.

We suggest *minimal filing*. Give the complaint-taker only dates, times, and a dispassionate account of the bully's actions. Obsessing over the details only gives them ammunition to fight you. Be brief. Save your thunder for making the case yourself in a setting you orchestrate (steps six and beyond) or to work with your attorney. Avoid giving witness names at this time to protect both you and them. Never give an emotional report about how your bully's assaults hurt your feelings or made you feel incompetent. Down the road, your supporting physician, psychologist, or psychiatrist can comment on psychological or physical health impact. Do not make yourself vulnerable in any way to the adversary in the early filing steps.

Filing takes away the employer's ability to deny that they were not aware of the bully's actions. Filing also satisfies the Supreme Court's requirement.

There may be talk of the employer launching an "investigation." Typically, this is comprised of one meeting or telephone call to the bully who says she did nothing, ending the investigation. Do not expect positive results. Expect the truth to not come out. Do not be surprised if disciplinary action begins against you as the result of filing the complaint. Do not cooperate with the employer's process except to repeat your account of the systematic mistreatment.

As one Target told us:

> I reported a co-worker after more than four personal, abusive attacks. I went to personnel and reported him. I was treated so nicely. I was sent home "on the clock" for two days so that "everything could be taken care of." I was called during the second day, Tuesday, and told "be patient, we are investigating and we will protect you. Enjoy your time off, you are on the clock." On Friday, I was fired with no reason given. Even when you think they are taking care of business, they may be taking care of YOU!!

Do not sign documents under duress. HR often gets Targets to sign away their rights to outside representation, to seeking private medical help, and to mandate examinations by employer-paid (and therefore, biased) physicians, psychologists, or psychiatrists. Insist on taking all documents you are asked to sign to private legal counsel for an opinion. If HR refuses to give you time or a copy for review, know that your situation would have worsened had you signed. Block out all threats the HR representative may make. Walk out of that meeting, noting date, time, and what threats were made. Get to a lawyer of your choosing immediately. If you have a union and HR attempts to coerce you without a union representative present, call the union immediately.

You must proceed with your own BullyBusting process despite promises made about the employer's investigation. Complaints filed with HR do not routinely receive the attention of senior management, executives, the Board of Directors, or the public. HR's actual role is to resolve apparent conflicts in "personality" at the lowest level so as not to take the precious time of higher-ups. They think this allows senior people to dodge accountability for in-the-trenches misconduct as long as they are unaware. The following steps prevent the ducking of responsibility and fix liability at the highest levels.

Step Six: Preparing of the Case Against the Bully

By the time you finish the BullyBusting process, your job will change dramatically. You will be part detective, part psychologist, part attorney, and part activist. The bully changed your life for the worse. When you choose to go BullyBusting, it will change even more. At least when BullyBusting, you are reclaiming your dignity and self-respect. Your career is back in your control.

As we said at the onset, the prospects for success are slim at best. However, if you quickly find an ally at a high enough level, the element of surprise is on your side. The employer might just do the right thing and purge or curtail the bully.

You must accomplish five preparatory tasks before staging the bully's in-house tribunal, or trial: (a) search for code violations, (b) identify allies, (c) revise documentation, (d) make the business case, and (e) clarify personal expectations.

Share your master plan and outline of activities with *no one at work*. Confide in only those with no vested interest or future role in your case against the bully and employer.

Search for Code Violations

Rather than post vague charges of cruelty, mistreatment, misconduct, harassment, or bullying against the bully, it is best when you can find where the bully broke a rule. Rules can be internal policies and procedures or societal laws.

Most employers, except the smallest family-run businesses, have personnel policies and procedures (P&P). They range from huge binders put together by HR staff, which gather dust on corporate cubicle shelves, to boilerplate documents small firms produce from generic software packages. Personnel P&P, supplemented by the occasional employment contract and job description, define the terms of employment. Though they always favor the employer, when present, the documents provide clarity about explicitly forbidden behaviors.

Politically savvy bullies know about prohibited actions. They can exploit the loopholes in formal employer documents. For instance, the arbitrary dumping of a punitive workload is permissible in that job description duty lists include an "additional duties as assigned" clause that licenses the abuse. Other bullies are too consumed by their insatiable desire to control Targets that they either never check P & P or ignore what they know, relying on the employer to also overlook the written codes.

Employers fearing litigation reluctantly create policies prohibiting illegal harassment—discrimination based on "protected class" status. These policies are narrowly focused, rarely going beyond what is required for compliance with federal or state law.

A rare exception is the anti-harassment policy written by the Office of Civil Rights at the Oregon Department of Transportation (ODOT). Implemented in 1998, it prohibits:

> ...an intimidating, hostile, or abusive work environment. It may be sexual, racial, based on national origin, age, disability, religion, or a person's sexual orientation. It may also encompass other forms of hostile, intimidating, threatening, humiliating, or violent behavior which are not necessarily illegal discrimination, but are nonetheless prohibited by this Policy...Workplace harassment can also be verbal or physical behavior which is derogatory, abusive, disparaging, "bullying," threatening, or disrespectful, even if unrelated to a legally protected status.

This is a bold approach to stop harassment of all kinds which extends protections to everyone regardless of race, age, religion, or disability. It is a "status-blind policy." In our conversation with the author of the ODOT policy, we learned that the impetus was an employee's frustration over his inability to hold another employee accountable for making a sexually harassing remark to his wife. The policy broadened coverage to include visitors to the worksite. And through the drafting process as an accidental byproduct of the response to one situation, the agency expanded civil rights protections beyond those mandated by the U.S. Supreme Court to include bullying, which is not yet necessarily illegal.

It would be wonderful if your employer's P&P was so broadly written. If that were the case, you could better trust the internal complaint system. Alas, few such encompassing policies exist.

You have to settle for references to "respect for the individual," "due process for all," or a "right to challenge a managerial assignment if the employee is asked to behave unethically or fraudulently." The point is to catch the bully violating a written code. The more specific, the better. At the very least, you can quote noble, lofty language from the organization's mission, vision, or values statements. Also, annual reports boast of enlightened labor practices and caring for the employer's most valued resource—its human capital, you.

Find a way to capture the hypocrisy between espoused (printed and aspired to goals) and enacted (bullying behavior practiced daily and actually encouraged) practices by your employer.

The ultimate policy is outside the company—societal law. We've stated frequently that the current legal remedies are limited. However, you have to consult an attorney to be sure. Locate a plaintiffs attorney, if possible. Most "employment lawyers" defend employers. Ask your attorney what percentage of her clients are employees. You need an employee advocate. The National Employment Lawyers Association (NELA), is a membership organization of three thousand individuals who represent employees.

You need a legal opinion before threatening action during a confrontation with your bully or to be accurate in the tribunal you are preparing. Know the law. Do not be disappointed if your situation has a weak legal standing. That is, if the attorney tells you that you have no case, ask for a second opinion from another attorney. If the law cannot support you, it is not the lawyer's fault. Help the Campaign introduce legislation in your state to plug the huge loophole through which most bullies slip.

Identify Allies

BullyBusting requires a little help from some friends and a lot from someone with the power to neutralize the bully. It's imperative to have help up the organization chart. We say to use the "Rule of 2." Go two levels above the bully or higher to find support. If you cannot find an ally, chances are good you will be the one leaving. It is not just or fair; it is simply a reality of how organizations work.

Targets in small firms where the bully is employer or owner have the least chance of escaping misery and holding a job. Face it, you will not likely get a family member to turn on the bully to help you. If the bully is their daughter or niece, it's better to cut your losses and leave, to avoid predictable emotional pain from "hanging in there" indefinitely and only losing more in the long run.

Allies fall into three categories: the bully's, yours who currently work there, and yours who used to work there. Knowing the difference between the first two types determines whether you can mount the case against the bully or be stopped before you begin. Too many Targets mistake the bully's allies for potential friends. Watch your backside.

The bully has many friends at work. This is not because she is wonderful, it is because she is good at kissing up the ladder while tormenting those below (our Two-Headed Snake bully type). She knows who can ensure her career security and cover up her mistakes (like bullying you). Unless the bully joined the firm after you, learn as much as you can about the circumstances surrounding the bully's recruitment and hiring. A terrible mistake is for you to solicit support for staging a bully tribunal from someone in management who is either related to the bully or was responsible for putting her in that position. That's why we propose the "Rule of Two." The bully's boss is too often connected at the hip. Going two levels up increases the chances of impartiality.

HR will discourage the pursuit of senior management. They feel their job is to protect executives from "messy personality conflicts." But insist on a private meeting. Don't take no for an answer. Cite a posted "open door" policy or communication policy that anyone can talk to anyone else about anything at anytime. Swear the secretary to confidentiality, if you must—and honor the promise. As before, find the P&P that serves your advantage.

Do your research. Ask around about how the bully was brought in and why. What did the other workers think? Who was passed over for the job? What does she know? Was the bully selected because she agreed to do the boss' bidding? Is the bully a "turnaround specialist?" That's code for firing all those who challenge top management. Only sycophants, kiss-ups, can expect to hold jobs there. As a

Target, your integrity probably gets in the way of fake, hypocritical loyalty. Do the bully and the bully's immediate boss play good cop, bad cop as a team? Stay out of situations where you alone face a team.

A great source of dirt about the bully is available when you bother to ask people who worked with your bully at her former jobs. She may have been driven out—she may have satisfied her need to harm there and sought a new territory. In either case, the bully is likely to have left a trail of shattered lives. Former employees then feel free to be honest with you, no longer fearing retaliation.

Schedule a lunch with one or two who offer to tell you all they know. Even if you don't uncover a past rife with criminal activities, you will most certainly learn about an exploitable weakness that the bully has not yet shown at your place. Ask specific questions about her exit. If it was involuntary, how did the employer muster the courage to expel the tyrant? The recipe for your success may have been discovered elsewhere. You need only to orchestrate the same steps with your employer to purge the cancerous tumor.

Revise Your Documentation

By now, you have recorded a long list of incidents with your bully. This is partly because the bully's pattern is to repeat the offenses over a long period of time until forced to stop. This narrative is important to you. It could form the basis of a movie about the heinous interlude in your life. But for that marvelous record to be useful in the fight to get the bully off your back, it has to be nearly completely revised.

First, depersonalize the record. The evidence is one of the pillars upon which your case against the bully is built. Treat it as evidence. Write a version that contains only dates, actions, witnesses, and probable triggering events— the bully was just chewed out by her boss, she just missed a deadline, she was caught not knowing her job, etc. Most of the bullying is inexplicable and completely surprising.

To depersonalize means to omit the effects the bizarre acts had on you. The sheer number of incidents will help you make a case that the wrongs constituted a "pattern and practice." You'll be able to argue that the record demonstrates the bullying was neither accidental nor the result of a single, justifiable overreaction.

The second important revision is to convert the massive record into a short list of bulleted items. Hard to believe that this is even possible, isn't it? It can be very difficult because you worry about what is not being said. Forgive yourself this once and let go of the obsessiveness that has gripped you throughout the bullying ordeal. There is power in a short list. The concentration of cruelty that leaps from such a list is just right for senior managers to hear in your company. If you say more, they will be overwhelmed.

A short bulleted list is also useful for faxing to attorneys who may be interested in your case. No one, not even your legal advocate will want the full narrative. When we sat down to prepare the narrative of Ruth's story for our attorney, we stayed up all night. Gary quizzed her for explicit dialogue that accompanied each episode. The tale of three months tyranny filled forty-eight single-space pages by morning. Do you think the attorney ever understood the big picture? The over-detailed record may have done more harm than good.

Another one-page visual tool that can clarify the record for all who need to know is a time line. As you create it, it might dawn on you that bullying incidents might coincide with specific dates. There might have been milestones in the company's history (acquisition, layoff notices, growth) or in the bully's life (divorce, promotion, bonus paid, etc.).

Though you may initially miss the verbose, richly detailed record of the bully's misconduct, you now have the verbal and visual tools by which others can learn about the torment foisted involuntarily on you and your co-workers.

Make a Liability-Focused Case Against the Bully

A company in denial tends to justify bullying and harassment as a necessary part of "motivating" people and encouraging production. Defenders of bullies say they can't afford to lose the bully. Your job is to argue that unchecked cruelty undermines productivity. You have to show that the employer can't afford to keep the bully.

When building the case, several of your natural impulses as a Target will have to be overcome. You will make a business case—not a moral one. You will challenge the employer's most senior representatives to be frugal in terms they understand but which may not come as easily to you. You will not include employee morale or satisfaction unless and until the senior person indicates that she or he values those outcomes as much as the bottom line. You will not threaten to sue unless and until you know you have legal standing to do so (only on the advice of an attorney).

Make your case with the following parts: (a) preventing or minimizing employment practices liability, (b) talent flight impairing recruitment of the most skilled employees, (c) downtime is expensive, and (d) the risk of losing reputation and credibility in the industry.

Introduce "Employment Practices Liability"

Know that employers are driven by fear, primarily of being sued. That fear drives them to purchase insurance to cover the costs of mistakes. Mistakes in the employment practices arena center around supervisory misconduct—wrongful termination, intentional infliction of emotional distress, and the well-known illegalities of sexual harassment and discrimination. They buy insurance to cover the costs of fighting accusations of employer abuse and to cover settlement costs when it no longer makes sense to fight. In 1995, the median award for damages given by courts to employees who sued for wrongful termination was more than $200,000.

An employer that pays premiums for this type of insurance feels that employee mistreatment is either out of their control at the lower levels (better to be safe than sorry) or is a necessary part of doing business. The latter type of employer is cynical toward employees, reducing each to a liability risk. This employer runs all pre-employment background checks currently available on the market to weed out the "bad seed" employee, while ignoring the poisonous types of bullies they continue to promote up the ranks.

In either case, the liability for employment practices is a genuine concern for employers. Your job is to convince the senior person alone or together with the risk manager that retaining the bully exposes the organization to risk that is easily prevented. The greater their fear, the greater your chances of success at moving the bully off her throne.

Let's say that you have been told that there is a legal basis for suing. Here's how to estimate some of the tangible litigation-related costs for your employer to defend themselves against you, the plaintiff:

- $300 per hour corporate defense attorneys
- $20,000–30,000 retainer to start the case against you
- court fees to file a requisite response to your filing a lawsuit
- $10,000 for a private investigator to explore every aspect of your past
- court reporter fees ($150 per hour) and attorney time to depose you during the pre-trial discovery phase
- corporate attorney fees for time to negotiate a settlement— phone calls, meetings, preparation of the settlement agreement (with the routine "gag clause" so you can tell no one about the mistreatment you endured)
- pre-trial negotiated settlement costs paid to you
- settlement costs during or after the trial but before the judge or jury decides
- court-awarded damages to you, if the employer loses the case

According to a 1998 *USA Today* report, annual premiums for employment practices insurance range from $5,000 to $100,000. The coverage typically comes with up to $50 million in coverage for compensatory damages (the actual losses plaintiffs suffer), settlements, and legal fees. Punitive damages, awarded by courts to send a message to the offending employer, are not covered.

An old TV ad campaign for Fram oil filters put the phrase "Pay me now or pay me later" in the American lexicon. That simple phrase encouraged paying a few dollars for prevention—the auto oil filter—as opposed to paying thousands of dollars later for a new or rebuilt engine.

Prevention of larger costs is a central theme in your business case for stopping the bully. It's a matter of minimizing further risks. The bully has already caused a lot of trouble, but the most severe losses still are preventable by taking action.

The best possible situation is where the bully has a record of trouble. Several people may have sued and settled. Talk to them. Promise confidentiality. Add the dollars spent to silence complainants all because of the single bully.

One particularly perverse twist on the litigation cost angle is the money the organization has paid to the bully. This happens when people file complaints against the bully through internal channels. The tyrant then goes directly to the risk management or legal departments (never content to deal with only human resources) and threatens them with legal action if a thorough investigation occurs. How can this be? It seems that devious bullies play their discrimination card provided by the federal Civil Rights Act.

This sick, twisted loophole is available when the bully is a member of a "protected class"—female, a minority member, gay (if the firm recognizes sexual orientation), or disabled. It's a world turned upside down. You could not sue if you were not a member of the opposite class, but the bully can claim that the organization would be guilty of discrimination if she is singled out for investigation. Crazy?

For your purpose here, try to find out how much money has been paid in settlements to the bully. One bully we know gets a new car each time she is accused of cruelty. Seems she makes a beeline to the legal folks and they cut checks within weeks. Complainers are banished; the tyrant buys a new car as a payoff for mismanagement and cruelty. Estimate the value of such a settlement. Emphasize the blood money paid, not your outrage over this paradoxical, ridiculous state of affairs. Remember, you're building a business case.

If the senior person argues stubbornly for the political protection of the bully, show her or him how the entire organization faces financial risk as a result of this misguided decision based on a perceived obligation to preserve the bully's job. An important ally is the Risk Manager who should immediately recognize the language of loss prevention. Talk about fiscal impact as would any cold-blooded

MBA consultant. The bully must be stopped before she bleeds the organization through litigation.

Talent Flight Impairs Recruitment and Retention of Highly Skilled Employees

Funny how the economic boom affects availability of the most desirable employees in every type of business. They are in short supply. It's to the sellers' advantage—employees can afford to pick and choose where they want to work. They can be less tolerant of "business as usual" tactics, like bullying, because there are options. Smart employers offer signing bonuses, quality of life perks, stock options, and other incentives to attract the best and brightest.

When word gets out on the street that tyrants are bred and sustained in certain workplaces, those employers will be avoided like the plague. Admittedly, most Targets depart in silence, gagged by their own shame or by a clause in a separation or settlement contract. However, if they speak out and tell the world, the harasser-rewarding employers can be blacklisted within the employee pool in any community.

To warn of an intangible loss such as reputation among physicians, engineers, nurses, teachers or other group is a good argument but weaker than to show how the loss of specific individuals at your workplace have cost the employer dollars.

We know that talented individuals are targeted by bullies. Competence threatens incompetents. By focusing on the job and its technical requirements while ignoring the political assassination by their bully, Targets do themselves a disservice. They lose the chance to turn back the bullies with immediate, discouraging responses. Instead, the Targets find themselves the ones driven out.

Turnover costs all organizations. Tangible and intangible costs can be estimated as follows:

- cost of recruiting replacements—headhunter fees, advertising costs, participation in job fairs (salaries of internal recruiters on junkets to far away cities, travel and lodging expenses, exhibit booth rental).

- fees paid to temporary worker service companies (sometimes nearly double the wage paid to the worker) until the Target is replaced.
- unemployment benefits paid to the departed Target (and any employer costs associated with fighting the appeal which follows the original denial of such benefits).
- pre-hire applicant review costs (travel expenses for candidates, background checking, testing by corporate psychologists, managers' time to meet with candidates).
- signing bonuses and perks for new hires.
- overtime expenses for overloaded staff asked to cover the load of departed staffers.
- resentment of those staffers whose morale suffers as well as loyalty to the employer.
- lost customer loyalty who valued the departed staffer and took the business to the competitor who hired the bullied staffer.
- customers' disgust over lost continuity ("the names and faces always change in the bully's department") and service disconnects, true for both external and internal customers.

Therefore, make the point that turnover costs the employer, and the turnover is directly attributable to the bully's unconscionable conduct. Do the math for the senior manager. When fifteen talented people making X dollars have left over the last two years, how can the employer justify the X dollars spent to replace them. It just doesn't make good business sense.

Estimate the Dollar Value of Downtime

First, estimate the lost dollars to sick days. If you personally know how many days you missed work simply to stay away from the bully to protect your mental health, take as your estimate 1.3 times your salary for all those days. If you know how many days of your co-workers were taken for the same reason, do the same math. Get an amount for the period of time the bully has been affecting the group. This will be quite an impressive amount of dollars lost, directly attributable to the bully. If you do not know about the utilization of sick days by others, then make a conservative estimate that one-third of the time was used to recover from bully assaults or in anticipation of an especially stressful meeting. In either case, try to produce a dollar amount.

Second, estimate the cost of paying injured Targets. Simply ask the person how much is paid out in workers' compensation or disability payments, both short-term and long-term.

Itemize, then total these expenses. This amount should rival the dollars spent on settling actual or potential legal cases.

Risk of Losing Reputation and Credibility

This final liability is the least tangible one. If your employer does not enjoy a great reputation either as a supplier of great products or services, forget this part of a standard liability argument.

Reputation and credibility within the industry and as expected by the general public sustain business for the employer who cares about them. If they care, then the risk of losing them will get senior management's attention. Loyalty by outsiders is fragile and fleeting in our supercharged, globalized, competitive world. It must be nourished constantly. Having a "loose cannon" within earshot of customers and the public needs to be portrayed as jeopardizing the prized relationship.

If your employer cares, then it is your job to demonstrate a cause-and-effect relationship between mistreatment within the ranks and the loss of these intangible qualities the employer only temporarily enjoys. Without knowing your work, it's hard to illustrate.

Take a small retail insurance office that sells policies—auto, home, life—to the public. It's clear that the office manager, the franchise owner, sets the tone for the office. When she historically denigrates all new agents, fails to train them adequately, constantly criticizes mistakes in front of potential policyholders and fires them arbitrarily, it is easy to argue that her irrational behavior impacts the bottom line. The central office could be shown that her maniacal actions drove away X numbers of customers who called or walked in for a policy quote and were repelled by what they witnessed. Furthermore, turnover is also a factor. See above for computing the associated costs. The wise Target also would find the most successful office of a competitor to compare the number and size of policies written by a fear-free staff.

Perhaps you can think of how to include this intangible attribute to list of risks the bully creates for your employer.

Clarify Your Expectations

Knowing what you want sounds simple. It is obviously a part of preparation for the BullyBusting showdown. However, Targets rarely give this the careful thought with family members it deserves. Articulate Targets spend an hour telling us every detail of their history of mistreatment only to stumble over how they want to be made whole.

You will have to make an explicit demand from your employer in one or more meetings.

The complete demand has:

(a) an organizational solution ensuring your safety and health;

(b) a cash value for damages and personal restoration if you stay; and

(c) a severance package for damages and restoration, if you are
    the one to leave.

A Safety and Health Solution

First, chase from your mind impossible solutions. The employer is not going to fire the bully. A slap on the wrist is about all that is ever done. You can ask, but know that this entire proposal you are bringing forward is very threatening to senior management. To ask for much more will push them over the top, causing them to freeze out the otherwise logical arguments you've spent weeks practicing.

It is also unrealistic, though noble, to ask the employer to make it a safer, better world for all those left behind to suffer with the bully after your depart. Given the dire circumstances you are facing, let us suggest that you try to negotiate the best solutions for yourself. If others want relief, they can participate with you in a team complaint. If they fear such involvement, then they will have to engineer their own freedom. Do not jeopardize your solution with altruism for your colleagues.

If your case is heard by a progressive, pragmatic senior person, the bully may be transferred or at least put in a position where she can no longer harm anyone (if such technical positions exist where you work). That would save the group.

A caring employer will offer to transfer you. This will offend those with a strong sense of equity and justice. After all, why should you have to move? You did nothing. However, if you think about it beforehand, you can see the benefits of being separated from your tormentor. Your personal health and sanity are paramount. So, this may be the best solution you'll ever be offered. Naturally, you have to decide whether to stay or not. We suggest taking the transfer, after insisting on no cut in pay or blocked promotion opportunities, and leaving the job later if you are too upset over the compromise. At least you can control the trauma rather than letting it control you.

In the thousands of tales we've heard, only once did the Target's boss say "you will not be fired because of this mess." Then she set out to find the Target different positions in the large company.

Nearly every Target uses up all her paid time off—sick, vacation, and holiday days as well as drawing from future years' PTO bank. At the very least, insist that all time off privileges be restored. This can be done with the simple stroke of the pen by senior management. Do not forget to make this part of your demand.

The final part of any solution if you agree to stay with the employer has to be freedom from the bully's reprisal guaranteed by the highest level of management. Retaliation occurred the first time you dared to complain about your bully. Bullies resent being "outed," of having their clandestine campaigns of terror revealed. Retaliation can be more difficult to bear than the original assaults.

Refuse to stay unless your next report of a bullying incident, either directly or indirectly traceable to the bully, results in the bully's immediate termination. You could negotiate a situation that has two steps. You agree to be transferred under certain conditions. Then, if retaliation occurs or the new supervisor continues the original bully's mistreatment, you automatically invoke a severance agreement. That is, you are giving the employer "one last chance" to refrain from cruelty or the relatively more punitive agreement is enforceable against the employer.

Cash for Damages and Personal Restoration

Affix a dollar value to the pain and suffering you've endured, without referring to it in those terms. What is two years of your worklife worth? This amount will be some fraction of your current compensation, counting both salary and the cash equivalent of benefits.

In a court case, compensatory damages are actual costs associated with the plaintiff's complaint. Punitive damages are awarded to send a message to hurtful defendants to deter future abusive mistreatment. You do not have to draw such distinctions in your informal BullyBusting case. Damages are what you suffered and cash can be paid in acknowledgment that you were subjected involuntarily to destructive bullying and harassment that adversely impacted your life and career.

Here are some tips about estimating compensation for damages:

- What salary would you be making if the bully had not come into your life and blocked opportunities? This amount will be a difference between what you make now and what you should be making internally.

- Next, what additional dollars are required to restore you to the self you were before the bullying? Fees for a private therapist for you and your partner or family counseling, stress-free vacations with the family that you ignored during the war with your bully, and anything else you can think of. This is padding to your demand that may be the first items given away in negotiations.

Design Your Severance Package

It is no accident that 75 percent of Targets claim the only way the bullying stopped for them was to leave their jobs, often after long, successful, loyal careers. For all the reasons described elsewhere, the wrong people are driven out of the workplace.

It is useful to pay for another attorney consultation here. You might need help with the language of a settlement agreement. If you attend the negotiations alone, you will be outgunned. Senior management will not act without consulting their legal eagles. Try to play only on a level playing field. If you don't want your attorney present, then get coaching on tricks and traps for employees in typical agreements. Know what rights can be forfeited and which ones are worth preserving.

In the meeting that you orchestrated, you planned elaborate appeals to a logical employer at the highest level you could arrange. However, you may be thrown off-course when you arrive.

It is important to prepare your demand knowing that during the discussion with senior management you may be asked to quit. This can be done with dignity and you need to be ready to insist on it. Negotiating in good faith is a sign of respect.

However, if the employer is angered that you have held them accountable for the bully's misconduct, your departure can be made very humiliating. The shaming starts at the scheduled meeting. HR often is consulted by the senior manager, despite your efforts to circumvent their involvement. You attend the long-awaited meeting expecting to find an impartial audience for the detailed case you're about to make only to see the HR rep, a security guard, a cardboard box, and a single piece of paper and pen on the executive's mahogany desk. Be prepared for this.

What follows is a predictable routine. You will be told to sign the document. With a gun to your head (though it's symbolic, it feels real at the time), you will be asked to confess to disrupting the workplace and agreeing to voluntarily leave your job, forfeiting all rights to pursue legal action after your removal. DO NOT SIGN anything under circumstances like these.

Whether or not you sign, the guard and HR rep will "escort" you to your workstation. This "exit parade," or "plank walk" is designed to humiliate you, nothing more. You will remove your personal belongings under the watchful eye of suspicious security, placing them in the company-provided box. Tears flow, co-workers whisper and wonder. The HR person smirks, trying to not show publicly how much she enjoys this. She's getting even for you going over her head. The most despised smirk is the one on the bully's face. Naturally, she makes an appearance during this episode. She just has to get in her "gotcha" before you are banished, signaling victory for tyranny in the workplace wars.

Of course, if you had sought legal advice well before this day, you would know what rights you have and do not have. How wonderful to pull out a letter on an attorney's stationery to greet the assassins that day, preventing all the nonsense.

Unfortunately, most Targets think of calling attorneys only after their coerced termination (which they sign) and hostile escort off the premises.

Now let's get back to the preparation for a meeting that does not go awry. It is still wise to plan the details of a severance package in case senior management is unresponsive to your logical, liability-focused argument.

A complete package includes: a clean recommendation, a transition period of a determined length, damages, and restoration expenses.

Most Targets have invested lots of years with their employers. There is usually a wealth of performance evaluation data attesting to the quality of their work. The positive record stopped abruptly when the bully came on the scene. What you want and deserve is a positive reference letter written by the senior manager. It can verify what a good worker you were, but they are more likely to agree only to provide the dates of employment—the minimum amount of information. This protects both them and you.

You have to clearly state that the bully is not to defame you to anyone who calls as part of a background check. She is bound by the conditions of the letter signed by senior management. Further, if the zealous bully interferes with your pursuit of subsequent employment and proof is provided that this occurs, the employer agrees to pay a substantial sum of money to preclude the filing of a defamation and breach of contract (the settlement agreement contract that you are now negotiating) lawsuit because of the bully's statements. Stipulate a stiff fine to encourage getting the message across to the bully—$500,000 or more would accomplish the task.

To ensure the bully's impulse control, use the services of a company that checks references in a way that catches lying bullies. One such firm is Documented Reference Check [(800) 742-3316]. If your former bully persists, DRC will provide the documentation you require to enforce the gag clause you inserted into the settlement agreement. DRC reports also are accepted by courts as evidence in the event that you have to sue later.

Assuming that you leave, what amount of damages will you require to survive until you begin the next position at another employer? First, decide how long the transition period should be. We suggest a minimum of eighteen months. It takes months to shake off the negative effects of displacement by severe bullying. You should consider yourself "transitioned" when you can work full-time again any-where with no lingering exhaustion or anticipatory anxiety associated with going to work.

If you are close to retirement age, then extrapolate the transition costs to your retirement age.

The dollar amount for your transition will include lost salary and money to purchase health insurance at COBRA rates. For most people, employers pay 80 to 100 percent of the monthly health insurance premium. Co-pay rates and monthly premiums are small compared to what you are charged when COBRA applies. COBRA, part of ERISA law, mandates employers to notify you that you have up to eighteen months of health insurance benefits after separation. The catch is that you now will have to pay for all of it. Ask the benefits guru in HR for the COBRA rate for the identical coverage you once enjoyed.

It makes sense to ask the employer to pay for those eighteen months or longer. Don't forget the other components of your employer-paid benefit package that you will want them to continue—dental, life, and disability insurance and retire-ment account contributions. If you were provided with a company car, then add in the cost of replacing that car—either purchase price or leasing costs for the transition period you choose.

Finally, create a deadline date by which you want the matter resolved. The employer will try to stall as much as possible. You lose money and time. Set a date and be ready to present it at the meeting.

Step Seven: The "Rule of 2" Meetings Presenting Your Case

The "Rule of 2" means that you should only bother to make an internal case if you can have the ear of someone two or more levels in the organization chart above the bully. In rare circumstances, the bully's boss will be sympathetic, but frequently that boss is the one who hired the bully for her desirable attributes in the first place.

The person is properly placed to hear your case if that person is:

- capable of being impartial,
- aware of the fiscal impact of the organization's exposure to risk,
- sufficiently powerful so as to terminate or discipline the bully,
- authorized to dictate terms to implement to HR, and
- authorized to negotiate settlement agreements to preclude lawsuits or to call in legal counsel and risk management to assist in the negotiations.

We'll refer to this person as the senior manager, the one with sufficient clout to right the wrongs committed by the bully. It could be the owner of a small firm or the office manager or a regional vice president or a deputy assistant deputy director in a government agency.

As noted before, you are most likely to present your case by yourself. If you are lucky enough to work with a brave group of similarly bullied co-workers, go in as a group. With luck, they will have participated in all steps of the elaborate research required to prepare for the meeting. We will assume you are going to present the case against the bully alone.

You should be prepared for two meetings: (a) one with the senior manager, and (b) the bully's tribunal in front of a larger group.

Meeting with the Senior Manager

Try to schedule a one-hour meeting.

You need to have a representative accompany you. It might be the attorney with whom you consulted before or the author of the threatening letter you hold back in the event you are attacked. It could be a courageous co-worker willing to witness the event and take notes. Your witness could be a tape recorder. Do this in the open at the onset declaring that taping is to avoid future misunderstandings or bad decisions based on hearing something that was not said. Offer to make a duplicate copy of the tape for the senior manager. Wise managers will have arranged to make their own copy.

Beforehand, ask the senior manager to invite the director of risk management to attend. In small firms, this person will work inside HR.

Thank them for attending. Work from your typed agenda. If confident enough, the briefest version of the outline of your presentation could be typed and given to the management reps to follow. As outlined above, they may have their own agenda and may ignore you. Let's proceed with the simple outline assuming they do plan to hear your case.

Present your case in chronological order.

Begin with a brief portrayal (about two minutes) of the workworld before the bully arrived. Then tell specifically how she disrupted normalcy for everyone. Use your abbreviated list of actions, dates and triggering events (about ten minutes). Emphasize impact on outsiders who were appalled by her conduct.

Detail the liability risks she poses (ten minutes). Present them in the order outlined above. Keep appealing to satisfying the organization's broadest needs—integrity, preserving good relations with customers, and the importance of a positive reputation within the industry.

Listen for the senior manager's response. Take cues from that response. Wait for both nonverbal cues and the words themselves to give you direction. Repeat risks that seem important; skip lightly or ignore completely risks that seem unimportant.

At some point, the senior manager will ask you bluntly what you propose they do. State that you believe employees deserve a safe workplace, one that ensures psychological as well as physical safety. Get on your soapbox about dignity at work and how this meshes with the mission, vision, and values espoused in several of the organization's documents.

Now turn to your list of demands. Initially act as if you are going to continue to work there. Ask to have the bully disciplined and moved. If that list is repulsed (and it might be), then wait for management to make you an offer for an inner-office transfer. State your conditions to approve a transfer. If those are not met, move without fuss into crafting a separation agreement that meets the needs of both parties. Since you will have prepared for all possible results, nothing can shock you at this time. Even the "plank walk" coerced termination was anticipated. If the employer's legal counsel is not present, then this discussion about separation terms can only be preliminary. List your demands and the senior manager may say, "I will have to get back with you." She or he is the courier to the legal department.

Give your deadline for action. That means schedule the next meeting in time to have matters finalized by your deadline. One week is reasonable. You do not have to be understanding about who is on vacation for how long; this kind of empathy for their needs got you into Targethood in the first place. It's time to put yourself first.

Business goes on every day, regardless of key players being away. Finalizing your separation is important to you. Make it important to them (the threat of litigation helps here). Respectful treatment, which the employer has not displayed up to this point through its representative—the bully—needs to begin now. After all, if they wanted to start the "exit parade" or "plank walk," your final paycheck and termination papers would have been cut within hours.

Possible outcomes:

- A promise is given that the bully will be transferred
  or disciplined.
- You are offered a transfer.
- You are unceremoniously dumped immediately.
  (Go to Step 8).
- The senior manager agrees to preside at the bully's tribunal.

The Bully's Tribunal

The tribunal is a meeting at which she will answer the charges against her, hear evidence, face witnesses and the senior manager, and be held accountable. It is the justice Targets long for but rarely becomes reality. Please know this is a long shot. Look at all the preliminary steps that had to have been decided in your favor to get here.

The senior manager will insist that the bully, the accused, deserves her day in court. Yes, she does, albeit in a "kangaroo court" arranged by you.

Your role at that meeting will be one of prosecutor, using the same evidence assembled for the initial meeting with the senior manager. The senior manager must attend as the judge. Human resources must attend to implement any progressive disciplinary action that may result. Witnesses need to be called.

Here's a checklist to make the meeting as positive for you as possible:

1. Announce the meeting to all participants separately
   (no disclosure of distribution list to bully) with the stated
   purpose of reviewing the performance of _____
   (the bully is named). Be sure HR sends a representative.
2. Make it a public meeting with witnesses in addition to
   the bully and Target.
3. It's your agenda. Sequence events as you wish. Keep it
   vague so the senior manager will approve without revision.
4. Have clearly defined, specific outcome expectations. What
   do you want? The bully transferred? Monitoring of the bully?

5. Hold the meeting at a site neutral or uncomfortable for the bully. The senior manager's conference room would be ideal.

6. Record the meeting with deliberate redundancy (in case one set of records mysteriously disappears). Have audio or video and written records.

7. Compel the senior manager to attend. It would be good to have risk management there, too.

8. Present your carefully prepared case as you did to the senior manager, only be briefer. The bully has to have the chance to justify her unjustifiable actions. Emphasize code or policy violations. Do not threaten legal action unless approved by your attorney.

9. Call witnesses. They may be reluctant to appear in person, so be ready to submit the written statements of facts gathered in your preparation in lieu of their presence.

10. Turn to the senior manager for a decision. She may want to consult HR. Be clear that you are holding the employer responsible for the bully's misconduct. It is her obligation to right the wrong.

11. Ideally, the bully will be disciplined according to a progressive system already in place. Even tyrants probably do not deserve a zero tolerance, "one strike, you're out," policy. However, be ready to hear that the bully did no wrong and will face no consequences. This is to be expected in the absence of a specific code or policy outlawing general harassment or cruelty directed at all persons. Sanctions or termination should be the consequences for the bully when subsequent violations are reported. Know to ask for these things or they will be ignored or forgotten by the senior manager. Make HR the implementers of the contract by having the senior manager agree that when you or anyone

next complains about the bully, HR has to act.
They will not be allowed to deny, delay, or deflect
the complaint as before.

12. Ensure written permanent immunity from retaliation
and protection from future harm (direct assaults, blatantly
negative and false performance evaluations, punitive work
assignments, involuntary transfer, coerced termination)
for all who brought or supported the case against the bully.
Have the senior manager warn the bully for all to hear.

Step Eight: Taking Your Case Public

All of the previous steps were created to appeal to logical, responsible senior management. We know that logic is tossed aside in favor of political alliances and buddy systems in fear-driven organizations. The internal departments and senior management circle the wagons to defend the indefensible bully.

The ultimate extension of this irrational system perpetrated by an employer is to brand you the troublemaker and banish you. That is, the organization levies the ultimate punishment it can think of, depriving you of your livelihood. Of course, it's the humiliation that led to the banishment that lingers beyond the job.

We say all this because it is difficult to have the internal meetings in Step 7 for which you so carefully prepared go the way we describe. Positive outcomes are rare. You may have been fired as a result. A worse scenario is that they block your escape from the bully, ordering your return to the tyrant. This is a prison sentence certain to affect your health. At least if you are fired, you can begin healing.

When meetings do not produce results or management refuses to meet at all, it may be time to take your case public. In order for justice to be served, the organization's tyranny may require the light of day.

There are three possible public audiences to consider:

- customers who could save your career
- the organization's governing Board of Directors
- the general public, reachable through the media

Loyal Customers

For this group to save your job requires them to absolutely love you. They would have to be more loyal to you than the market price for your product or service, more loyal to you than the company that helps them stay in business with a product or service, and downright rebellious with a willingness to buck the status quo and tell the top person at their supplier that their continued business depends on retaining you and keeping you happy. It's a long shot, but those things would all have to occur to count on help from customers.

Board of Directors

Just before you run to the press, give the organization one last chance to behave responsibly at the highest level, to atone for the bully's sins. After all, the Board tells the CEO what to do (in theory, anyway). Turn to the Board as soon as the internal channels betray you. Know beforehand whether or not you can threaten litigation if you don't get your way. Prepare a five-minute version of your complaint. (The one-page bullet list is useful again.)

Governmental Boards and those of publicly held corporations should meet regularly and have space on the agenda for public comment. Research the directors as individuals. Attend a meeting as an unidentified observer to watch how the group interacts among themselves and with the CEO. Who takes charge and controls the agenda and discussion of the scheduled items? Can the CEO slip in unscheduled matters simply to get her way? Who is capable of moral outrage? Who is sensitive to the organization's public image? Try to meet with individual board members where they work. Find an ally who you think would be sympathetic to your plight. Use the same rules to identify an ally on the board as you did within the organization.

You want to fill the public board time with a concise, strongly worded appeal to the board's rationality in light of how management botched or ignored your complaint. Public accountability and scrutiny are key elements of your argument here. If you are whistleblowing, then describe how you are compelled to shed light on a hidden, dangerous practice at the company. Most boards, which think and vote in concert with the CEO, will dismiss your charges as noise from a "disgruntled" worker who has "personality conflicts" with her boss. They will say the matter has to be settled by HR. Boards, they say, do not involve themselves in "personnel matters." This less-than-acceptable outcome is likely, but attending with a member of the press there to record the board's reaction to the situation of facing liability may get the board's attention.

Tell the Media, Tell the World

Before you approach the press, know exactly what benefit the newspaper, radio, or TV station will derive from covering your story. While you want to educate the public, most media outlets want stories with entertainment value. TV imposes the additional burden of wanting a story that makes "good pictures." Fortunately, bullying stories can educate the public by touching those who suffer in silence from the same plight as you. And most readers and viewers find stories like yours compelling. Make sure you get your goals accomplished from the coverage. Otherwise, you will be simply fodder for selling papers and airtime. You will not have the luxury of obsessing as is the habit of Target storytellers. At most, you can give the highlights.

As part of your preparation, view the film *The Insider* (1999) that shows the true-story portrayal of the price a whistleblower paid for telling all about Brown & Williamson Tobacco. He had the "support" of America's premier TV network investigative newsmagazine, 60 *Minutes*, but it couldn't help him keep his family intact nor scare off the corporate goons who trailed him and threatened his life. Every Target who goes public and incurs the wrath of her employer risks similar losses, perhaps on a smaller scale, but disruptive and painful nevertheless.

Here's how to get your story told. Start with the local newspaper because you want the employer to face challenging scrutiny in its own backyard, the community of constituents they risk angering because of how they treated you. Ask for the reporter who covers workplace issues or for a general assignment reporter. If the reporter treats you with indifference, go to a larger regional newspaper. You will find print reporters will have long talks with you, but newspaper non-advertising space is limited. Only a few excerpts can ever appear in a story. Ask how many words the article will be and tailor your story to accommodate the length of the story.

Magazine articles are typically longer than those in newspapers, giving your complicated tale a shot at fairer treatment. You can propose an article yourself. Several magazines seek first-person accounts. You should familiarize yourself with the desired magazine. Envision where your story would fit. Then, write a query letter to the editor proposing the story. Don't write the article until you know the length and writer guidelines. Consult the *Writers' Market* annual guide for specifics. The 1999 version, which you can buy or read in your public library's reference section, has a wonderful tutorial on writing query letters. The second way to appear in a magazine is to be contacted by a freelance writer who will research the topic and try to include several interviews in a balanced piece.

Nothing draws attention like TV. The drawback is that they are biased toward pictures and very few words. If you think newspaper stories are brief, TV segments are scant! The longest, "in-depth" feature-type stories runs almost four minutes.

> *One outraged Twin Cities teacher who works with high-risk, special children was outraged that she had to discover on her own that her bully had attempted to kill both his parents over a decade earlier. Her school board and administration ignored her constant complaints about the inappropriately aggressive co-worker. A sympathetic TV reporter did the bravest thing the Campaign has ever heard of. He filmed an "ambush" interview with the bully, catching him unaware that he had been found out. A state legislator was also on tape suggesting a law to close the loophole that enabled the would-be murderer to work with children. The Target said her maternal instincts kicked in and drove her personal campaign to remove the man who had demonstrated his violent tendencies.*

The Campaign is approached constantly by print and broadcast media reporters—local and national—as well as by freelance writers and radio talk show hosts. As the clearinghouse of tales about bullying, we are able to provide local Targets for interviews. Simply contact the Campaign if you are willing to go "on record" with your story. We will keep your name and contact information in a private, secure database (neither shared with, nor sold to, anyone) and we might be able to help your story reach the public.

Chapter Twenty:

Moving On, Up, or Out

. . . .

I decided it is better to scream…the last vestige of human dignity.
It's a man's way of leaving a trace….He asserts his right to live, sends a
message to the outside world demanding help and calling for resistance….
Silence is the real crime against humanity. —Nadez Hda Mandelstam

W e end the book where most Targets begin, with a question. "Should I stay or leave?"

The Campaign Survey Says . . .

Bullies Stay, Targets Are Driven Out

✓75 percent of Targets end bullying by leaving

Only you know the answer. Only you know how the quality of your work and personal life have fallen as the result of bullying.

You get no medals for "hanging in there." For you, toughness may be one of those unattainable personal standards over which you beat yourself up.

We suggest doing a cost-benefit analysis on a two-column sheet. Review the Impact Assessment results from Chapter 10. Let that information enter your decision-making discussions. Leaving a job is a private decision to be made only by you and your life partner. Do the required math yourself.

Sacrifice Health & Sanity For A Paycheck? It Simply Doesn't Add Up!

For what it's worth, we coach people as long and as hard as we can to get them to save their jobs. However, the kiss of death for potential BullyBusters is when the bully has support all the way to the top of the organization. Targets facing unanimous opposition like that do not stand a chance. If no allies can be found above the bully (using the "Rule of 2"), you'll never gain the leverage against her that you need to have her stopped.

If your workplace is a convenience store and the bully is a co-worker but the owner hired her, polish your resume and hit the road.

However, if you decide to stay and you work in a large organization, you owe it to yourself to follow one or more steps described in the BullyBusting Strategies chapter.

Targets seriously underestimate the consequences for their health. The cumulative nature of the bullying, combined with the tendency to procrastinate about seeing a doctor or telling others out of shame, lulls the individual into a barely perceptible decline. However, the strain may have already begun cardiovascular and gastrointestinal problems, several of which may be irreversible. Make your health a significant factor in the decision-making process.

The major conflict for Targets is wanting to get out to save their sanity and wanting to stay so as to not seem to turn tail and run. Trust us, you can control the story of your departure if you don't accept a quiet exit. Leaving with dignity seems to quicken the healing process.

Let's assume you've decided to leave. You can leave the way your employer wants or you can try our suggested routine.

A Quiet Exit

Thousands of traditional career counselors out there can advise you about leaving gracefully. They can tell you how to transition to the next job without ruffling feathers. To summarize their approach: burn no bridges, kiss the behind of the bully boss so she won't say bad things about you (she will anyway, don't they know), never be negative (which we guess means to avoid the truth) about the job-ending turmoil you are leaving behind when interviewing for the next job, smile, and put your future in the hands of those who have ruined your life to date.

The Alternative Good-bye

Accepting the humiliation inflicted by the bully, personnel, and upper management, culminating in the "exit parade" or "plank walk," essentially leaving with your "tail between your legs," jeopardizes your ability to move on with your life, to start anew somewhere else. The circumstances under which you leave seem to predict the length of your time to completely heal and be able to function at 100 percent in another job. When you control the terms, damage is minimized. When the bully and employer set the agenda, Targets are left doubting for months about what they could or should have done differently.

We suggest an alternative. It involves guile, cynicism, and paranoia. But the bully pushed you into this mess in the first place. Never forget that.

1. Arrange for Positive References and a Great Letter

Ask for a positive reference from colleagues, allies up the chain, and customers who will verify that your performance record was impeccable. You need people to confirm that you are a skilled competent person. Some employers insist on talking with your ex-supervisor (often the bully) regardless of the glowing reference list you produce. If that next employer is more obsessed with your subordination and willingness to sell your soul to a tyrant, would you want to work there? Choose carefully where you work next. Go with open eyes.

Write your own letter of recommendation and make the employer sign it before you leave. Even if they hate you, just maybe their fear of confrontation will convince them to sign. Plus, this might balance the practice of making you sign forms against your will (such as stating that your departure was voluntary to cut you out of unemployment benefits). Then you can threaten them with legal action if they renege on the letter or choose to state anything more than employment dates if and when contacted. If they go along with this letter, you can skip the next suggestion. Use Documented Reference Check to verify compliance.

Warn the bully and all bully supporters, including HR, that they are to provide the next employer with dates of employment only or face legal action. Use the legal language about defamation.

2. Know the Law Regarding Defamation of Character

Goad the bully into defaming you to others. Get it on the record. (Most bullies will actually boast of the smear campaign they launch against you.)

David Hurd, attorney and author of the *California Employee Survival Handbook*, states that it is illegal for an employer to make a "misrepresentation which prevents or attempts to prevent a former employee from getting a new job.... A misrepresentation can include any act, suggestion or inference that leads the listener to believe something untruthful or misleading...(even) gestures, or tone of voice, or a raising of an eyebrow could qualify as an illegal misrepresentation." Proof can be provided by DRC.

According to Hurd, if an employer "volunteers to another person or another employer, the reason or reasons, for an employee's discharge or reason for quitting, that employer is guilty of a crime....The past employer is only permitted to disclose the truthful reasons for the discharge or voluntary termination of the employee if the past employer is specifically asked without prompting."

Because warnings don't stop liars and cowards, consider using a unique pro-employee service from DRC [(800) 742-3316]. The company calls your ex-employer as would someone checking your references. Since they are working for you, for a modest fee, they transcribe exactly what is said. The defaming statements give an attorney ammunition to exact your pound of flesh from them for continuing the bullying after your departure. Using this service doesn't stop them, but it might help you get a settlement from them large enough to cushion the economic blow from being "constructively discharged" from the job you once loved.

3. If the Employer Insists on an "Exit Interview," Deliver or Send an Attorney's Letter Instead

You are leaving. So, you control the meeting agenda for once. Be prepared for Gestapo-like tactics. Produce a letter from an attorney representing you (pay for one hour's time) to the employer in a way that proves receipt. The letter warns all those listed that they, as individuals and as representatives of the employer liable for the mistreatment you endured, will be held liable for the release to future employers of any information prohibited by law regarding your employment there.

4. Worst-case Scenario—Launch a Pre-emptive Strike about Your Version of the Bullying Fiasco at the Interview for the Next Job

Prospective employers are always desperate to talk to your ex-employer. Convince them to not do this. Tell them there was conflict and positive news from the bully is not likely. If you then let them know how you expect to be smeared, then you will have "self-published" the defamation you anticipate. According to Hurd, your statement would be admissible in court to show you have been defamed by disclosing the false statement made against you by the ex-employer. Direct their attention to the positive comments from others. Emphasize the skills you bring. Compliment them on their reputation as a humane, progressive employer who cares about employees, if they enjoy this reputation.

5. Review Your Record of Bullying Incidents and the Response By the Employer. Consider Legal Action against the Company

Scan the record and your memory for potential invasions of your privacy while there. There is no explicit right to privacy. Courts always question whether or not the person watched or recorded had the "reasonable expectation" of privacy. In the workplace you should expect that the employer's property would be considered public (except for toilet stalls, and even then, there seems to be some doubt). Call the Privacy Rights Clearinghouse in San Diego [(619) 298-3396] for advice on privacy questions.

Pursue legal or EEOC complaints, if applicable. Your departure is imminent when complaints are filed. As a rule, retaliation is swift, severe, and persistent for those who dare to complain. If your rights have been violated as a member of a "protected class" under Title VII Civil Rights Act, call the EEOC for a free consultation and preliminary determination of your status.

If you are not Title VII eligible, consult a plaintiffs-only attorney or an attorney concerned about employee rights. There may be "tort" law that applies— e.g., intentional infliction of emotional distress (see IIED in Legalities chapter), constructive discharge, defamation, wrongful termination, breach of contract, reckless indifference, employer negligence. We're not lawyers, so ask one about the various alternatives. Now that you are out, the power of a lawsuit would be to create a nuisance for the ex-employer to let them know they messed with the wrong person. Justice happened the day you stepped away from your tormentor's grasp. Lawsuits can make public the dirty tactics they tried to accomplish behind closed doors. Do not expect to get rich from bringing a suit. Also consider how your current employer feels about someone on staff who has sued a boss. You must expect retaliation.

Admittedly, these steps sound like hardball, but doesn't that describe accurately what the employer and bully conspired to do to you? It's an alternative to the quiet exit. It's time to live the richly rewarding life you were enjoying before the uninvited bully distracted you temporarily.

Work Shouldn't Hurt!

Join the Campaign Against Workplace Bullying:
(707) 745-6630

Appendix

. . . .

The Campaign Survey

Three online surveys were posted at the website as part of the initial research of, and for, bullied workers. Targets of bullying were invited to complete part one, the "Target" survey, and part two, the "Aftermath" survey, to describe some of the consequences of bullying that have lingered. A third survey for witnesses of the bullying of others was designed for co-workers.

The initial two hundred completed surveys were analyzed. The summary of our findings appear below. In all, 154 Targets and 46 witnesses completed surveys. Sixty-six Targets also completed the Aftermath questionnaire.

Though the sample was not a randomly representative group, thus rendering the study a "non-scientific" one, it was a rare look inside many of our sick workplaces.

Bullying was defined at the website as "the hurtful, repeated mistreatment of a Target (the recipient) by a bully (the perpetrator) whose actions are characterized as controlling."

Gary Namie, Ph.D.
Research Coordinator
Campaign Against Workplace Bullying

Summary

1. Bullying is different from the more recognizable issues that plague the workplace—sexual harassment, racial discrimination, and violence. Both women and men are victimized as Targets and serve as perpetrators.
2. Falling prey to a bully's destructive tactics is a career hazard; it is not about gamesmanship or a fair competition among equals. Bullies commonly adopt surprise and secrecy to gain leverage over Targets.
3. Targets are a diverse group of normal, talented people.
4. Bullying devastates the Target's emotional stability and can last a long time.
5. The employer, as an organization, bears partial responsibility for the systematic disassembly of a once productive employee by a mean-spirited, one-person wrecking crew.

Detailed Findings

1. Bullying is different from other issues that plague the workplace— sexual harassment, racial discrimination, and violence.

Both women and men are victimized as Targets and serve as perpetrators. It is a type of harassment that ignores the legal condition of disparate treatment based on gender. Female Targets were nearly equally likely to be bullied by women (46 percent) as men (54 percent). Though men were a minority of the respondents (27.2 percent), they, too, were bullied. For them, the bully was usually male (72 percent of the time). Legality is not required for acknowledging its existence. Furthermore, less than 10 percent of the respondents felt that legal charges could be brought against the bully based on EEOC (Title VII) criteria—gender, race, etc.

Bullying is unconscionable meanness, but rarely related to physical violence or threats of it. Bullying is characterized by verbal assaults and sabotage. Results confirmed that in only 6.5 percent of the cases were physical threats made.

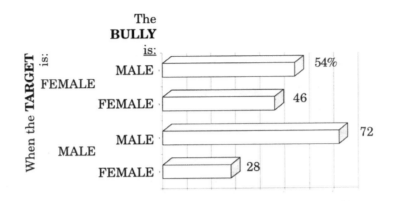

2. Falling prey to a bully's destructive tactics is a career hazard; it is not about gamesmanship or a fair competition among equals.

Bullies commonly adopt surprise and secrecy to gain leverage over Targets.

What exactly did bullies do? The top ten tactics ranked from most to least frequent were: blame for errors; unreasonable demands; criticism of work ability; inconsistent application of made-up rules; threats of job loss; insults and put-downs; discounting accomplishments; social exclusion; yelling and screaming; and stealing credit for Target's work. Bullies all adopted more than one spirit-crushing technique. Witnesses tended to see making unreasonable demands, stealing credit, blaming, and threatening job loss as bigger problems than did Targets themselves.

The top four causes of the bullying, as seen by Targets and witnesses, were: a refusal to accept the subservience the bully sought (31 percent), "bully envy" of the Target's competence and abilities (21 percent), nothing [the assaults were unprovoked] (18 percent), and top-down company policies, or the workplace culture (14.3 percent). If bullying was a civil interaction, independence would be rewarded instead of having attack as a consequence. Bullying is as capricious and surprising as the bully's personality is unpredictable.

Most important was that three out of four (75 percent) of those who reported that bullying had stopped said it did so only because they left the job. Terminations were engineered by bullies with falsified facts or without bothering

Targets' Rationale For Being Bullied

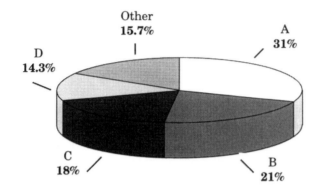

to concoct a reason (which is rarely illegal). Others quit after being driven out. Bullies stay; Targets leave.

The bullies' favorite arena for misconduct was in front of others (53.2 percent). Public actions not only humiliate the Target but serve notice to the group that anyone could next fall into the predator's path. The other half of the bullies divided their preference between private, truly secret settings (24 percent) and encounters behind closed doors but overheard (22.8 percent). Privacy enables deniability. Disputes become a "she said/she said" dialogue which discourages people to whom the Target turns for help from taking remedial action.

3. Targets are a diverse group of normal, talented people.

Targets and witnesses who completed the surveys were predominantly female (73 percent). The age range was 15 to 58, with a mean age of 36, and 78 percent of the respondents between the ages of 24 and 46.

Education: 43 percent had less than a four-year college degree; 27.5 percent had a four-year degree; 29.5 percent had a graduate or professional degree.

Most employers were in the private, for-profit sector (59.3 percent); 15.4 percent were nonprofit organizations, and 25.3 percent were government employees.

Typical employers: legal office, toy manufacturer, aerospace, chamber of commerce, private elementary school, casino, physician's medical group, substance abuse counseling center, accounting/consulting firm, national magazine, university, community action agency, state prison, hospital, semiconductor manufacturer, software design, bookseller, satellite communications, resort hotel, pharmaceuticals, pipeline construction, book publisher, market research, chiropractor.

Representative jobs: "a checkout chick, a register dog," nutritionist, professor, janitor, training officer, corrections officer, machinist, researchers, beverage supervisor, fraud investigator, heavy equipment operator, tech support, clinic director, engineer, child care worker, nurse, bank teller, teacher, purchasing, security officer, design engineering, sales, quality control assistant.

4. Bullying devastates the Target's emotional stability and can last a long time.

As rated by Targets, the list of most prevalent eight effects bullies had on Targets were: stress, anxiety (79.4 percent); depression (64.7 percent); exhaustion (64 percent); insecurity, self-doubt (59 percent); shame, embarrassment, and guilt (58 percent); obsessive thinking, nightmares (58 percent); poor concentration (56 percent); and sleeplessness (53 percent).

Those who completed the Aftermath survey were evenly divided into two groups. The shorter-term group was removed from their bullies for one year or less. A second, longer-term group had a "recovery time" that spanned eighteen months to ten or more years. The short-term group reported frequent or constant intrusive negative thoughts about the bullying in 81.25 percent of the cases. This alone is horrific.

More disturbing is that 23.5 percent of respondents in the long-term group were bothered by frequent or constant thinking about the bullying. Remarkably, for those removed from the bullying for ten years or more, 80 percent said they "sometimes" still thought about it.

Subsequent to the bullying episode to which respondents referred in their questionnaires, 58 percent reported that they were still troubled by bullying (that it was either an infrequent or debilitating part of their current job). Freedom from bullying is obviously difficult to achieve once wounded.

These data confirm the anecdotal evidence gathered as part of the Campaign's advising service.

5. The employer, as an organization, bears partial responsibility for the systematic disassembly of a once productive employee by a mean-spirited, one-person wrecking crew.

The bully's rank in the workplace was higher than the Target's in 89 percent of the cases. Of the others, 6.7 percent were co-worker bullies and 4.5 percent bullied up the organization chart.

Recall that the fourth-ranked perceived cause of bullying was the employer's culture (top-down policies). Further support for the employer's condoning, rather than condemnation, of bullying came from the question asking who supported bullies. Management was the principal source of support (76 percent) while the bully's peers ranked second (56.3 percent).

Sadly, the Target's co-workers were seen as pro-bully, though at a level less than half that of management (32.4 percent). This could reflect the success of a "divide and conquer" tactic that bullies sometimes adopt to turn co-workers against peers. The final noteworthy supporter of bullies was human resources, according to 30 percent of survey respondents.

When asked to rate the helpfulness of company representatives, the two least helpful were human resources (an average of .423 on a scale of 0 to 2, and only 3 percent saying they were helpful) and senior management (an average of .424 and 7.6 percent crediting them as helpful).

Witnesses tended to discredit HR and management more harshly than did Targets, though the differences were not statistically significant. It is reasoned that, as outsiders, they saw more objectively how the Target's downward spiral could be attributed to HR and management's indifference or deliberate obstruction of a compassionate resolution on behalf of the Target.

Who Supports the Bully?

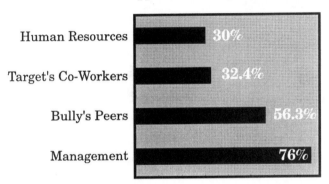

The question of responsibility for bullying was raised by having respondents distribute 100 percent of accountability across four groups. The average percentage assigned to Targets for their own fate was 8.2 percent. Bullies bore the brunt of responsibility, an average 59.5 percent. However, the organization was given an average 24 percent and the law (society or unknown external factor) was assigned slightly more culpability (8.3 percent) than Targets. Clearly the bully and her accomplice, the organization, were seen as the culprits.

Again, witnesses tended to view the bully more harshly than Targets (64.5 percent versus 58 percent), but the difference was not significant.

Some good news about co-workers came from the list of sources of support for Targets. Co-workers topped the list, but co-workers saw themselves as more frequently supportive than did Targets (95 percent versus 72 percent). Next most supportive as seen by Targets were friends away from work (62 percent), a spouse

Targets Divide Responsibility for Bullying

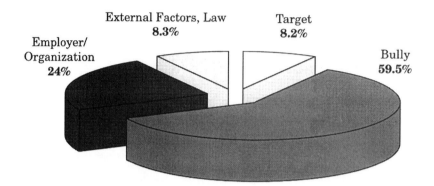

or partner (58 percent), and family (51 percent). Note how friends are consulted more frequently than mates. We infer that the shameful nature of assault victims drives them to shield loved ones rather than burden them first.

Management provided the least support to Targets (8.5 percent). Management loyalty is showered on bullies.

Who Supports Targets?

Percentages reported for groups

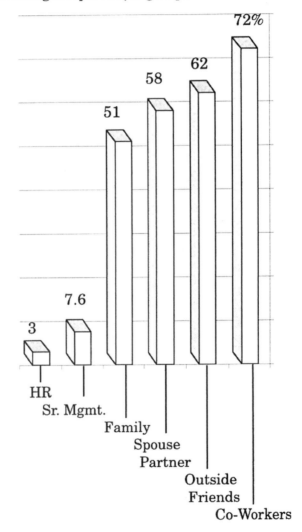

Bibliography

Brink, Betty. "Transforming the truth: How TU Electric twisted the medical facts after an employee working with PCB got sick." *Fort Worth Weekly,* 26 March 1998.

Brown, Stephanie. *Safe Passage: Recovery for Adult Children of Alcoholics.* New York: John Wiley & Sons, 1992.

Frank, Robert H. & Cook, Philip J. *The Winner-Take-All Society: Why the Few at the Top Get So Much More Than the Rest of Us.* New York: Penguin, 1995.

Harvey, Jerry. *The Abilene Paradox and Other Meditations on Management.* New York: Lexington Books, 1989.

Hornstein, Harvey. *Brutal Bosses and Their Prey: How to Identify and Overcome Abuse in the Workplace.* Riverhead Books, 1996

Hurd, David J. *The California Employee Survival Handbook.* 3rd ed. Pro Per Publications, 1998.

Keashly, Loraleigh. "Emotional abuse at work: conceptual and empirical issues." *Journal of Emotional Abuse* 1(1998).

Keashly, Loraleigh, and Jagatic, Karen. "Workplace abuse and aggression." Paper presented at Workplace Bullying 2000: Redefining Harrassment. Oakland, Calif., 27 January 2000.

Labor Occupational Health Program. "Violence on the Job: A Guidebook for Labor and Management." University of California, Berkeley, 1997.

Levine, Daniel S. *Disgruntled: The Darker Side of the World of Work*. Berkley, Calif.: Berkley Boulevard, 1998.

Marais, Susan, and Herman, Magriet. *Corporate Hyenas at Work: How to Spot and Outwit Them by Being Hyenawise*. Pretoria, South Africa: Kagiso, 1997.

McCarthy, Paul, Sheehan, Michael, and Wilkie, William. *Bullying: From Backyard to Boardroom*. Alexandria, NSW, Australia: Millennium Books, 1996.

Michenbaum, Donald, Ph.D. *A Clinical Handbook/Practical Therapist Manual for Assessing and Treating Adults with PTSD*. Waterloo, Ontario: Institute Press, 1994.

Nader, Ralph, and Smith, Wesley. *No Contest: Corporate Lawyers and the Perversion of Justice in America*. New York: Random House, 1996.

Neuman, Joel H., and Baron, Robert A. "Workplace violence and workplace aggression: evidence concerning specific forms, potential causes, and preferred targets." *Journal of Management* 24 (1998): 391-419.

Nisbett, R. E., C. Caputo, P. Legant, and J. Marechek. "Behavior as seen by the actor and as seen by the observer." *Journal of Personality and Social Psychology* 27 (1973): 154-64.

Office of Civil Rights, Oregon Department of Transportation. "Anti-Harassment Policy." Salem, Oregon, 1999.

Privacy Rights Clearinghouse, Dale Fetherling (Ed.). *The Privacy Rights Handbook: How to Take Control of Your Personal Information*. New York: Avon Books, 1997.

Queensland Government, Division of Workplace Health and Safety, Department of Employment, Training & Industrial Relations. "An Employer's Guide to Workplace Bullying." Queensland, Australia.

Richman, Judith, et al. "Sexual harassment and generalized workplace abuse among university employees: prevalence and mental health correlates." *American Journal of Public Health* 89, no. 3 (1999): 358-363.

Schaef, Anne Wilson, and Fassel, Diane. *The Addictive Organization: Why We Overwork, Cover Up, Pick Up the Pieces, Please the Boss & Perpetuate Sick Organizations*. Harper & Row, 1988.

Scott, Michael J, and Stradling, Stephen G. "Post-traumatic stress disorder without the trauma." *British Journal of Clinical Psychology* 33 (1994): 71-74.

Solomon, Norman. *The Trouble with Dilbert: How Corporate Culture Gets the Last Laugh*. Monroe, Maine: Common Courage Press, 1997.

Storms, N. D. "Videotape and the attribution process: Reversing actors' and observers' points of view." *Journal of Personality and Social Psychology* 27 (1973): 165-75.

Tobias, Paul, and Sauter, Susan. *Job Rights & Survival Strategies: A Handbook for Terminated Employees*. NERI, 1997.

Waggoner, Martha. "Study: workplace incivility rising." Associated Press, May 29, 1998.

Yamada, David. "The phenomenon of 'workplace bullying' and the need for status-blind hostile work environment protection." *Georgetown Law Journal* 88, no. 3 (2000).

Index

About the Authors

Gary Namie, Ph.D., is a social organizational psychologist. He is the President of the Campaign Against Workplace Bullying. He brings experience as a Training/OD manager (for two hospital systems), consultant, university professor (at the University of Southern California and Scripps College), and steelworker. Gary won national and University of California awards for his quality teaching. He has delivered more than five hundred seminars, courses, and speeches on every imaginable workplace topic.

Ruth Namie, Ph.D., is the CEO of the Campaign Against Workplace Bullying. Dr. Namie has been a psychotherapist since 1986 with a doctorate in clinical psychology. She maintains a private practice in Benicia, California, and facilitates support groups for working women. She also has experience as a corporate training director in retail human resources management. It was her personal experience with bullying that led to the Campaign and subsequent publications.